Praise for *Becoming a Better Programmer*

Becoming a Better Programmer oozes experience and communicates the wisdom drawn from a career in the software business. Snappy, single-topic chapters make the book really readable with common themes being tackled from every angle. If you are a software engineer looking to go from good to great, this book is for you. I will be using it with the junior developers I'm responsible for mentoring.

— *Andrew Burrows*
lead developer

Goodliffe takes the very broad subject of computer programming and manages to break it down into a clear, compelling, and engaging narrative. He has a particular flair for saying things that seem obvious, but I hadn't realised before he said them. Any programmer who aspires to be a great programmer should read this book.

— *Greg Law*
cofounder and CEO of Undo Software

Pete Goodliffe successfully blends the theoretical with the practical. Where things must be done in a particular way, he pulls no punches. Where grey areas exist, he clearly explains different points of view. If you consider and apply what he says you'll benefit and be better; you'll become a better programmer. Overall this book is full of distilled real-world experience, mixed with humor, to provide gentle wisdom.

— *Dr. Andrew Bennett*
BEng/PhD/MIET/MIEEE

This book will fuel your passion for the art and science of programming. Pete understands that great software comes from good people doing their best work. He illustrates how to do this through good coding practices, a good attitude, and good relationships, with lots of examples. Bonus: it's really fun to read!

— *Lisa Crispin*
coauthor of *Agile Testing: A Practical Guide
for Testers and Agile Teams*

Pete's got a wealth of experience being a programmer and mentor. In this book, he's applied the same attention to detail categorising and describing those experiences as he does to the task of actually being a programmer. Knowing about programming is only one part of "being a programmer," and whether you're new to the Code Factory, an old hand, or starting to mentor someone, this is a treasure trove of advice about how to go about it—from someone who really knows. It's a manual about many of the hurdles you'll encounter, and how to negotiate them safely and effectively.

— *Steve Love*
editor of *C Vu* magazine

All too often, programmers are divided into average programmers and rockstar or ninja developers. Where there's a rockstar, there's a trashed codebase with broken classes and spaced-out control flow. Where there's a ninja, there's mysterious bugs and build problems that appear in the middle of the night. Where there's an average, there's a distribution. In the longterm, what matters is less where on the distribution someone is than where they are headed. If you want to divide programmers into two groups, there are programmers who get better and programmers who don't. You care about the first group. This book is for them.

— *Kevlin Henney*
consultant, speaker, and author of *97 Things Every Programmer Should Know*

This book is quite dull, and I'm not convinced by the fish on the cover.

— *Alice Goodliffe*
age 12

Becoming a Better Programmer

Pete Goodliffe

Beijing · Cambridge · Farnham · Köln · Sebastopol · Tokyo

Becoming a Better Programmer

by Pete Goodliffe

Copyright © 2015 Pete Goodliffe. All rights reserved.

Printed in the United States of America.

Published by O'Reilly Media, Inc., 1005 Gravenstein Highway North, Sebastopol, CA 95472.

O'Reilly books may be purchased for educational, business, or sales promotional use. Online editions are also available for most titles (*http://safaribooksonline.com*). For more information, contact our corporate/institutional sales department: 800-998-9938 or *corporate@oreilly.com*.

Editors: Mike Loukides and Brian MacDonald
Production Editor: Melanie Yarbrough
Copyeditor: Jasmine Kwityn
Proofreader: Sonia Saruba

Indexer: Pete Goodliffe
Cover Designer: Karen Montgomery
Interior Designer: David Futato
Illustrator: Pete Goodliffe

October 2014:   First Edition

Revision History for the First Edition:

2014-10-01:   First release

See *http://oreilly.com/catalog/errata.csp?isbn=9781491905531* for release details.

ISBN: 978-1-491-90553-1

[LSI]

For my wife, Bryony, who I adore.

And our three wonderful girls.

Psalm 150.

Table of Contents

Part II.   Practice Makes Perfect

Part III.   Getting Personal

Part IV.   Getting Things Done

Also by Pete Goodliffe

Code Craft: The Practice of Writing Excellent Code
(No Starch Press)

97 Things Every Programmer Should Know
(O'Reilly, contributed three chapters)

Beautiful Architecture
(O'Reilly, contributed one chapter)

Introduction

You care about code. You're passionate about programming. You're the kind of developer who likes to craft truly great software. And you've picked up this book because you want to do it *even better*. Good call.

This book will help you.

The aim is to do exactly what it says on the cover: help you become a better programmer. But what does that mean exactly?

Pretty early in any programmer's career comes the realisation that there's more to being a great coder than a simple understanding of syntax and a mastery of basic design. The awesome programmers, those productive people who craft beautiful code and work effectively with other people, know far more. There are methods of working, attitudes, approaches, idioms, and techniques you learn over time that increase your effectiveness. There are useful social skills, and a whole pile of tribal knowledge to pick up.

And, of course, you need to learn syntax and design.

That is exactly what this book is about. It's a catalogue of useful techniques and approaches to the art and craft of programming that will help you become better.

I won't pretend that this is an exhaustive treatise. The field is vast. There's always more to learn, with new ground being claimed every day. These chapters are simply the fruit of more than 15 years of my work as a professional programmer. I've seen enough code, and made enough mistakes. I won't claim I'm an expert; I'm just well seasoned. If you can learn from the mistakes I've made and garner inspiration from what I've experienced, then you'll gain a leg up in your own development career.

What's Covered?

The topics covered in this book run the whole gamut of the software developer's life:

- Code-level concerns that affect how you write individual lines of code, as well as how you design your software modules.
- Practical techniques that will help you work better.
- Illustrations of effective attitudes and approaches to adopt that will help you become both super effective and well grounded.
- Procedural and organisational tricks and tips that will help you flourish whilst you are incarcerated in the software factory.

There's no particular language or industry bias here.

Who Should Read This?

You!

Whether you're an industry expert, a seasoned developer, a neophyte professional, or a hobbyist coder—this book will serve you.

Becoming a Better Programmer aims to help programmers at any level improve. That's a grand claim, but there's always something we can learn, and always room for improvement, no matter how experienced a programmer you are. Each chapter provides the opportunity to review your skills and work out practical ways to improve.

The only prerequisite for making use of this book is that you must *want* to become a better programmer.

The Structure

The information in this book is presented in a series of simple, self-contained chapters, each covering a single topic. If you're a traditionalist, you can read them in order from front to back. But feel free to read chapters in any order you want. Go straight to what seems most pertinent to you, if that makes you most happy.

The chapters are presented in five parts:

you.write(code);
> We start right at the bottom, at the codeface, where programmers feel most comfortable. This section reveals important code-writing techniques, and shows ways to write the best code possible. It covers code writing, code reading, code design, and mechanisms to write robust code.

Practice Makes Perfect
> Stepping back from the codeface, this part covers the important programming *practices* that help make you a better programmer. We'll see healthy attitudes and

approaches to the coding task, and sound techniques that will help you craft better code.

Getting Personal

These chapters dig deep to build excellence into your personal programming life. We'll look at how to learn effectively, consider behaving ethically, find stimulating challenges, avoid stagnation, as well as improve physical well-being.

Getting Things Done

These chapters talk about practical ways to *get things done:* to deliver code on time without getting sidetracked or delayed.

The People Pursuit

Software development is a social activity. These chapters show how to work well with the other inhabitants of the software factory.

More important than the order you consume these chapters is how you approach the material. In order to actually improve, you have to apply what you read practically. The structure of each chapter is designed to help you with this.

In each chapter, the topic at hand is unpacked in flowing prose with stark clarity. You'll laugh; you'll cry; you'll wonder why. The conclusion of each chapter includes the following subsections:

Questions

A series of questions for you to consider, and to answer. *Do not* skip these! They do not ask you to regurgitate the information you've just read. They are there to make you think deeper, beyond the original material, and to work out how the topic weaves into your existing experience.

See also

Links to any related chapters in the book, with an explanation of how the chapters fit together.

Try this...

Finally, each chapter is rounded off with a simple challenge. This is a specific task that will help you improve and apply the topic to your coding regimen.

Throughout each chapter, there are particularly important *key points*. They are highlighted so you don't miss them.

> KEY ➤ This is a key point. Take heed.

As you work through each chapter, please do spend time considering the questions and the *Try this...* challenges. Don't gloss over them. They're an important part of *Becoming a Better Programmer*. If you just flick through the information in each chapter, then it will be just that: information. Hopefully interesting. No doubt informative. But unlikely to make you a much better programmer.

You need to be challenged, and absorb what you read to your programming skillset. These closing exercises won't take you too long. Honestly. And they will really help cement each chapter's theme in your mind.

A Note for Mentors

This book has been designed to work as a valuable tool for mentoring fellow programmers. You can use it one-on-one or in a study group.

The best approach to this material is *not* to methodically work through each section together. Instead, read a chapter separately, and then get together to discuss the contents. The questions really work as a springboard for discussion, so it's a good idea to start there.

Safari® Books Online

Safari Books Online is an on-demand digital library that delivers expert content in both book and video form from the world's leading authors in technology and business.

Technology professionals, software developers, web designers, and business and creative professionals use Safari Books Online as their primary resource for research, problem solving, learning, and certification training.

Safari Books Online offers a range of product mixes and pricing programs for organizations, government agencies, and individuals. Subscribers have access to thousands of books, training videos, and prepublication manuscripts in one fully searchable database from publishers like O'Reilly Media, Prentice Hall Professional, Addison-Wesley Professional, Microsoft Press, Sams, Que, Peachpit Press, Focal Press, Cisco Press, John Wiley & Sons, Syngress, Morgan Kaufmann, IBM Redbooks, Packt, Adobe Press, FT Press, Apress, Manning, New Riders, McGraw-Hill, Jones & Bartlett, Course Technology, and dozens more. For more information about Safari Books Online, please visit us online.

How to Contact Us

Please address comments and questions concerning this book to the publisher:

O'Reilly Media, Inc.
1005 Gravenstein Highway North
Sebastopol, CA 95472

800-998-9938 (in the United States or Canada)
707-829-0515 (international or local)
707-829-0104 (fax)

We have a web page for this book, where we list errata, examples, and any additional information. You can access this page at *http://bit.ly/becoming_a_better_programmer*.

To comment or ask technical questions about this book, send email to *bookques tions@oreilly.com*.

For more information about our books, courses, conferences, and news, see our website at *http://www.oreilly.com*.

Find us on Facebook: *http://facebook.com/oreilly*

Follow us on Twitter: *http://twitter.com/oreillymedia*

Watch us on YouTube: *http://www.youtube.com/oreillymedia*

Acknowledgments

Writing a book is a surprisingly large undertaking: one that tends to take over your life and suck other people into the maelstrom on the way. There are many people who have in some way contributed to the state of this book, from the very early drafts of this material right through until it became the complete tome that rests on your (potentially digital) bookshelf.

My wonderful wife, Bryony, has patiently supported (and put up with) me whilst my finger has been in this pie, alongside the many other pies my other fingers find. I love you, and I appreciate you very much. Alice and Amelia have provided many welcome distractions; you make life fun!

Some parts of this book originated in articles I wrote over the last few years. Steve Love, the esteemed editor of ACCU's *C Vu* magazine, has contributed valuable feedback on many of these, and his encouragement and sage opinion has always been appreciated. (If you don't know about ACCU (*http://www.accu.org*), it is an awesome organisation for programmers who care about code.)

Many friends and colleagues have contributed valuable inspiration, feedback, and critique. These include my Akai family: Dave English, Will Augar, Łukasz Kozakiewicz, and Geoff Smith. Lisa Crispin and Jon Moore provided insight from the QA perspective, Greg Law taught me facts about bugs, whilst Seb Rose and Chris Oldwood offered much-appreciated and timely reviews.

The technical reviewers—Kevlin Henney, Richard Warburton, and Jim Brikman—provided much valuable feedback and helped shape the text you're reading. I am grateful for their expert input.

The excellent O'Reilly team of editors and production geniuses have worked hard on this book, and I'm grateful for their skillful attention. In particular, Mike Loukides and Brian MacDonald's early formative work helped shape the material considerably.

Lorna Ridley drew a chicken, single-handedly preventing this book from being fowl.

CHAPTER 1

Care About the Code

From caring comes courage.

— Lao Tzu

It doesn't take Sherlock Holmes to work out that good programmers write good code. Bad programmers... don't. They produce elephantine monstrosities that the rest of us have to clean up. You want to write the good stuff, right? You want to be a good programmer.

Good code doesn't pop out of thin air. It isn't something that happens by luck when the planets align. To get good code you have to work at it. Hard. And you'll only get good code if you actually *care* about good code.

> KEY ➤ To write good code, you have to *care* about it. To become a better programmer you must invest time and effort.

Good programming is not born from mere technical competence. I've seen highly intellectual programmers who can produce intense and impressive algorithms, who know their language standard by heart, but who write the most awful code. It's painful to read, painful to use, and painful to modify. I've seen more humble programmers who stick to very simple code, but who write elegant and expressive programs that are a joy to work with.

Based on my years of experience in the software factory, I've concluded that the real difference between mediocre programmers and great programmers is this: *attitude*. Good programming lies in taking a professional approach, and *wanting* to write the best software you can, within the real-world constraints and pressures of the software factory.

The code to hell is paved with good intentions. To be an excellent programmer you have to rise above good intentions and actually *care* about the code—foster positive perspectives and develop healthy attitudes. Great code is carefully crafted by master artisans, not thoughtlessly hacked out by sloppy programmers or erected mysteriously by self-professed coding gurus.

You want to write good code. You want to be a good programmer. So, you care about the code. This means you act accordingly; for example:

- In any coding situation, you refuse to hack something that only *seems* to work. You strive to craft elegant code that is clearly correct (and has good tests to show that it is correct).

- You write code that *reveals intent* (that other programmers can easily pick up and understand), that is *maintainable* (that you, or other programmers, will be able to easily modify in the future), and that is *correct* (you take all steps possible to determine that you *have* solved the problem, not just made it look like the program works).

- You work well alongside other programmers. No programmer is an island. Few programmers work alone; most work in a team of programmers, either in a company environment or on an open source project. You consider other programmers, and construct code that others can read. You want the team to write the best software possible, rather than to make yourself look clever.

- Any time you touch a piece of code, you strive to leave it better than you found it (better structured, better tested, and more understandable…).

- You care about code and about programming, so you are constantly learning new languages, idioms, and techniques. But you only apply them when appropriate.

Fortunately, you're reading this book because you *do* care about code. It interests you. It's your passion. You like doing it well. Read on, and we'll see how to turn this code concern into practical action.

As you do this, never forget to have fun programming. Enjoy cutting code to solve tricky problems. Produce software that makes you proud.

> KEY ➤ There is nothing wrong with an emotional response to code. Being proud of your great work, or disgusted at bad code, is healthy.

Questions

1. Do you *care* about code? How does this manifest in the work you produce?

2. Do you want to improve as a programmer? What areas do you think you need to work on the most?

3. If you don't care about code, why are you reading this book?!

4. How accurate is the statement *Good programmers write good code. Bad programmers... don't*? Is it possible for good programmers to write bad code? How?

See also

- *Software Development Is...* What *is* this thing we care about?
- *Speak Up!* We care about working with good code. We should also care about working with good *people*.

Try this....

Commit now to improving your programming skills. Resolve to engage with what you read in this book, answer the questions, and attempt all of the *Try this...* challenges.

PART I

you.write(code);

This first part deals with life on the front lines: our daily battle with code.

We'll look at low-level details that programmers revel in: how to write individual lines of code, how to improve sections of code, and how to plan a route into existing code. We'll also spend some time preparing for the unexpected: handling errors, writing robust code, and the black art of tracking down bugs. Finally, we look at the bigger picture: considering the design aspects of our software systems and investigating the technical and practical consequences of those designs.

CHAPTER 2

Keeping Up Appearances

Appearances are deceptive.

— Aesop

No one likes working with messy code. No one wants to wallow in a mire of jagged, inconsistent formatting, or battle with gibberish names. It's not fun. It's not productive. It's the programmer's purgatory.

We care about good code. And so we naturally care about code aesthetics; it is the most immediate determinant of how easy a section of code will be to work with. Practically every book about programming has a chapter on presentation. Oh look, this one does, too. Go figure.

Sadly, programmers care so much about code presentation that they end up bickering about it. This is the stuff that holy wars are made of. That, and which editor is best.[1] Tabs *versus* spaces. Brace positioning. Columns per line. Capitalisation. I've got my preferences. You have yours.

Godwin's law states that as any discussion on the Internet grows longer, the probability of a comparison to the Nazis or Hitler approaches one. *Goodliffe's law* (unveiled here) states that as any discussion about code layout grows, the probability of it descending into a fruitless argument approaches one.

Good programmers care deeply about good code presentation. But they rise above this kind of petty squabble. Let's act like grown-ups.

> KEY ➤ Stop fighting over code layout. Adopt a healthy attitude to your code presentation.

---

1. Vim is. That is all.

Our myopic focus on layout is most clearly illustrated by the classic dysfunctional code review. When given a section of code, the tendency is to pick myriad holes in the presentation. (Especially if you only give it a cursory skim-read, then layout is all you'll pick up on.) You feel like you've made many useful comments. The design flaws will be completely overlooked because the position of a bracket is wrong. Indeed, it seems that the larger the code review, and the faster it's done, the more likely this blindness will strike.

Presentation Is Powerful

We can't pretend that code formatting is unimportant. But understand why it matters. A good code format is *not* the one you think looks prettiest. We do not lay out code in order to exercise our deep artistic leanings. (Can you hear the code-art critics? *Daaaah-ling, look at the wonderful Pre-Raphaelite framing on that nested switch statement. Or: you have to appreciate the poignant subtext of this method.* I think not.)

Good code is clear. It is consistent. The layout is almost invisible. Good presentation does not draw attention or distract; it serves only to reveal the code's intent. This helps programmers work with the code effectively. It reduces the effort required to maintain the code.

> KEY ➤ Good code presentation reveals your code's intent. It is not an artistic endeavour.

Good presentation techniques are important, not for beauty's sake, but to *avoid mistakes* in your code. As an example, consider the following C snippet:

```
bool ok = thisCouldGoWrong();
if (!ok)
    fprintf(stderr, "Error: exiting...\n");
    exit(0);
```

You can see what the author intended here: `exit(0)` was only to be called when the test failed. But the presentation has hidden the real behaviour: the code will always `exit`. The layout choices have made the code a liability.[2]

Names have a similarly profound effect. Bad naming can be more than just distracting, it can be downright dangerous. Which of these is the bad name?

```
bool numberOfGreenWidgets;
string name;
void turnGreen();
```

---

2. This is not just an academic example to fill books! Serious real-life bugs stem from these kinds of mistakes. Apple's infamous 2014 *goto fail* security vulnerability in its SSL/TLS implementation was caused by exactly this kind of layout error.

The `numberOfGreenWidgets` is a variable, right? Clearly a counter is not represented by a boolean type. No; it's a trick question. They're all bad. The string does not actually hold a name, but the name of a colour; it is set by the `turnGreen()` function. So that variable name is misleading. And `turnGreen` was implemented thus:

```
void turnGreen()
{
    name = "yellow";
}
```

The names are all lies!

Is this a contrived example? Perhaps; but after a little careless maintenance, code can quickly end up in this state. What happens when you work with code like this? Bugs. Many, many bugs.

> KEY ➤ We need good presentation to avoid making code errors. Not so we can create pretty ASCII art.

Encountering inconsistent layout and hodgepodge naming is a sure sign that code quality is not high. If the authors haven't looked after the layout, then they've probably taken no care over other vital quality issues (like good design, thorough testing, etc.).

It's About Communication

We write code for two audiences. First: for the compiler (or the language runtime). This beast is perfectly happy to read any old code slop and will turn it into an executable program the only way it knows how. It will impassionately do this without passing judgment on the quality of what you've fed it, nor on the style it was presented in. This is more a conversion exercise than any kind of code "reading."

The other, more important, audience is *other programmers*. We write code to be executed by a computer, but to be *read* by humans. This means:

- You right now, as you're writing it. The code has to be crystal clear so you don't make implementation mistakes.
- You, a few weeks (or months) later as you prepare the software for release.
- The other people on your team who have to integrate their work with this code.
- The maintenance programmer (which could be you or another programmer) years later, when investigating a bug in an old release.

Code that is hard to read is hard to work with. This is why we strive for clear, sympathetic, supporting presentation.

> KEY ➤ Remember who you're writing code for: other people.

We've already seen that code can look pretty but obscure its intent. It can also look pretty, but be unreasonably hard to maintain. A great example of this is the "comment box." Some programmers like to present banner comments in pretty ASCII-art boxes:

```
/*************************************************
 * This is a pretty comment.                     *
 * Note that there are asterisks on the          *
 * righthand side of the box. Wow; it looks neat. *
 * Hope I never have to fix this tiypo.          *
 *************************************************/
```

It's cute, but it's not easy to maintain. If you want to change the comment text, you'll have to manually rework the right-hand line of comment markers. Frankly, this is a sadistic presentation style, and the people who choose it do not value the time and sanity of their colleagues. (Or they hope to make it so crushingly tedious to edit their comments that no one dare adjust their prose.)

Layout

If any man wishes to write a clear style, let him first be clear in his thoughts.

— Johann von Goethe

Code layout concerns include indentation, use of whitespace around operators, capitalisation, brace placement (be it K&R style, Allman, Whitesmith, or the like), and the age-old tabs *versus* spaces indent debate. In each of these areas there are a number of layout decisions you can make, and each choice has good reasons to commend it. As long as your layout choices enhance the structure of your code and help to reveal the intent, then they're good.

A quick glance at your code should reveal the shape and structure. Rather than argue about brace positioning, there are more important layout considerations, which we'll explore in the following sections.

Structure Well

Write your code like you write prose.

Break it up into chapters, paragraphs, and sentences. Bind the like things together; separate the different things. Functions are akin to chapters. Within each chapter may be a few distinct but related parts of code. Break them up into paragraphs by inserting blank lines between them. Do not insert blank lines unless there is a natural "paragraph" break. This technique helps to emphasise flow and structure.

For example:

```
void exampleFunction(int param)
{
    // We group things related to input
```

```
        param = sanitiseParamValue(param);
        doSomethingWithParam(param);

        // In a separate "paragraph" comes other work
        updateInternalInvariants();
        notifyOthersOfChange();
    }
```

The order of code revelation is important. Consider the reader: put the most important information first, not last. Ensure APIs read in a sensible order. Put what a reader cares about at the top of your class definition. That is, all public information comes before private information. Creation of an object comes before use of an object.

This grouping might be expressed in a class declaration like this:

```
class Example
{
public:
    Example();                      // lifetime management first
    ~Example();

    void doMostImportantThing(); // this starts a new "paragraph"
    void doSomethingRelated();   // each line here is like a sentence

    void somethingDifferent();   // this is another paragraph
    void aRelatedThing();

private:
    int privateStuffComesLast;
};
```

Prefer to write shorter code blocks. Don't write one function with five "paragraphs." Consider splitting this up into five functions, each with a well-chosen name.

Consistency

Avoid being precious about layout styles. Pick one. Use it consistently. It is best to be idiomatic—use what fits best with your language. Follow the style of standard libraries.

Write code using the same layout conventions as the rest of your team. Don't use your own style because you think it's prettier or better. If there is no consistency on your project then consider adopting a *coding standard* or *style guide*. This does not need to be a lengthy, draconian document; just a few agreed upon layout princples to pull the team together will suffice. In this situation, coding standards must be agreed on mutually, not enforced.

If you're working in a file that doesn't follow the layout conventions of the rest of your project, follow the layout conventions in that file.

Ensure that the entire team's IDEs and source code editors are configured the same way. Get the tab stop size the same. Set the brace position and comment layout options identically. Make the line ending options match. This is particularly important on cross-platform projects where very different development environments are used simultaneously. If you aren't diligent in this, then the source code will naturally become fractured and inconsistent; you will breed bad code.

War Story: The Whitespace Wars

I joined a project where the programmers had paid no attention to presentation. The code was messy, inconsistent, and unpleasant. I petitioned to introduce a coding standard.

All developers agreed that this was a good idea, and were willing to agree on conventions for naming, layout, and directory hierarchy. This was a huge step forward. The code began to grower neater.

However, there was one point we simply couldn't reach consensus on. You guessed it: *tabs or spaces*. Almost everyone preferred four-space indents. One guy swore tabs were superior. He argued, complained, and refused to change his coding style. (He probably still argues about it to this very day.)

Because we'd made some significant improvements, and in the interest of avoiding unnecessarily divisive arguments, we let this issue slide. We all used spaces. He used tabs.

The result was that the code remained frustrating and hard to work with. Editing was surprisingly inconsistent; sometimes your cursor moved one space at a time, sometimes it leapt around. Some tools would display the code reasonably well if you set an appropriate tab stop. Other tools (including our version control viewer and our online code review system) could not be adjusted and displayed ragged, awful looking code.

Names

> When I use a word, Humpty Dumpty said, in a rather scornful tone,
> it means just what I choose it to mean—neither more nor less.
>
> — Lewis Carroll

We name many things: variables, functions and methods, types (e.g., enumerations, classes), namespaces, and packages. Equally important are larger things, like files, projects, and programs. Public APIs (e.g., library interfaces or web service APIs) are perhaps the most significant things we choose names for, as "released" public APIs are most often set in stone and particularly hard to change.

A name conveys the identity of an object; it describes the thing, indicates its behaviour and intended use. A misnamed variable can be *very* confusing. A good name is descriptive, correct, and idiomatic.

You can only name something when you know *exactly* what it is. If you can't describe it clearly, or don't know what it will be used for, you simply can't name it well.

Avoid Redundancy

When naming, avoid redundancy and exploit context. Consider:

```
class WidgetList {
    public int numberOfWidgets() { ... }
};
```

The *numberOfWidgets* method name is unnecessarily long, repeating the word *Widget*. This makes the code harder, and more tedious, to read. Because this method returns the size of the list, it can simply be called `size()`. There will be no confusion, as the context of the enclosing class clearly defines what *size* means in this case.

Avoid redundant words.

I once worked on a project with a class called `DataObject`. That was a masterpiece of baffling, redundant naming.

Be Clear

Favour clarity over brevity. Names don't need to be short to save you key presses—you'll *read* the variable name far more times than you'll type it. But there is, however, a case for single-letter variable names: as counter variables in short loops, they tend to read clearly. Again, context matters!

Names don't need to be cryptic. The poster child for this is Hungarian Notation. It's not useful.

Baroque acronyms or "amusing" plays on words are not helpful.

Be Idiomatic

Prefer idiomatic names. Employ the capitalisation conventions most often used in your language. These are powerful conventions that you should only break with good reason. For example:

- In C, macros are usually given uppercase names.
- Capitalised names often denote types (e.g., a class), where uncapitalised names are reserved for methods and variables. This can be such a univerally accepted idiom that breaking it will render your code confusing.

Be Accurate

Ensure that your names are accurate. Don't call a type `WidgetSet` if it behaves like an array of widgets. The inaccurate name may cause the reader to make invalid assumptions about the behaviour or characteristics of the type.

Making Yourself Presentable

We come across badly formatted code all the time. Be careful how you work with it.

If you must "tidy it up" never alter presentation at the same time as making functional changes. Check in the presention change to source control as a separate step. *Then* alter the code's behaviour. It's confusing to see commits mixing the two things. The layout changes might mask mistakes in the functionality.

> KEY ➤ Never alter presentation and behaviour at the same time. Make them separate version-controlled changes.

Don't feel you have to pick a layout style and stick with it faithfully for your entire life. Continually gather feedback from how layout choices affect how you work with code. Learn from the code you read. Adapt your presentation style as you gain experience.

Over my career, I have slowly migrated my coding style, moving ever towards a more consistent and easier to modify layout.

From time to time, every project considers running automated layout tools over the source tree, or adding them as a pre-commit hook. This is always worth investigating, and rarely worth using. Such layout tools tend to be (understandably) simplistic, and are never able to deal with the subtlties of code structure in the real world.

Conclusion

Stop fighting about code presentation. Favour a common convention in your project, even if it's not your personal preferred layout style.

But do have an informed opinion on what constitutes a good layout style, and why. Continually learn and gain more experience from reading other code.

Strive for conistency and clarity in your code layout.

Questions

1. Should you alter layout of legacy code to match the company coding standard? Or is it better to leave it in the author's original style? Why?

2. How valuable are code reformatting tools? How much does this depend on the language you're using?

3. Which is more important: good code presentation or good code design?

4. How consistent is your current project's code? How can you improve this?

5. Tabs or spaces? Why? Does it matter?

6. Is it important to follow a language's layout and naming conventions? Or is it useful to adopt a different "house style" so you can differentiate your application code from the standard library?

7. Does our use of colourful syntax-highlighting code editors mean that there is less requirement for certain presentation concerns because the colour helps to reveal code structure?

See also

- *Speak Up!* Writing and presenting code is all about communication. This chapter discusses how a programmer communicates, in both code and the written word, and in speech.

- *The Ghost of a Codebase Past* Discusses how your programming style develops over time. Code presentation style is likely something you'll adapt as you gain experience.

Try this....

Review your layout preferences. Are they idiomatic, low ceremony, clear, and consistent? How can you improve them? Do you disagree with teammates about presentation? How can these differences be resolved?

10,000 MONKEYS

(OR THEREABOUTS)

NAMING
AND SHAMING

TRY THESE GREAT NAMING IDEAS

PALINDROMIC LOOP COUNTERS

BECAUSE LOOPING IS JUST ONE
THING AFTER ANOTHER

```
for (a : 0..10)
    for (ana : a..an[a])
        an[a*ana] = an[a]*ana;
```

ACROSTIC CODE

THE FIRST LETTER OF EACH LINE
SPELLS OUT A MESSAGE

```
namespace {
    enum fruit {a,b};
    volatile fruit juice;
    extern bool orange(fruit);
    run();
}

do {
  orange(juice); } while (1);

template <typename S> class
Henry {
    int i = 0;
    S s;
};
```

CHAPTER 3

Write Less Code!

A well-used minimum suffices for everything.

— Jules Verne
Around the World in Eighty Days

It's sad, but it's true: in our modern world there's just too much code.

I can cope with the fact that my car engine is controlled by a computer. There's obviously software cooking the food in my microwave. And it wouldn't surprise me if my genetically modified cucumbers had an embedded microcontroller in them. That's all fine; it's not what I'm obsessing about. I'm worried about all of the *unnecessary* code out there.

There's simply too much unnecessary code kicking around. Like weeds, these evil lines of code clog up our precious bytes of storage, obfuscate our revision control histories, stubbornly get in the way of our development, and use up precious code space, choking the good code around them.

Why is there so much unnecessary code?

Some people like the sound of their own voice. You've met them; you just can't shut them up. They're the kind of people you don't want to get stuck with at parties. *Yada yada yada.* Other people like their own code too much. They like it so much they write reams of it: `{ yada->yada.yada(); }`.

Or perhaps they're the programmers with misguided managers who judge progress by how many thousands of lines of code have been written a day.

Writing lots of code does *not* mean that you've written lots of software. Indeed, some code can actually negatively affect the amount of software you have—it gets in the way, causes faults, and reduces the quality of the user experience. The programming equivalent of antimatter.

> KEY ➤ Less code *can* mean more software.

Some of my best software improvement work has been by removing code. I fondly remember one time when I lopped thousands of lines of code out of a sprawling system, and replaced it with a mere 10 lines of code. What a wonderfully smug feeling of satisfaction. I suggest you try it some time.

Why Should We Care?

So why is this phenomenon *bad*, rather than merely annoying?

There are many reasons why unnecessary code is the root of all evil. Here are a few bullet points:

- Writing a fresh line of code is the birth of a little life form. It will need to be lovingly nurtured into a useful and profitable member of software society before you can release a product using it.

  Over the life of your software system, that line of code needs maintenance. Each line of code costs a little. The more code you write, the higher the cost. The longer a line of code lives, the higher its cost. Clearly, unnecessary code needs to meet a timely demise before it bankrupts us.

- More code means there is more to read and more to understand—it makes our programs harder to comprehend. Unnecessary code can mask the purpose of a function, or hide small but important differences in otherwise similar code.

- The more code there is, the more work is required to make modifications—the program is harder to modify.

- Code harbours bugs. The more code you have, the more places there are for bugs to hide.

- Duplicated code is particularly pernicious; you can fix a bug in one copy of the code and, unbeknown to you, still have another 32 identical little bugs kicking around elsewhere.

Unnecessary code is nefarious. It comes in many guises: unused components, dead code, pointless comments, unnecessary verbosity, and so on. Let's look at some of these in detail.

Flappy Logic

A simple and common class of pointless code is the unnecessary use of conditional statements and tautological logic constructs. Flappy logic is the sign of a flappy mind. Or, at least, of a poor understanding of logic constructs. For example:

```
if (expression)
    return true;
```

```
else
    return false;
```

can more simply, and directly, be written:

```
return expression;
```

This is not only more compact, it is easier to read, and therefore easier to understand. It looks more like an English sentence, which greatly aids human readers. And do you know what? The compiler doesn't mind one bit.

Similarly, the verbose expression:

```
if (something == true)
{
    // ...
}
```

would read much better as:

```
if (something)
```

Now, these examples are clearly simplistic. In the wild we see much more elaborate constructs created; never underestimate the ability of a programmer to complicate the simple. Real-world code is riddled with things like this:

```
bool should_we_pick_bananas()
{
    if (gorilla_is_hungry())
    {
        if (bananas_are_ripe())
        {
            return true;
        }
        else
        {
            return false;
        }
    }
    else
    {
        return false;
    }
}
```

which reduces neatly to the one-liner:

```
return gorilla_is_hungry() && bananas_are_ripe();
```

Cut through the waffle and say things clearly, but succinctly. Don't feel ashamed to know how your language works. It's not dirty, and you won't grow hairy palms. Knowing, and exploiting, the order in which expressions are evaluated saves a lot of unnecessary logic in conditional expressions. For example:

```
if ( a
    || (!a && b) )
{
    // what a complicated expression!
}
```

can simply be written:

```
if (a || b)
{
    // isn't that better?
    // didn't hurt, did it?
}
```

> **KEY** ➤ Express code clearly and succinctly. Avoid unnecessarily long-
> winded statements.

Refactoring

The term *refactor* entered the programmer lexicon in the 1990s. It describes a particular kind of software modification, and was popularised by Martin Fowler's book, *Refactoring: Improving the Design of Existing Code*.[1]

The term, in my experience, is frequently misused.

It specifically describes a change made to the structure of existing code (i.e., its *factoring*) that *does not* change its exhibited behaviour. It's that last part that's often forgotten. A refactor is *only* a refactor if it is a transformation of the source code, preserving behaviour. An "improvement" that changes how the program reacts (no matter how subtly) is not a refactor; it's an improvement. A "tidy-up" that adjusts the UI is not a refactor; it's a tidy-up.

We refactor to increase the readability of the code, to improve the internal structure, to make the code more maintainable, and—most often—to prepare the code for some later functional enhancement.

There are catalogues of simple refactorings which can be applied in sequence to the code. Many language's IDEs provide automated support for these. Such transforms include: *Extract Class* and *Extract Method*, which break up functionality into better logic pieces, and *Rename Method* and *Pull Up/Pull Down*, which help move it to the right place.

Proper refactoring requires discipline and is greatly simplified by a good suite of unit tests that cover the code in question. These help to prove that any transformation has indeed preserved behaviour.

---

1. Martin Fowler, *Refactoring: Improving the Design of Existing Code* (Boston: Addison-Wesley, 1999).

Duplication

Unnecessary code duplication is evil. We mostly see this crime perpetrated through the application of *cut-and-paste* programming: when a lazy programmer chooses not to factor repeated code sections into a common function, but physically copies it from one place to another in their editor. Sloppy. The sin is compounded when the code is pasted with minor changes.

When you duplicate code, you hide the repeated structure, and you copy all of the existing bugs. Even if you repair one instance of the code, there will be a queue of identical bugs ready to bite you another day. Refactor duplicated code sections into a single function. If there are similar code sections with slight differences, capture the differences in one function with a configuration parameter.

> KEY ➤ Do not copy code sections. Factor them into a common function. Use parameters to express any differences.

This is commonly known as the *DRY* principle: *Don't Repeat Yourself!* We aim for "DRY" code, without unnecessary redundancy. However, be aware that factoring similar code into a shared function introduces tight coupling between those sections of code. They both now rely on a shared interface; if you change that interface, both sections of code must be adjusted. In many situations this is perfectly appropriate; however, it's not always a desirable outcome, and can cause more problems in the long run than the duplication—so DRY your code responsibly!

Not all code duplication is malicious or the fault of lazy programmers. Duplication can happen by accident too, by someone reinventing a wheel that they didn't know existed. Or it can happen by constructing a new function when a perfectly acceptable third-party library already exists. This is bad because the existent library is far more likely to be correct and debugged already. Using common libraries saves you effort, and shields you from a world of potential faults.

There are also microcode-level duplication patterns. For example:

```
if (foo) do something();
if (foo) do_something_else()
if (foo) do_more();
```

could all be neatly wrapped in a single `if` statement. Multiple loops can usually be reduced to a single loop. For example, the following code:

```
for (int a = 0; a < MAX; ++a)
{
    // do something
}
// make hot buttered toast
for (int a = 0; a < MAX; ++a)
{
```

```
        // do something else
    }
```

probably boils down to:

```
    for (int a = 0; a < MAX; ++a)
    {
        // do something
        // do something else
    }
    // make hot buttered toast
```

if the making of hot buttered toast doesn't depend on either loop. Not only is this simpler to read and understand, it's likely to perform better, too, because only one loop needs to be run. Also consider redundant duplicated conditionals:

```
    if (foo)
    {
        if (foo && some_other_reason)
        {
            // the 2nd check for foo was redundant
        }
    }
```

You probably wouldn't write that on purpose, but after a bit of maintenance work a lot of code ends up with sloppy structure like that.

> KEY ➤ If you spot duplication, remove it.

I was recently trying to debug a device driver that was structured with two main processing loops. Upon inspection, these loops were almost entirely identical, with some minor differences for the type of data they were processing. This fact was not immediately obvious because each loop was 300 lines (of very dense C code) long! It was tortuous and hard to follow. Each loop had seen a different set of bugfixes, and consequently the code was flaky and unpredictable. A little effort to factor the two loops into a single version halved the problem space immediately; I could then concentrate on one place to find and fix faults.

Dead Code

If you don't maintain it, your code can rot. And it can also die. *Dead code* is code that is never run, that can never be reached. That has no life. Tell your code to get a life, or get lost.

These examples both contain dead code sections that aren't immediately obvious if you quickly glance over them:

```
    if (size == 0)
    {
        // ... 20 lines of malarkey ...
```

```
    for (int n = 0; n < size; ++n)
    {
        // this code will never run
    }
    // ... 20 more lines of shenanigans ...
}
```

and

```
void loop(char *str)
{
    size_t length = strlen(str);
    if (length == 0) return;
    for (size_t n = 0; n < length; n++)
    {
        if (str[n] == '\0')
        {
            // this code will never run
        }
    }
    if (length) return;
    // neither will this code
}
```

Other manifestations of dead code include:

- Functions that are never called
- Variables that are written but never read
- Parameters passed to an internal method that are never used
- Enums, structs, classes, or interfaces that are never used

Comments

Sadly, the world is riddled with awful code comments. You can't turn around in an editor without tripping over a few of them. It doesn't help that many corporate coding standards are a pile of rot, mandating the inclusion of millions of brain-dead comments.

Good code does *not* need reams of comments to prop it up, or to explain how it works. Careful choice of variable, function, and class names, and good structure should make your code entirely clear. Duplicating all of that information in a set of comments is unnecessary redundancy. And like any other form of duplication, it is also dangerous; it's far too easy to change one without changing the other.

Stupid, redundant comments range from the classic example of byte wastage:

```
++i; // increment i
```

to more subtle examples, where an algorithm is described just above it in the code:

```
// loop over all items, and add them up
int total = 0;
for (int n = 0; n < MAX; n++)
{
    total += items[n];
}
```

Very few algorithms when expressed in code are complex enough to justify that level of exposition. (But some *are*—learn the difference!) If an algorithm does need commentary, it may be better supplied by factoring the logic into a new, well-named function.

> KEY ➤ Make sure that every comment adds value to the code. The code itself says *what* and *how*. A comment should explain *why*—but only if it's not already clear.

It's also common to enter a crufty codebase and see "old" code that has been surgically removed by commenting it out. Don't do this; it's the sign of someone who wasn't brave enough to perform the surgical extraction completely, or who didn't really understand what they were doing and thought that they might have to graft the code back in later. Remove code completely. You can always get it back afterwards from your source control system.

> KEY ➤ Do not remove code by commenting it out. It confuses the reader and gets in the way.

Don't write comments describing what the code *used* to do; it doesn't matter anymore. Don't put comments at the end of code blocks or scopes; the code structure makes that clear. And don't write gratuitous ASCII art.

Verbosity

A lot of code is needlessly chatty. At the simplest end of the verbosity spectrum (which ranges from infra-redundant to ultra-voluble) is code like this:

```
bool is_valid(const char *str)
{
    if (str)
        return strcmp(str, "VALID") == 0;
    else
        return false;
}
```

It is quite wordy, and so it's relatively hard to see what the intent is. It can easily be rewritten:

```
bool is_valid(const char *str)
{
    return str && strcmp(str, "VALID") == 0;
}
```

Don't be afraid of the ternary operator if your language provides one; it really helps to reduce code clutter. Replace this kind of monstrosity:

```
public String getPath(URL url) {
    if (url == null) {
        return null;
    }
    else {
        return url.getPath();
    }
}
```

with:

```
public String getPath(URL url) {
    return url == null ? null : url.getPath();
}
```

C-style declarations (where all variables are declared at the top of a block, and used much, much later on) are now officially passé (unless you're still forced to use officially defunct compiler technology). The world has moved on, and so should your code. Avoid writing this:

```
int a;
// ... 20 lines of C code ...
a = foo();
// what type was an "a" again?
```

Move variable declarations and definitions together, to reduce the effort required to understand the code, and reduce potential errors from uninitialised variables. In fact, sometimes these variables are pointless anyway. For example:

```
bool a;
int b;
a = fn1();
b = fn2();
if (a)
    foo(10, b);
else
    foo(5, b);
```

can easily become the less verbose (and, arguably clearer):

```
foo(fn1() ? 10 : 5, fn2());
```

Bad Design

Of course, unnecessary code is not just the product of low-level code mistakes or bad maintenance. It can be caused by higher-level design flaws.

Bad design may introduce many unnecessary communication paths between components—lots of extra data marshalling code for no apparent reason. The further data flows, the more likely it is to get corrupted en route.

Over time, code components become redundant, or can mutate from their original use to something quite different, leaving large sections of unused code. When this happens, don't be afraid to clear away all of the deadwood. Replace the old component with a simpler one that does all that is required.

Your design should consider whether off-the-shelf libraries already exist that solve your programming problems. Using these libraries will remove the need to write a whole load of unnecessary code. As a bonus, popular libraries will likely be robust, extensible, and well used.

Whitespace

Don't panic! I'm not going to attack whitespace (that is, spaces, tabs, and newlines). Whitespace is a good thing—do not be afraid to use it. Like a well-placed pause when reciting a poem, sensible use of whitespace helps to frame our code.

Use of whitespace is not usually misleading or unnecessary. But you can have too much of a good thing, and 20 newlines between functions probably is too much.

Consider, too, the use of parentheses to group logic constructs. Sometimes brackets help to clarify the logic even when they are not necessary to defeat operator precedence. Sometimes they are unnecessary and get in the way.

So What Do We Do?

To be fair, often such a buildup of code cruft isn't intentional. Few people set out to write deliberately laborious, duplicated, pointless code. (But there are some lazy programmers who continually take the low road rather than invest extra time to write great code.) Most frequently, we end up with these code problems as the legacy of code that has been maintained, extended, worked with, and debugged by many people over a large period of time.

So what do we do about it? We must take responsibility. Don't write unnecessary code, and when you work on "legacy" code, watch out for the warning signs. It's time to get militant. Reclaim our whitespace. Reduce the clutter. Spring clean. Redress the balance.

Pigs live in their own filth. Programmers needn't. Clean up after yourself. As you work on a piece of code, remove all of the unnecessary code that you encounter.

This is an example of how to follow Robert Martin's advice and honour "the Boy Scout Rule" in the coding world: Always leave the campground cleaner than you found it.[2]

> KEY ➤ Every day, leave your code a little better than it was. Remove redundancy and duplication as you find it.

But take heed of this simple rule: make "tidying up" changes separately from other functional changes. This will ensure that it's clear in your source control system what's happened. Gratuitous structural changes mixed in with functional modifications are hard to follow. And if there is a bug then it's harder to work out whether it was due to your new functionality, or because of the structural improvement.

Conclusion

Software functionality does not correlate with the number of lines of code, or to the number of components in a system. More lines of code do not necessarily mean more software.

So if you don't need it, don't write it. Write less code, and find something more fun to do instead.

Questions

1. Do you naturally write succinct logical expressions? Are your succinct expressions so terse as to be incomprehensible?

2. Does the C-language-family's *ternary operator* (e.g., `condition ? true_value : false_value`) make expressions more or less readable? Why?

3. We should avoid *cut-and-paste* coding. How different does a section of code have to be before it is justifiable to not factor into a common function?

4. How can you spot and remove dead code?

5. Some coding standards mandate that every function is documented with specially formatted code comments. Is this useful? Or is it an unnecessary burden introducing a load of worthless extra comments?

See also

- *Improve Code by Removing It* Describes techniques for identifying larger sections of redundant, dead code and removing it.

---

2. Robert C. Martin, *Clean Code: A Handbook of Agile Software Craftsmanship* (Upper Saddle River, NJ: Prentice Hall, 2008).

CHAPTER 4

Improve Code by Removing It

We ascribe beauty to that which is simple;
which has no superfluous parts; which exactly answers its end...

— Ralph Waldo Emerson

Less is more. It's a trite maxim, but sometimes it really is true.

Some of the most exciting improvements I remember making to code involved *removing* vast chunks of it. Let me tell you, it's a good feeling.

War Story: No Need for the Code

As an Agile software development team, we'd been following the hallowed eXtreme Programming tenets, including *YAGNI*. That is, *You Aren't Gonna Need It*: a caution to not write unnecessary code—even code you *think* is going to be needed in future versions. Don't write it now if you don't need it now. Wait until you do have a genuine need.

This sounds like eminently sensible advice. And we'd all bought in to it.

But human nature being what it is, we fell short in a few places. At one point, I observed that the product was taking too long to execute certain tasks—simple tasks that should have been near instantaneous. This was because they had been over-implemented, festooned with extra bells and whistles that were not required, and littered with hooks for later extension. None of these things were being used, but at the time they each had seemed sensible additions.

So I simplified the code, improved the product performance, and reduced the level of global code entropy by simply removing all of the offending "features" from the codebase. Helpfully, my unit tests told me that I hadn't broken anything else during the operation. A simple and thoroughly satisfying experience.

> KEY ➤ You can improve a system by adding new code. You can also improve a system by removing code.

Code Indulgence

So why did all that unnecessary code get written? Why did one programmer feel the need to write extra code, and how did it get past review or the pairing process?

It was almost certainly the programmers' indulging their own personal vices. Something like:

- It was a fun bit of extra code, and the programmer wanted to write it. *(Hint: Write code because it adds value, not because it amuses you, or you'd enjoy trying to write it.)*

- Someone thought it was a feature that would be needed in the future, so decided to code it now, whilst they thought about it. *(Hint: That isn't YAGNI. If you don't need it right now, don't write it right now.)*

- But it was only a small thing; not a massive "extra" feature. It was easier to just implement it now, rather than go back to the customer to see whether it was really required. *(Hint: It always takes longer to write and to maintain extra code. And the customer is actually quite approachable. A small extra bit of code snowballs over time to a large piece of work that needs maintenance.)*

- The programmer invented extra requirements that were not documented in the story that justified the extra feature. The requirement was actually bogus. *(Hint: Programmers do not set system requirements; the customer does.)*

Now, we had a well-understood lean development process, very good developers, and procedural checks in place to avoid this kind of thing. And unnecessary extra code still snuck in.

That's quite a surprise, isn't it?

It's Not Bad, It's Inevitable

Even if you can avoid adding unnecessary *new* features, dead pieces of code will still spring up naturally during your software development. Don't be embarrassed about it! They come from a number of unavoidable accidental sources, including:

- Features are removed from an application's user interface, but the backend support code is left in. It's never called again. Instant code necrosis. Often it's not removed "because we might need it in the future, and leaving it there isn't going to hurt anyone."

- Data types or classes that are no longer being used tend to stay put in the project. It's not easy to tell that you're removing the last reference to a class when working in a separate part of the project. You can also render *parts* of a class obsolete: for example, reworking methods so a member variable is no longer needed.

- Legacy product features are *rarely* removed. Even if your users no longer want them and will never use them again, removing product features never looks good. It would put a dent in the awesome list of tick-box features. So we incur perpetual product testing overhead for features that will never be used again.

- The maintenance of code over its lifetime causes sections of a function to not be executable. Loops may never iterate because code added above them negates an invariant, or conditional code blocks are never entered. The older a codebase gets, the more of this we see. C helpfully provides the preprocessor as a rich mechanism for writing non-executable spaghetti.

- Wizard-generated UI code inserts hooks that are frequently never used. If a developer accidentally double-clicks on a control, the wizard adds backend code, but the programmer never goes anywhere near the implementation. It's more work to remove these kinds of autogenerated code blocks than to simply ignore them and pretend that they don't exist.

- Many function return values are never used. We all know that it's morally reprehensible to ignore a function's error code, and we would *never* do that, would we? But many functions are written to *do something* and return a result that someone *might* find useful. Or might not. It's not an error code, just a small factoid. Why go through extra effort to calculate the return value, and write tests for it, if no one ever uses it?

- Much "debug" code is necrotic. A lot of support code is not needed once the initial implementation has been completed. It is unsightly scaffolding that hides the beautiful architecture underneath. It's not unusual to see reams of inactive diagnostic printouts and invariant checks, testing hook points, and the like, that will never be used again. They clutter up the code and make maintenance harder.

So What?

Does this really matter? Surely we should just accept that dead code is inevitable, and not worry about it too much if the project still works. What's the cost of unnecessary code?

- It is undeniable that unnecessary code, like any other code, requires maintenance over time. It costs time and money.

- Extra code also makes it harder to learn the project, and requires extra understanding and navigating.

- Classes with one million methods that may, or may not, be used are impenetrable and only encourage sloppy use rather than careful programming.
- Even if you buy the fastest machine money can buy, and the best compiler toolchain, dead code will slow down your builds, making you less productive.
- It is harder to refactor, simplify, or optimise your program when it is bogged down by zombie code.

Dead code won't kill you, but it will make your life harder than it needs to be.

> KEY ▶ Remove dead code wherever possible. It gets in the way and slows you down.

Waking the Dead

How can you find dead code?

The best approach is to pay attention whilst working in the codebase. Be responsible for your actions, and ensure that you always clean up after your work. Regular code reviews do help to highlight dead code.

If you're serious about rooting out unused code sections, there are some great code coverage tools that will show you exactly where the problems are.[1] Good IDEs, especially when used with statically typed languages, can automatically highlight unused code. For public APIs, many IDEs have a "find references" feature that can show whether a function is ever called.

To identify dead features, you can instrument your product and gather metrics on what customers actually use. This is useful for making all sorts of business decisions, rather than just identifying unused code.

Surgical Extraction

There is no harm in removing dead code. Amputate it. It's not like you're throwing it away. Whenever you realise that you need an old feature again, it can easily be fetched from your version control system.

> KEY ▶ It is safe to remove code that you *might* need in the future. You can always get it back from version control.

There is a counter argument to that simple (and true) view, though: how will a new recruit know that the removed code is available in version control if they don't know

---

1. You might even already have them—look at the warning options provided by your compiler.

that it existed in the first place? What's going to stop them writing their own (buggy or incomplete) version instead? This is a valid concern. But similarly, what would stop them rewriting their own version if they simply didn't notice the code fragment was already located elsewhere?

As in previous chapters, remember to remove dead code as a single step; do not conflate it in a version control check-in that also adds functionality. Always separate your "spring cleaning" work from other development tasks. This makes the version history clearer, and also makes revivifying removed code a breeze.

> KEY ➤ Code cleanup should always be made in separate commits to functional changes.

Conclusion

Dead code happens in even the best codebases. The larger the project, the more dead code you'll have. It's not a sign of failure. But not doing something about it when you find dead code *is* a sign of failure. When you discover code that is not being used, or find a code path that cannot be executed, remove that unnecessary code.

When writing a new piece of code, don't creep the specification. Don't add "minor" features that you think are interesting, but no one has asked for. They'll be easy enough to add later, if they are required. Even if it *seems* like a good idea. Don't do it.

Questions

1. How can you identify "dead code" that is not run in your program?
2. If you temporarily remove code that is not currently required (but may be needed in the future) should you leave it commented out (so it is still visible) in the source tree, or just delete it completely (as it will be stored in the revision history)? Why?
3. Is the removal of legacy (unused) features always the right thing to do? Is there any inherent risk in removing sections of code? How can you determine the right time to remove unused features?
4. What percentage of your current project's codebase do you think is unnecessary? Does your team have a culture of adding things they *like* or that they *think* will be useful?

See also

- *Write Less Code!* Talks about removing duplication at the micro level: whittling away unncessary lines of code.
- *Wallowing in Filth* How to navigate a route into problematic code so you can spot what needs to be removed.
- *Coping with Complexity* Removing dead code reduces complexity in your software.

- *Effective Version Control* Removing dead code does not mean it's lost forever. You can retrieve it from version control if you make a mistake.

> Try this....
>
> Look for dead and unnecessary code in the files you are working in. Remove it!

10,000 MONKEYS
(OR THEREABOUTS)

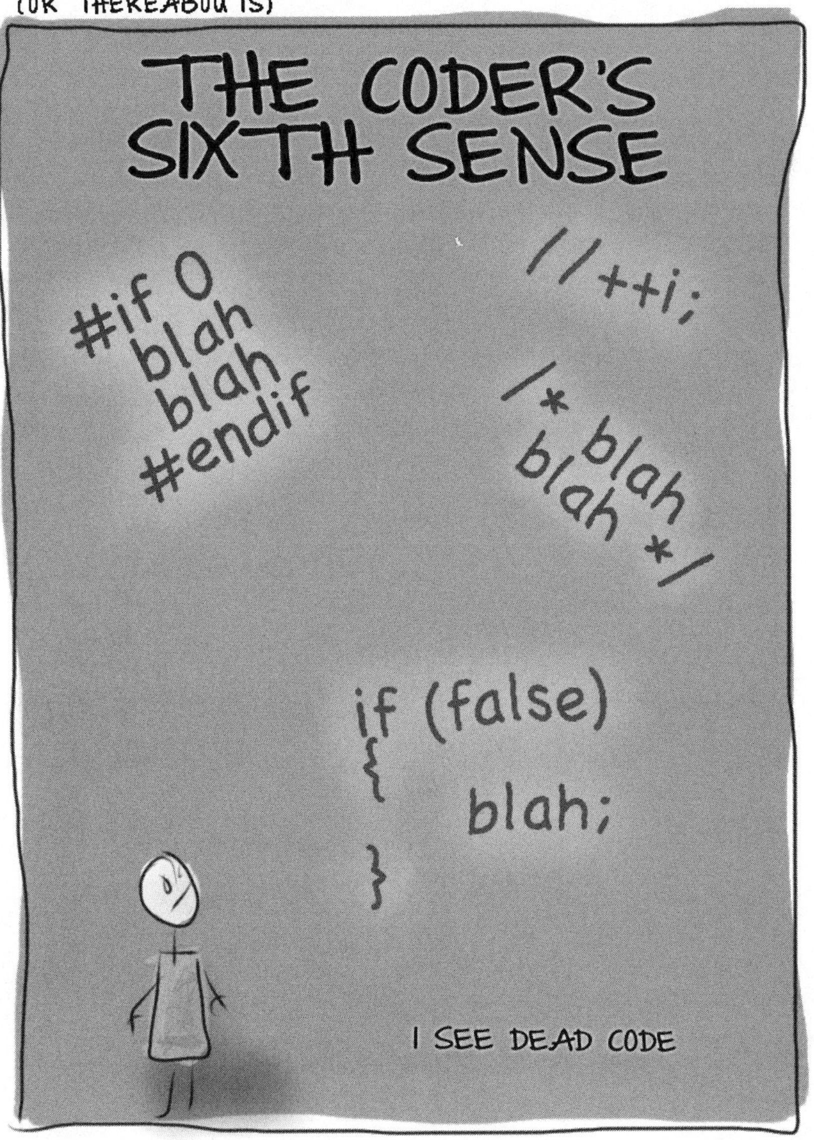

CHAPTER 5

The Ghost of a Codebase Past

I will live in the Past, the Present, and the Future.
The Spirits of all Three shall strive within me.
I will not shut out the lessons that they teach!

— Charles Dickens
A Christmas Carol

Nostalgia isn't what it used to be. And neither is your old code. Who knows what functional gremlins and typographical demons lurk in your ancient handiwork? You thought it was perfect when you wrote it—but cast a critical eye over your old code and you'll inevitably bring to light all manner of code gotchas.

Programmers, as a breed, strive to move onwards. We love to learn new and exciting techniques, to face fresh challenges, and to solve more interesting problems. It's natural. Considering the rapid turnover in the job market, and the average duration of programming contracts, it's hardly surprising that very few software developers stick with the same codebase for a prolonged period of time.

But what does this do to the code we produce? What kind of attitude does it foster in our work? I maintain that exceptional programmers are determined more by their attitude to the code they write and the way they write it, than by the actual code itself.

The average programmer tends not to maintain *their own* code for too long. Rather than roll around in our own filth, we move on to new pastures and roll around in *someone else's* filth. Nice. We even tend to let our own "pet projects" fall by the wayside as our interests evolve.

Of course, it's fun to complain about other people's poor code, but we easily forget how bad our own work was. And you'd never *intentionally* write bad code, would you?

Revisiting your old code can be an enlightening experience. It's like visiting an ageing, distant relative you don't see very often. You soon discover that you don't know them as well as you think. You've forgotten things about them, about their funny quirks and irritating ways. And you're surprised at how they've changed since you last saw them (perhaps, for the worst).

> KEY ▶ Looking back at your older code will inform you about the improvement (or otherwise) in your coding skills.

Looking back at old code you've produced, you might shudder for a number of reasons.

Presentation

Many languages permit artistic interpretation in the indentation layout of code. Even though some languages have a de facto presentation style, there is still a large gamut of layout issues which you may find yourself exploring over time. Which ones stick depends on the conventions of your current project, or on your experiences after years of experimentation.

Different tribes of C++ programmers, for example, follow different presentation schemes. Some developers follow the standard library scheme:

```
struct standard_style_cpp
{
    int variable_name;
    bool method_name();
};
```

Some have more Java-esque leanings:

```
struct JavaStyleCpp
{
    int variableName;
    bool methodName();
};
```

And some follow a C# model:

```
struct CSharpStyleCpp
{
    int variableName;
    bool MethodName();
};
```

A simple difference, but it profoundly affects your code in several ways.

Another C++ example is the layout of member initialiser lists. One of my teams moved from this traditional scheme:

```
Foo::Foo(int param)
: member_one(1),
  member_two(param),
  member_three(42)
{
}
```

to a style that places the comma separators at the beginning of the following line, thus:

```
Foo::Foo(int param)
: member_one(1)
, member_two(param)
, member_three(42)
{
}
```

We found a number of advantages with the latter style (it's easier to "knock out" parts in the middle via preprocessor macros or comments, for example). This prefix-comma scheme can be employed in a number of layout situations (e.g., many kinds of lists: members, enumerations, base classes, and more), providing a nice consistent shape. There are also disadvantages, one of the major cited issues being that it's not as "common" as the former layout style. IDEs' default auto-layout also tends to fight with it.

I know over the years that my own presentation style has changed wildly, depending on the company I'm working for at the time.

As long as a style is employed consistently in your codebase, this is really a trivial concern and nothing to be embarrassed about. Individual coding styles rarely make much of a difference once you get used to them, but inconsistent coding styles in one project make everyone slower.

The State of the Art

Most languages have rapidly developed their in-built libraries. Over the years, the Java libraries have grown from a few hundred helpful classes to a veritable plethora of classes, with different skews of the library depending on the Java deployment target. Over C#'s revisions, its standard library has also burgeoned. As languages grow, their libraries accrete more features.

And as those libraries grow, some of the older parts become deprecated.

Such evolution (which is especially rapid early in a language's life) can unfortunately render your code anachronistic. Anyone reading your code for the first time might presume that you didn't understand the newer language or library features, when those features simply did not exist when the code was written.

For example, when C# added generics, the code you would have written like this:

```
ArrayList list = new ArrayList(); // untyped
list.Add("Foo");
list.Add(3); // oops!
```

with its inherent potential for bugs, would have become:

```
List<string> list = new List<string>();
list.Add("Foo");
list.Add(3); // compiler error - nice
```

There is a very similar Java example with surprisingly similar class names!

The state of the art moves much faster than your code. Especially your old, untended code.

Even the (relatively conservative) C++ library has grown considerably with each new revision. C++11 language features and library support have made much old C++ code look old-fashioned. The introduction of a language-supported threading model renders third-party thread libraries (often implemented with rather questionable APIs) redundant. The introduction of lambdas removes the need for a lot of verbose handwritten "trampoline" code. The range-based `for` helps remove a lot of syntactical trees so you can see the code-design wood. Once you start using these facilities, returning to older code without them feels like a retrograde step.

Idioms

Each language, with its unique set of language constructs and library facilities, has a particular "best practice" method of use. These are the *idioms* that experienced users adopt, the modes of use that have become honed and preferred over time.

These idioms are important. They are what experienced programmers expect to read; they are familiar shapes that enable you to focus on the overall code design rather than get bogged down in macro-level code concerns. They usually formalise patterns that avoid common mistakes or bugs.

It's perhaps most embarrassing to look back at old code, and see how un-idiomatic it is. If you now know more of the accepted idioms for the language you're working with, your old non-idiomatic code can look quite, quite wrong.

Many years ago, I worked with a team of C programmers moving (well, shuffling slowly) towards the (then) brave new world of C++. One of their initial additions to a new codebase was a max helper macro:

```
#define max(a,b) ((a)>(b)) ? (a) : (b))
// do you know why we have all those brackets?

void example()
{
    int a = 3, b = 10;
    int c = max(a, b);
}
```

In time, someone revisited that early code and, knowing more about C++, realised how bad it was. They rewrote it in the more idiomatic C++ shown here, which fixed some very subtle lurking bugs:

```
template <typename T>
inline T max(const T &a, const T &b)
```

```
{
    // Look mum! No brackets needed!
    return a > b ? a : b;
}

void better_example()
{
    int a = 3, b = 10;

    // this would have failed using the macro
    // because ++a would be evaluated twice
    int c = max(++a, b);
}
```

The original version also had another problem: wheel reinvention. The best solution is to just use the built-in `std::max` function that always existed. It's obvious in hindsight:

```
// don't declare any max function

void even_better_example()
{
    int a = 3, b = 10;
    int c = std::max(a,b);
}
```

This is the kind of thing you'd cringe about now, if you came back to it. But you had no idea about the right idiom back in the day.

That's a simple example, but as languages gain new features (e.g., lambdas) the kind of idiomatic code you'd write today may look very different from previous generations of the code.

Design Decisions

Did I *really* write that in Perl; what was I thinking?! Did I *really* use such a simplistic sorting algorithm? Did I *really* write all that code by hand, rather than just using a built-in library function? Did I *really* couple those classes together so unnecessarily? Could I *really* not have invented a cleaner API? Did I *really* leave resource management up to the client code? I can see many potential bugs and leaks lurking there!

As you learn more, you realise that there are better ways of formulating your design in code. This is the voice of experience. You make a few mistakes, read some different code, work with talented coders, and pretty soon find you have improved design skills.

Bugs

Perhaps this is the reason that drags you back to an old codebase. Sometimes coming back with fresh eyes uncovers obvious problems that you missed at the time. After you've been bitten by certain kinds of bugs (often those that the common idioms steer you away from) you naturally begin to see potential bugs in old code. It's the programmer's *sixth sense*.

Conclusion

> *No space of regret can make amends for one life's opportunity misused.*
>
> — Charles Dickens
> *A Christmas Carol*

Looking back over your old code is like a code review for yourself. It's a valuable exercise; perhaps you should take a quick tour through some of your old work. Do you like the way you used to program? How much have you learnt since then?

Does this kind of thing actually *matter*? If your old code isn't perfect, but it works, should you do anything about it? Should you go back and "adjust" the code? Probably not—*if it ain't broke don't fix it*. Code does not rot, unless the world changes around it. Your bits and bytes don't degrade, so the meaning will likely stay constant. Occasionally a compiler or language upgrade or a third-party library update might "break" your old code, or perhaps a code change elsewhere will invalidate a presumption you made. But normally, the code will soldier on faithfully, even if it's not perfect.

It's important to appreciate how times have changed, how the programming world has moved on, and how your personal skills have improved over time. Finding old code that no longer feels "right" is a good thing: it shows that you have learnt and improved. Perhaps you don't have the opportunity to revise it now, but knowing where you've come from helps to shape where you're going in your coding career.

Like the Ghost of Christmas Past, there are interesting cautionary lessons to be learnt from our old code if you take the time to look at it.

Questions

1. How does your old code shape up in the modern world? If it doesn't look too bad, does that mean that you haven't learnt anything new recently?

2. How long have you been working in your primary language? How many revisions of the language standard or built-in library have been introduced in that time? What language features have been introduced that have shaped the style of the code you write?

3. Consider some of the common idioms you now naturally employ. How do they help you avoid errors?

See also

- *Keeping Up Appearances* Contains more discussion of code layout.
- *Nothing Is Set in Stone* Code never stands still, nor does your understanding of it.

- *A Tale of Two Systems* An example of revisiting old code; learning from mistakes and appreciating successes.

Try this....

Take a quick tour through some of your old work. Do you like the way you used to program? How much have you learnt since then?

CHAPTER 6

Navigating a Route

...the Investigation of difficult Things by the Method of Analysis,
ought ever to precede the Method of Composition.

— Sir Isaac Newton

A new recruit joined my development team. Our project, whilst not vast, was relatively large and contained a number of different areas. There was a lot to learn before he could become effective. How could he plot a route into the code? From a standing start, how could he rapidly become productive?

It's a common situation; one which we all face from time to time. If you don't, then you need to see more code and move on to new projects more often. (It's important not to get stale from working on one codebase with one team forever.)

Coming into any large existing codebase is hard. You have to rapidly:

- Discover where to start looking at the code
- Work out what each section of the code does, and how it achieves it
- Gauge the quality of the code
- Work out how to navigate around the system
- Understand the coding idioms, so your changes will fit in sympathetically
- Find the likely location of any functionality (and the consequent bugs caused by it)
- Understand the relationship of the code to its important satellite parts (e.g., its tests and documentation)

You need to learn this quickly, as you don't want your first changes to be too embarrassing, accidentally duplicate existing work, or break something elsewhere.

A Little Help from My Friends

My new colleague had a wonderful head start in this learning process. He joined an office with people who already knew the code, who could answer innumerable small questions about it, and point out where existing functionality could be found. This kind of help is simply invaluable.

If you are able to work alongside someone already versed in the code, then exploit this. Don't be afraid to ask questions. If you can, take opportunities to pair program and/or to get your changes reviewed.

> KEY ➤ Your best route into code is to be led by someone who already knows the terrain. Don't be afraid to ask for help!

If you can't pester people nearby, don't fear; there may still be helpful people further afield. Look for online forums or mailing lists that contain helpful information and helpful people. There is often a healthy community that grows around popular open source projects.

The trick when asking for help is to always be polite, and to be grateful. Ask sensible, appropriate questions. "Can you do my homework for me?" is never going to get a good response. Always be prepared to help others out with information in return.

Employ common sense: make sure that you've Googled for an answer to your question first. It's simple politeness to not ask foolish questions that you could easily research yourself. You won't endear yourself to anyone if you continually ask basic questions and waste people's precious time. Like the boy who cried wolf and failed to get help when he really needed it, a series of mind-numbingly dumb questions will make you less likely to receive more complex help when you need it.

Look for Clues

If you are rooting in the murky depths of a software system without a personal guide, then you need to look for the clues that will orient you around the code.

These are good indicators:

Ease of getting the source
> How easy is it to obtain the source?
>
> Is it a single, simple checkout from version control that can be placed in any directory on your development machine? Or must you check out multiple separate parts, and install them in specific locations on your computer?
>
> Hardcoded file paths are evil. They prohibit you from easily building different verisons of the code.

> **KEY** ➤ Healthy projects require a single checkout to obtain the whole codebase, and the code can be placed in *any* directory on your build machine. Do not rely on multiple checkout steps, or code in hardcoded locations.

As well as availabilty of the source code itself, consider availability of *information about* the code's health. Is there a CI (*continuous integration*) build server that continually ensures that all parts of the code build successfully? Are there published results of any automated tests?

Ease of building the code

This can be very telling. If it's hard to build the code, it's often hard to work with it.

Does the build depend on unusual tools that you'll have to install? (How up-to-date are those tools?)

How easy is it to build the code from scratch? Is there adequate and simple documentation in the code itself? Does the code build straight out of source control, or do you first have to manually perform many small configuration tweaks before it will build?

Does one simple, single step build the entire system, or does it require many individual build steps? Does the build process require manual intervention?[1] Can you work on a small part of the code, and only build that section, or must you rebuild the whole project repeatedly to work on a small component?

> **KEY** ➤ A healthy build runs in one step, with no manual intervention during the build process.

How is a release build made? Is it the same process as the development builds, or do you have to follow a very different set of steps?

When the build runs, is it quiet? Or are there many, many warnings that may obscure more insidious problems?

Tests

Look for tests: unit tests, integration tests, end-to-end tests, and the like. Are there any? How much of the codebase is under test? Do the tests run automatically, or do they require an additional build step? How often are the tests run? How much coverage do they provide? Do they appear appropriate and well constructed, or are there just a few simple stubs to make it look like the code has test coverage?

There is an almost universal link here: code with a good suite of tests is usually also well factored, well thought out, and well designed. These tests act as a great route

---

1. A single, automatic build step means your build can be placed into a CI harness and run automatically.

into the code under test, helping you understand the code's interface and usage patterns. It's also a great place from which to start working on a bugfix (you can start by adding a simple, failing unit test—then fix that test, without breaking the others).

File structure

Look at the directory structure. Does it match the code shape? Does it clearly reveal the areas, subsystems, or layers of the code? Is it neat? Are third-party libraries neatly separated from the project code, or is it all messily intermingled?

Documentation

Look for the project documentation. Is there any? Is it well written? Is it up-to-date? Perhaps the documentation is written in the code itself using *NDoc, Javadoc, Doxygen*, or a similar system. How comprehensive and up-to-date does this documentation appear?

Static analysis

Run tools over the code to determine the health and to plot out the associations. There are some great source navigation tools available, and Doxygen can also produce very usable class diagrams and control flow diagrams.

Requirements

Are there any original project requirements documents or functional specifications? (In my experience, these often tend to bear little relation to the final product, but they are interesting historical documents nonetheless.) Is there a project wiki where common concepts are collected?

Project dependencies

Does the code use specific frameworks and third-party libraries? How much information do you need to know about them? You can't learn every aspect of all of them initially, especially because some libraries are huge (Boost, I'm looking at you). But it pays to get a feel for what facilities are provided for you, and where you can look for them.

Does the code make good use of the language's standard library? Or do many wheels get reinvented? Be wary of code with its own set of custom collection classes or homegrown thread primitives. System-supplied core code is more likely to be robust, well tested, and bug-free.

Code quality

Browse through the code to get a feel for the quality. Observe the amount and the quality of code comments. Is there much dead code—redundant code commented out but left to rot? Is the coding style consistent throughout?

It's hard to draw a conclusive opinion from a brief investigation like this, but you can quickly get a reasonable feel for a codebase from some basic reading.

Architecture

By now you should be able to get a reasonable feel for the shape and the modularisation of the system. Can you identify the main layers? Are the layers cleanly separated, or are they all rather interwoven? Is there a database layer? How sensible does it look? Can you see the schema? Is it sane? How does the app talk to the outside world? What is the GUI technology? The file I/O tech? The networking tech?

Ideally, the architecture of a system is a top-level concept that you learn before digging in too deeply. However, this is often not the case, and you *discover* the real architecture as you delve into the code.

> KEY ➤ Often the *real* architecture of a system differs from the *ideal* design. Always trust the code, not the documentation.

Perform *software archaeology* on any code that looks questionable. Drill back through version control logs and "svn blame" (or the equivalent) to see the origin and evolution of some of the messes. Try to get a feel for the number of people who worked on the code in the past. How many of them are still on the team?

Learn by Doing

A woman needs a man like a fish needs a bicycle.

— Irina Dunn

You can read as many books as you like about the theory of riding a bicycle. You can study bicycles, take them apart, reassemble them, investigate the physics and engineering behind them. But you may as well be learning to ride a fish. Until you get on a bicycle, put your feet on the pedals and try to ride it for real, you'll never advance. You'll learn more by falling off a few times than from days of reading about how to balance.

It's the same with code.

Reading code will only get you so far. You can only really learn a codebase by getting on it, by trying to ride it, by making mistakes and falling off. Don't let inactivity prevent you from moving on. Don't erect an intellectual barrier to prevent you from working on the code.

I've seen plenty of great programmers initially paralysed through their own lack of confidence in their understanding.

Stuff that. Jump in. Boldly. Modify the code.

> KEY ➤ The best way to learn code is to modify it. Then learn from your mistakes.

So what should you modify?

As you are learning the code, look for places where you can immediately make a benefit, but that will minimise the chances you'll break something (or write embarrassing code).

Aim for anything that will take you around the system.

Low-Hanging Fruit

Try some simple, small things, like tracking down a minor bug that has a very direct correlation to an event you can start hunting from (e.g., a GUI activity). Start with a small, repeatable, low-risk fault report, rather than a meaty intermittent nightmare.

Inspect the Code

Run the codebase through some code validators (like *Lint, Fortify, Cppcheck, FxCop, ReSharper*, or the like). Look to see if compiler warnings have been disabled; re-enable them, and fix the messages. This will teach you the code structure and give you a clue about the code quality.

Fixing this kind of thing is often not tricky, but very worthwhile; a great introduction. It often gets you around most of the code quickly. This kind of nonfunctional code change teaches you how things fit together and about what lives where. It gives you a great feel for the diligence of the existing developers, and highlights which parts of the code are the most worrisome and will require extra care.

Study, Then Act

Study a small piece of code. Critique it. Determine if there are weak spots. Refactor it. Mercilessly. Name variables correctly. Turn sprawling code sections into smaller well-named functions.

A few such exercises will give you a good feel for how malleable the code is and how yielding to fixes and modifications. (I've seen codebases that really fought back against refactoring).

Be wary: writing code is easier than reading it. Many programmers, rather than putting in the effort to read and understand existing code, prefer to say "it's ugly" and rewrite it. This certainly helps them get a deep understanding of the code, but at the expense of lots of unnecessary code churn, wasted time, and in all likelihood, new bugs.

Test First

Look at the tests. Work out how to add a new unit test, and how to add a new test file to the suite. How do the tests get run?

A great trick is to try adding a single, one-line, failing test. Does the test suite immediately fail? This *smoke test* proves that the tests are not actively being ignored.

Do the tests serve to illustrate how each component works? Do they illustrate the interface points well?

Housekeeping

Do some spit-and-polish on the user interface. Make some simple UI improvements that don't affect core functionality, but do make the app more pleasant to use.

Tidy the source files: correct the directory hierarchy. Make it match the organisation in the IDE or project files.

Document What You Find

Does the code have any kind of top-level *README* documentation file explaining how to start working on it? If not, create one and include the things that you have learned so far.

Ask one of the more experienced programmers to review it. This will show how correct your knowledge is, and also help future newbies.

As you gain understanding of the system, maintain a layer diagram of the main sections of code. Keep it up-to-date as you learn. Do you discover that the system is well layered, with clear interfaces between each layer and no unnecessary coupling? Or do you find the sections of code are needlessly interconnected? Look for ways of introducing interfaces to bring about separation without changing the existing functionality.

If there are no architectural descriptions so far, yours can serve as the documentation that will lead the new recruit into the system.

Conclusion

Scientific investigations are a sort of warfare carried on in the closet
or on the couch against all one's contemporaries and predecessors.

— Thomas Young

The more you exercise, the less pain you feel and the greater the benefit you receive. Coding is no different. The more you work on new codebases, the more you are able to pick up new code effectively.

Questions

1. Do you often enter new codebases? Do you find it easy to work your way around unfamiliar code? What are the common tools you use to investigate a project? What tools can you add to this arsenal?

2. Describe some strategies for adding new code to a system you don't understand fully yet. How can you put a firewall around the existing code to protect it (and you)?

3. How can you make code easier for a new recruit to understand? What should you do now to improve the state of your current project?

4. Does the likely time you will spend working on the code in the future affect the effort and manner in which you learn existing code? Are you more likely to make a "quick and dirty" fix to code that you will no longer have to maintain, even though others will have to later on? Is this appropriate?

See also

- *Wallowing in Filth* How to gauge the quality of code, and make safe adjustments.

- *Live to Love to Learn* Learning a new codebase is like learning any new subject. These techniques will help.

- *Nothing is Set in Stone* Learn by doing: make changes to the code to understand it better.

Try this….

The next time you approach new code, plan a mindful route into it. Use these techniques to build a good understanding.

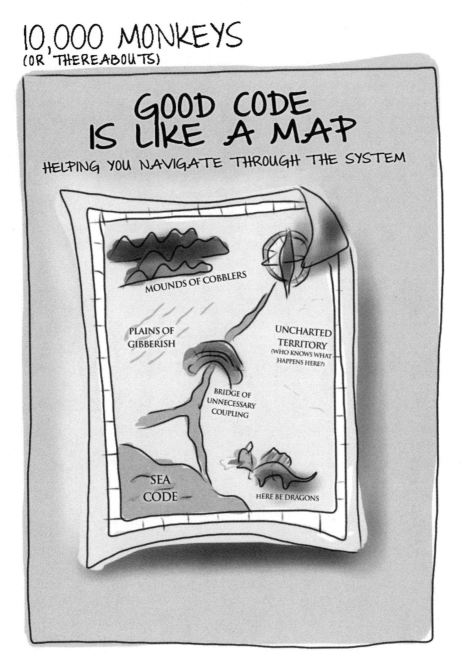

CHAPTER 7

Wallowing in Filth

As a dog returns to its vomit, so fools repeat their folly.

— Psalms 26:11

We've all encountered it: *quicksand code*. You wade into it unawares, and pretty soon you get that sinking feeling. The code is dense, not malleable, and resists any effort made to move it. The more effort you put in, the deeper you get sucked in. It's the man-trap of the digital age.

How does the effective programmer approach code that is, to be polite, *not so great*? What are our strategies for *coping with crap*?

Don't panic, don your sand-proof trousers, and we'll wade in…

Smell the Signs

Some code is great, like fine art, or well-crafted poetry. It has discernible structure, recognisable cadences, well-paced meter, and a coherence and beauty that make it enjoyable to read and a pleasure to work with.

But, sadly, that is not always the case.

Some code is messy and unstructured: a slalom of gotos that hide any semblance of algorithm. Some is hard to read: with poor layout and shabby naming. Some code is cursed with an unnecessarily rigid structure: nasty coupling and poor cohesion. Some code has poor factoring: entwining UI code with low-level logic. Some code is riddled with duplication: making the project larger and more complex than it need be, whilst harbouring the exact same bug many times over. Some code commits "OO abuse": inheriting, for all the wrong reasons, tightly associating parts of code that have no real need to be bound. Some code sits like a pernicious cuckoo in the nest: C# written in the style of JavaScript.

Some code has even more insidious badness: brittle behaviour where a change in one place causes a seemingly unconnected module to fail—the very definition of *code chaos theory*. Some code suffers from poor threading behaviour: employing inappropriate thread primitives or exercising a total lack of understanding of the safe concurrent use of resources. This problem can be very hard to spot, reproduce, and diagnose, as it manifests so intermittently.

(I know I shouldn't moan, but sometimes I swear that programmers shouldn't be allowed to type the word *thread* without first obtaining a license to wield such a dangerous weapon.)

> KEY ➤ Be prepared to encounter bad code. Fill your toolbox with sharp tools to deal with it.

To work effectively with alien code, you need to able to quickly spot these kinds of problems, and understand how to respond.

Wading into the Cesspit

The first step is to take a realistic survey of the coding crime scene. You arrive at the shores of new code. What *are* you wading into?

The code may have been given to you with a pre-attached stigma. No one wants to touch it because they know it's foul. Some quicksand code you discover yourself when you feel yourself sinking.

It's all too easy to pick up new code and dismiss it because it's not written in the style you'd prefer. Is it really dire work? Is it truly *quicksand code*, or is it merely unfamiliar? Don't make snap judgments about the code, or the authors who produced it, until you've spent some time investigating.

Take care not to make this personal.

Understand that few people set out to write shoddy code. Some filthy code was simply written by a less capable programmer. Or by a capable programmer on a bad day. Once you learn a new technique or pick up a team's preferred idiom, code that seemed perfectly fine a month ago is an embarrassing mess now and requires refactoring.

You can't expect any code, even your own, to be perfect.

> KEY ➤ Silence the feeling of revulsion when you encounter "bad" code. Instead, look for ways to practically improve it.

The Survey Says...

We've already looked at techniques for navigating a new codebase in Chapter 6.

As you build a mental model of a new piece of code, you can begin to gauge its quality using benchmarks like:

- Are the external APIs clean and sensible?

- Are the types used well chosen, and well named?

- Is the code layout neat and consistent? (Whilst this is certainly not a guarantee of underlying code quality, I do find that inconsistent, messy code tends also to be poorly structured and hard to work with. Programmers who aim for high-quality, malleable code also tend to care about clean, clear presentation. But don't base your judgment on presentation alone.)

- Is the structure of cooperating objects simple and clear to see? Or does control flow unpredictably around the codebase?

- Can you easily determine where to find the code that produces a certain effect?

It can be hard to perform this initial survey. Maybe you don't know the technology involved, or the problem domain. You may not be familiar with coding style.

Consider employing *software archaeology* in your survey: mine your revision control system logs for hints about the quality. Determine: how old is this code? How old is it in relation to the entire project? How many people have worked on it over time? When was it last changed? Are any recent contributors still working on the project? Can you ask them for information about the code? How many bugs have been found and fixed in this area? Many bugfixes centered here indicates that the code is poor.

Working in the Sandpit

You've identified quicksand code, and you are now on the alert. You need a sound strategy to work with it.

What is the appropriate plan of attack?

- Should you repair the bad code?

- Should you perform the minimal adjustment necessary to solve your current problem, and then run away?

- Should you cut out the necrotic code and replace it with new, better work?

Gaze into your crystal ball. Often the right answer will be informed by your future plans. How long will you be working with this section of code? Knowing that you will be pitching camp and working here for a while influences the amount of investment you'll put in. Don't attempt a sweeping rewrite if you haven't the time.

Also, consider how frequently this code has been modified up to now. Financial advisors will tell you that *past performance is not an indicator of future results*. But often it is.

Invest your time wisely. This code might be unpleasant, but if it has been working adequately for years without tinkering, it is probably inappropriate to "tidy it up" now, especially if you're unlikely to need to make many more changes in the future.

> KEY ➤ Pick your battles. Consider carefully whether you should invest
> time and effort in "tidying up" bad code. It may be pragmatic to
> leave it alone right now.

If you determine that it is not appropriate to embark on a massive code rework right now, that doesn't mean you are necessarily left to drift in a sea of sewage. You can wrestle back some control of the code by cleaning progressively.

Cleaning Up Messes

Whether you're digging in for the long haul, or just making a simple fix-and-run, heed Robert Martin's advice and follow the "the Boy Scout Rule": *Always leave the campground cleaner than you found it.* It might not be appropriate to make a sweeping improvement today, but that doesn't mean you can't make the world a slightly less awful place.

> KEY ➤ Follow the Boy Scout Rule. Whenever you touch some code leave
> it *better* than you found it.

This can be a simple change: address inconstant layout, correct a misleading variable name, simplify a complex conditional clause, or split a long method into smaller, well-named sub-functions.

If you regularly visit a section of code, and each time leave it slightly better than it was, then before long you'll wind up with something that might be classified as *good*.

Making Adjustments

The single most important advice when working with messy code is this:

> KEY ➤ Make code changes slowly, and carefully. Make one change at a
> time.

This is so important that I'd like you to stop, go back, and read it again.

There are many practical ways to follow this advice. Specifically:

- Do not change code layout whilst adjusting functionality. Tidy up the layout, if you must. Then commit your code. Only *then* make functional changes. (However, it's preferable to preserve the existing layout unless it's so bad that it gets in the way.)

- Do everything you can to ensure that your "tidying" preserves existing behaviour. Use trusted automated tools, or (if they are not available) review and inspect your changes carefully; get extra sets of eyeballs on it. This is the prime directive of *refactoring*: the well-known set of techniques for improving code structure.

  This goal can only be reached effectively if the code is wrapped in a sound set of unit tests. It is likely that messy code will not have any tests in place, so consider whether you should first write some tests to capture important code behaviour.

- Adjust the APIs that wrap the code without directly modifying the internal logic. Correct naming, parameter types, and ordering; generally introduce consistency. Perhaps introduce a new outer interface—the interface you wish that code had. Implement it in terms of the existing API. Then at a later date you can rework the code behind that interface.

Have courage in your ability to change the code. You have a safety net: source control. If you make a mistake, you can always go back in time and try again. It's probably not wasted effort, as you will have learnt about the code and its adaptability in doing so.

Sometimes it is worth boldly ripping out code in order to replace it. Badly maintained code that has seen no tidying or refactoring can be too painful and hard to correct piecemeal. There is an inherent danger in replacing code wholesale, though: the unreadable mess of special cases *might* be like that for a reason. Each bodge and code hack encodes an important piece of functionality that has been uncovered through bitter experience. Ignore these subtle behaviours at your peril.

An excellent book that deals with making appropriate changes in quicksand code is Micheal Feathers' *Working Effectively with Legacy Code*.[1] In it, he describes sound techniques to introduce seams into the code—places where you can introduce test points and most safely introduce sanity.

War Story: The Curious Case of the Container Code

There was a container class. It was central to our project. Internally, it was foul. The API stank, too. The original coder had worked hard to wreak code mischief. The bugs in it were hidden by the already confusing behaviour. Indeed, the confusing behaviour *was* a bug itself.

One of our programmers, a highly skilled developer, tried to refactor and repair this container. He kept the external interface intact, and improved many internal qualities: the correctness of the methods, the buggy object lifetime behaviour, performance, and code elegance.

---

1. Michael Feathers, *Working Effectively with Legacy Code* (Upper Saddle River, NJ: Prentice Hall, 2004).

He took out nasty, ugly, simplistic, stupid code and replaced it with the polar opposite. But in his effort to maintain the old API, this new version was internally far too contrived, more like a science project than useful code. It was hard to work with. Although it succinctly expressed the old (bizarre) behaviour, there was no room for extension.

We struggled to work with this new version, too. It had been a wasted effort.

Later on, another developer simplified the way we used the container: removing the weirder requirements, therefore simplifying the API. This was a relatively simple adjustment to the project. Inside the container, we removed swaths of code. The class was simpler, smaller, and easier to verify.

Sometimes you have to think laterally to see the right improvement.

Bad Code? Bad Programmers?

Yes, it's frustrating to be slowed down by bad code. The effective programmer does not only deal well with the bad code, but also with the people that wrote it. It is not helpful to apportion blame for code problems. People don't tend to purposefully write drivel.

> KEY ▶ There is no need to apportion blame for "bad" code.

Perhaps the original author didn't understand the utility of code refactoring, or see a way to express the logic neatly. It's just as likely there are other similar things you do not yet understand. Perhaps they felt under pressure to work fast and had to cut corners (believing the lie that it helps you get there faster; it rarely does).

But of course, you know better.

If you can, *enjoy* the chance to tidy. It can be very rewarding to bring structure and sanity to a mess. Rather than see it as a tedious exercise, look at it as a chance to introduce higher quality.

Treat it as a lesson. Learn. How will you avoid repeating these same coding mistakes yourself?

Check your attitude as you make improvements. You might think that you know better than the original author. But do you always know better?

I've seen this story play out many times: a junior programmer "fixed" a more experienced programmer's work, with the commit message "refactored the code to look neater." The code indeed looked neater. But he had removed important functionality. The original author later reverted the change with the commit message: "refactored code back to working."

Questions

1. Why does code frequently get so messy?

2. How can we avoid this from happening in first place? Can we?

3. What are the advantages of making layout changes separately from code changes?

4. How many times have you been confronted with distasteful code? How often was this code *really* dire, rather than "not to your taste"?

See also

- *Navigating a Route* Techniques to familiarise yourself with a new codebase.

- *Improve Code by Removing It* Improve "filthy" programs by exorcising dead code.

- *An Ode to Code* An unnecessarily extreme reaction to bad code.

Try this....

Employ the Boy Scout Rule. Leave every piece of code you touch better, if even only fractionally.

CHAPTER 8

Don't Ignore That Error!

All you need is ignorance and confidence and the success is sure.

— Mark Twain

Settle yourself down for an apocryphal bedtime story. A programmer's parable, if you will....

I was walking down the street one evening to meet some friends in a bar. We hadn't shared a beer in some time and I was looking forward to seeing them again. In my haste, I wasn't looking where I was going. I tripped over the edge of a curb and ended up flat on my face. Well, it serves me right for not paying attention, I guess.

It hurt my leg, but I was in a hurry to meet my friends. So I pulled myself up and carried on. As I walked further the pain was getting worse. Although I'd initially dismissed it as shock, I rapidly realised there was something wrong.

But, I hurried on to the bar regardless. I was in agony by the time I arrived. I didn't have a great night out, because I was terribly distracted. In the morning I went to the doctor and found out I'd fractured my shinbone. Had I stopped when I felt the pain, I'd've prevented a lot of extra damage that I caused by walking on it. Probably the worst morning-after of my life...

Too many programmers write code like my disastrous night out.

Error? What error? It won't be serious. Honestly. I can ignore it. This is *not* a winning strategy for solid code. In fact, it's just plain laziness. (The bad sort.) No matter how unlikely you think an error is in your code, you should always check for it, and always handle it. Every time. If you don't, you're not saving time, you're storing up potential problems for the future.

> KEY ➤ Do not ignore possible errors in your code. Don't put off handling errors until "later" (you won't get around to it).

The Mechanism

We report errors in our code in a number of ways, including:

Return codes

A function returns a value. Some of which mean "it didn't work." Error return codes are far too easy to ignore. You won't see anything in the code to highlight the problem. Indeed, it's become standard practice to ignore some standard C functions' return values. How often do you check the return value from `printf`?

Return codes are perhaps the most popular error-report channel: we see *functions* return values, operating system *processes* return values, in some systems even *threads* can return values.

Often this code is an integer value; conventionally, zero means success and non-zero is an error code. In modern code it's a rather strange idiom, and we can write far more expressive code by either returning a *tuple* of values or an "optional" type encoding success and the value in one type (e.g., the `boost::optional` type in C++ or `Nullable<T>` in C#). Functional programming languages may indicate errors through the return *type* of the function rather than a magical value; Haskell provides the `Maybe` class, Scala provides `Option` and `Either`.

Side effects

`errno`, the poster child for side effects, is a curious C language aberration: a separate global variable used to signal an error. It's easy to ignore, hard to use, and leads to all sorts of nasty problems—for example, what happens when you have multiple threads calling the same function?

You may see other side channels or side effects used to signal error. For example, you may see another function that must be called to check the "success state," or an object going into an "invalid" state when something goes wrong.

Exceptions

Exceptions are a more structured, language-supported way of signalling and handling errors. And you can't possibly ignore them. Or can you? I've seen lots of code like this:

```
try
{
    // ...do something...
}
catch (...) {} // ignore errors
```

The saving grace of this awful construct is that it highlights the fact you're doing something morally dubious.

Exceptions aren't perfect. Their detractors complain that they hide the error-path. An exception could unwind through a method with awful repercussions (e.g., leaking resources or failing to satisfying a function contract). But because that method contains no error-handling code itself, you'd not realise these problems.

Like many other technologies, effective use of exceptions requires much discipline. This is far outside the scope of this chapter.

> KEY ➤ Use exceptions well, with discipline. Understand your language's idioms and requirements for effective exception use.

The Madness

Not handling errors leads to:

Brittle code
    This type of code is full of hard-to-find crashes.

Insecure code
    Crackers often exploit poor error handling to break into software systems.

Bad structure
    If there are errors from your code that are tedious to deal with continually, you probably have a bad interface. Express it better, so the errors are not so onerous.

Just as you should check all potential errors in your code, you must expose all potentially erroneous conditions in your interfaces. Do not hide them, and pretend that your services will always work.

Programmers must be made aware of programmatic errors. Users must be made aware of usage errors.

It's not good enough to *log* the error (somewhere), and hope that a diligent operator will notice an error and do something about it one day. Who knows about the log? Who checks the log? Who is likely to do anything about it? If program termination is not an option, ensure that problems are flagged up in an unobtrusive, but obvious and unignorable manner.

The Mitigation

Why don't we check for errors? There are a number of common excuses. Which of these do you agree with? How would you counter each of them?

- Error handling clutters up the flow of the code, making it harder to read, and harder to spot the "normal" flow of execution.
- It's extra work and I have a deadline looming.

- I know that this function call will *never* return an error (`printf` always works, `malloc` always returns new memory, and if it fails we have bigger problems, anyway…).

- It's only a toy program, and needn't be written to a production-worthy level.

- My language encourages me not to. (E.g., Erlang's philosophy is "let it fail": erroneous code should fail *fast* and cause its Erlang process to terminate. Good Erlang systems are designed to be robust to failing processes, so error handling is not such a big deal.)

Conclusion

This is a very short chapter. It could be much, much longer. But doing so would be an error. The message is simple: Do. Not. Ignore. Errors.

Questions

1. How can you ensure your code does not ignore errors that are reported by lower levels? Consider code-level solutions and process-related techniques.

2. Exceptions cannot be ignored as easily as return codes. Does that make them a safer mechanism for reporting errors?

3. What approaches are required when working on code that mixes error codes and exceptions?

4. What testing techniques will help identify code that fails due to inadequate error handling?

See also

- *A Love for Languages* The appropriate style of error reporting and handling depends on the language in use.

- *Expect the Unexpected* Error conditions are one example of the kind of "unexpected" situations that we must consider for our code to be robust.

Try this….

Set up a review of the most frequently worked-on code in your system. Determine how many error conditions have been left unhandled. Next, review some infrequently maintained code and compare the results.

CHAPTER 9

Expect the Unexpected

Be Prepared...the meaning of the motto is that a scout must prepare
himself by previous thinking out and practicing how to act on any accident
or emergency so that he is never taken by surprise.

— Robert Baden-Powell

They say that some people see the glass half full, some see it half empty. But most programmers don't see the glass at all; they write code that simply does not consider unusual situations. They are neither optimists nor pessimists. They are not even realists. They're *ignore-ists*.

When writing your code, don't consider only the thread of execution that you expect to happen. At every step, consider all of the *unusual* things that might occur, no matter how *unlikely* you think they'll be.

Errors

Any function you call may not work as you expect.

- If you are lucky, it will return an error code to signal this. If so, you should check that value; never ignore it.

- The function might throw an exception if it cannot honor its contract. Ensure that your code will cope with an exception bubbling up through it. Whether you catch the exception and handle it, or allow it to pass further up the call stack, ensure that your code is correct. Correctness includes not leaking resources or leaving the program in an invalid state.

- Or the function might return no indication of failure, but silently not do what you expected. You ask a function to print a message. Will it always print it? Might it sometimes fail and consume the message?

Always consider errors that you can recover from, and write appropriate recovery code. Consider also the errors that you cannot recover from. Write your code to do the best thing possible—don't just ignore it.

Ensure that your error handling is idiomatic, and uses the appropriate language mechanisms. Erlang, for example, has a "let it crash" philosophy, where defensive coding is discouraged in favour of letting errors cause loud and visible failures, to be handled at a process level.

Threading

The world has moved from single-threaded applications to more complex, often highly threaded, environments. Unusual interactions between pieces of code are staple here. It's hard to enumerate every possible interweaving of code paths, let alone reproduce one particular problematic interaction more than once.

To tame this level of unpredictability, make sure you understand basic concurrency principles, and how to decouple threads so they cannot interact in dangerous ways. Understand mechanisms to reliably and quickly pass messages between thread contexts without introducing race conditions or blocking the threads unnecessarily.

Shutdown

We plan how to construct a system: how to create all the objects, how to get all the plates to spin, and how to keep those objects running and those plates spinning. Less attention is given to the other end of the life cycle: how to bring the code to a graceful halt without leaking resources, locking up, or crashing.

Shutting down your system and destroying all the objects is especially hard in a multi-threaded system. As your application shuts down and destroys its worker objects, make sure you can't leave one object attempting to use another that has already been disposed of. Don't enqueue threaded callbacks that target objects already discarded by other threads.

The Moral of the Story

The "unexpected" is not the unusual. It's the stuff bugs are made of. You need to write your code in the light of this.

It's important to think about these issues early on in your code development. You can't tack on this kind of correctness as an afterthought; the problems are insidious and run deeply into the grain of your code. Such demons are very hard to exorcise after the code has been fleshed out.

> **KEY** ➤ Consider all potential code paths *as you write* your code. Do not plan to handle "unusual" cases later: you'll forget and your code will be buggy.

Writing good code is not about being an optimist or a pessimist. It's not about how much water is in the glass right now. It's about making a watertight glass so that there will be no spillages, no matter how much water the glass contains.

Questions

1. What kinds of problems have you observed from code that did not adequately handle "unexpected" situations?

2. Do you always include robust error handling in all your code?

3. When is it acceptable to forego rigorous error handling?

4. What other sources of surprise scenarios can you think of that would affect the quality and robustness of your code?

See also

- *Don't Ignore That Error!* Advice for handling error conditions—and an admonition to *expect* them.

- *Wallowing in Filth* You must consider all potential conditions in your code, even *unlikely* ones or it will end up a filthy, brittle mess.

- *Bug Hunting* If you don't handle all cases appropriately, you're introducing bugs. This is what you'll be doing as a consequence.

- *Testing Times* A good testing regimen can help you enumerate and keep track of unexpected conditions.

Try this....

Inspect the last section of code you worked on. Audit the code for diligence in error handling and potential unusual interactions. How can you improve it?

CHAPTER 10

Bug Hunting

If debugging is the process of removing software bugs,
then programming must be the process of putting them in.

— Edsger Dijkstra

It's open season; a season that lasts all year round. There are no permits required, no restrictions levied. Grab yourself a shotgun and head out into the open software fields to root out those pesky varmints, the elusive *bugs*, and squash them, dead.

OK, reality is not as saccharin as that. But sometimes you end up working on code in which you swear the bugs are multiplying and ganging up on you. A shotgun is the only response.

The story is an old one, and it goes like this: Programmers write code. Programmers aren't perfect. The programmer's code isn't perfect. It therefore doesn't work perfectly the first time. So we have bugs.

If we bred better programmers we'd clearly breed better bugs.

Some bugs are simple mistakes that are obvious to spot and easy to fix. When we encounter these, we are lucky.

The majority of bugs—the ones we invest hours of effort tracking down, losing our follicles and/or hair pigment in the search—are the nasty, subtle issues. These are the odd, surprising interactions; the unexpected consequences of our algorithms; the seemingly non-deterministic behaviour of software that looked so very simple. It can only have been infected by gremlins.

This isn't a problem limited to newbie programmers who don't know any better. Experts are just as prone. The pioneers of our craft suffered; the eminent computer scientist Maurice Wilkes wrote: *"I well remember [...] on one of my journeys between the EDSAC room and the punching equipment that hesitating at the angles of stairs the realisation came over me with full force that a good part of the remainder of my life was going to be spent in finding errors in my own programs.*"[1]

So face it. You'll be doing a lot of debugging. You'd better get used to it. And you better get good at it. (At least you can console yourself that you'll have plenty of chances to practice.)

An Economic Concern

How much time do you think is spent debugging? Add up the effort of all of the programmers in every country around the world. Go on, guess.

A staggering $312 billion per year is spent on the wage bills for programmers debugging their software. To put that in perspective, that's two times all Eurozone bailouts since 2008! This huge, but realistic, figure comes from research carried out by Cambridge University's Judge Business School.[2]

You have a responsibility to fix bugs faster: *to save the global economy.* The state of the world is in your hands.

It's not just the wage bill, though. Consider all the other implications of buggy software: shipping delays, cancelled projects, the reputation damage from unreliable software, and the cost of bugs fixed in shipping software.

An Ounce of Prevention

It would be remiss of a chapter about debugging to not stress how much better it is to actively prevent bugs manifesting in the first place, rather than attempt a post-bug fix. *An ounce of prevention is worth a pound of cure.* If the cost of debugging is astronomical, we should primarily aim to mitigate this by not creating bugs in the first place.

This, in a classic editorial sleight of hand, is material for a different chapter, and so we won't investigate the theme exhaustively here. Do remember the advice in Chapter 9 and always Chapter 17.

Suffice to say, we should always employ sound engineering techniques that minimise the likelihood of unpleasant surprises. Thoughtful design, code review, pair programming, and a considered test strategy (including TDD practices and fully automated unit test suites) are all of the utmost importance. Techniques like assertions, defensive programming, and code coverage tools will all help minimise the likelihood of errors sneaking past.

1. Maurice Wilkes, *Memoirs of a Computer Pioneer* (Cambridge, MA: The MIT Press, 1985).

2. "Cambridge University Study States Software Bugs Cost Economy $312 Billion per Year" (*http://undo-software.com/company/press/press-release-8*)

We all know these mantras. Don't we? But how diligent are we in employing such tactics?

> KEY ➤ Avoid injecting bugs into your code by employing sound engineering practices. Don't expect quickly hacked-out code to be of high quality.

The best bug-avoidance advice is to not write incredibly "clever" (which often equates to complex) code. Brian Kernighan states: *Debugging is twice as hard as writing the code in the first place. Therefore, if you write the code as cleverly as possible, you are, by definition, not smart enough to debug it.* Martin Fowler reminds us: *Any fool can write code that a computer can understand. Good programmers write code that humans can understand.*

Bug Hunting

Beware of bugs in the above code; I have only proved it correct, not tried it.

— Donald Knuth

Being realistic, no matter how sound your code-writing regimen, some of those pernicious bugs will always manage to squeeze through the defences and require you to don the coder's hunting cap and an anti-bug shotgun. How should we go about finding and eliminating them? This can be a Herculean task, akin to finding a needle in a haystack. Or, more accurately, a needle in a needle stack.

Finding and fixing a bug is like solving a logic puzzle. Generally the problem isn't too hard when approached methodically; the majority of bugs are easily found and fixed in minutes. However, some are nastier and take longer. Those hard bugs are few in number, but given their nature, that's where we will spend most of our time.

Two factors usually determine how hard a bug is to fix:

- How reproducible it is.
- The time between the cause of the bug entering the code, the "software fault" itself —the bad line of code, or faulty integration assumption—and you actually noticing.

When a bug scores highly on both counts, it's almost impossible to track down without sharp tools and a keen intellect. There are a number of practical techniques and strategies we can employ to solve the puzzle and locate the fault.

The first, and most important thing, is to methodically investigate and characterise the bug. Give yourself the best raw material to work with:

- Reduce it to the simplest set of *reproduction steps* possible. This is vital. Sift out all the extraneous fluff that isn't contributing to the problem, and only serves to distract.

- Ensure that you are focusing on a single problem. It can be very easy to get into a tangle when you don't realise you're conflating two separate—but related—faults into one.

- Determine how repeatable the problem is. How frequently do your repro steps demonstrate the problem? Is it reliant on a simple series of actions? Does it depend on software configuration or the type of machine you're running on? Do peripheral devices attached make any difference? These are all crucial data points in the investigation work that is to come.

In reality, when you've constructed a single set of reproduction steps, you really have won most of the battle.

The following sections cover some of the most useful debugging strategies.

Lay Traps

You have errant behaviour. You know a point when the system seems correct; maybe it's at start-up, but hopefully a lot later through the reproduction steps. You can get it to a point where its state is invalid. Find places in the code path *between* these two points, and set traps to catch the fault.

Add assertions or tests to verify the system *invariants*—the facts that must hold for the state to be correct. Add diagnostic printouts to see the state of the code so you can work out what's going on.

As you do this, you'll gain a greater understanding of the code, reasoning more about its structure, and will likely add many more assertions to the mix to prove your assumptions hold. Some of these will be genuine assertions about invariant conditions in the code, others will be assertions relevant to this particular run. Both are valid tools to help you pinpoint the bug. Eventually a trap will snap, and you'll have the bug cornered.

> KEY ➤ Assertions and logging (even the humble `printf`) are potent debugging tools. Use them often.

Diagnostic logs and assertions may be valid to leave in the code after you've found and fixed the problem. But be careful you don't litter the code with useless logging that hides what's really going on, making unnecessary debug noise.

Learn to Binary Chop

Aim for a *binary chop* strategy, to focus in on bugs as quickly as possible.

Rather than single-stepping through code paths, work out the start of a chain of events, and the end. Then partition the problem space into two, and work out if the middle point is good or bad. Based on this information, you've narrowed the problem space to something half the size. Repeat this a few times, and you'll soon have honed in on the problem.

This is a very powerful approach—allowing you to get to a solution in order $O(\log n)$ time, rather than $O(n)$. That is significantly faster.

> KEY ➤ Binary chop problem spaces to get results faster.

Employ this technique with trap laying. Or with the other techniques described next.

Employ Software Archaeology

Software archaeology describes the art of mining through the historical records in your version control system. This can provide an excellent route into the problem; it's often a surprisingly simple way to hunt a bug.

Determine a point in the near past of the codebase when this bug didn't exist. Armed with your reproducible test case, step forward in time to determine which code change-set caused the breakage. Again, a binary chop strategy is the best bet here.[3]

Once you find the breaking code change, the cause of the fault is usually obvious, and the fix is self-evident. (This is another compelling reason to make series of small, frequent, atomic check-ins, rather than massive commits covering a range of things at once.)

Test, Test, Test

As you develop your software, invest time to write a suite of unit tests. This will not only help shape how you develop and verify the code you've initially written. It acts as a great early warning device for changes you make later; much like the miner's canary, the test fails long before the problem becomes complex to find and expensive to fix.

These tests can also act as great points from which to begin debugging sessions. A simple, reproducible unit test case is a far simpler scaffold to debug than a fully running program that has to spin up and have a series of manual actions run to reproduce the fault. For this reason, it's advisable to write a unit test to demonstrate a bug, rather than start to hunt it from a running "full system."

Once you have a suite of tests, consider employing a *code coverage* tool to inspect how much of your code is actually covered by the tests. You may be surprised. A simple rule of thumb is: if your test suite does not exercise it, then you can't believe it works. Even if it looks like it's OK now, without a test harness then it'll be very likely to get broken later.

---

3. The `git bisect` tool automates this binary chop for you, and is worth keeping in your toolbox if you're a Git user.

When you finally determine the cause of a bug, consider writing a simple test that clearly illustrates the problem, and add it to the test suite *before* you really fix the code. This takes genuine discipline, as once you find the code culprit, you'll naturally want to fix it ASAP and publish the fix. Instead, first write a test harness to demonstrate the problem, and use this harness to prove that you've fixed it. The test will serve to prevent the bug coming back in the future.

Invest in Sharp Tools

The are many tools that are worth getting accustomed to, including memory checkers like Electric Fence, and Swiss Army knife tools like Valgrind. These are worth learning about *now* rather than reaching for them at the last minute. If you know how to use a tool before you have a problem that demands it, you'll be far more effective.

Learning a range of tools will prevent you from cracking a nut with a pneumatic drill.

Of course, the tool of debugging champions is the *debugger*. This is the king of tools that allows you to break into the execution of a running program, step forward by a single instruction, or step in and out of functions. Other very handy facilities include the ability to watch variables for changes, set conditional breakpoints (e.g., "break if x > y"), and change variable values on the fly to quickly experiment with different code paths. Some advanced debuggers even allow you to step backward (now that's real voodoo).

Most IDEs come with a debugger built in, so you're never far from deploying a breakpoint. But you may find it worth investing in a higher quality alternative, don't rely on the first tool that falls to hand.

In some circles there is a real disdain for the debugger. *Real programmers don't need a debugger.* To some extent this is true; being overly reliant on the debugger is a bad thing. Single-stepping through code mindlessly can trick you into focusing on the micro level, rather than thinking about the macro, overall shape of the code.

But it's not a sign of weakness. Sometimes it's just far easier and quicker to pull out the big guns. Don't be afraid to use the right tool for the job.

Remove Code to Exclude It from Cause Analysis

When you can reproduce a fault, consider removing everything that doesn't appear to contribute to the problem to help focus in on the offending lines of code. Disable other threads that *shouldn't* be involved. Remove subsections of code that do not look like they're related.

It's common to discover objects indirectly attached to the "problem area"—for example, via a message bus or a notifier-listener mechanism. Physically disconnect this coupling (even if you're *convinced* it's benign). If you still reproduce the fault, you have proven your hunch about isolation, and have reduced the problem space.

Then consider removing, or skipping over, sections of code leading up to the error (as much as makes practical sense). Delete, or comment out blocks that don't appear to be involved.

Cleanliness Prevents Infection

Don't allow bugs to stay in your software for longer than necessary. Don't let them linger.

Don't dismiss niggling problems as *known issues*. This is a dangerous practice. It can lead to *broken window syndrome*,[4] making it gradually feel normal and acceptable to have buggy behaviour. This lingering bad behaviour can mask the causes of other bugs you're hunting.

> KEY ➤ Fix bugs as soon as you can. Don't let them pile up until you're stuck in a code cesspit.

One project I worked on was demoralisingly bad in this respect. When given a bug report to fix, before managing to reproduce the initial bug you'd encounter 10 different issues that all also needed to be fixed, and may (or may not) have contributed to the bug in question.

Oblique Strategies

Sometimes you can bash your head against a gnarly problem for hours and get nowhere. Try an oblique strategy to avoid getting stuck in a debugging rut.

Take a break
> It's important to learn when you should simply stop and walk away. A break can give you fresh perspective.
>
> This can help you to think more carefully. Rather than running headlong back into the code, take a break to consider the problem description and code structure.

---

4. *Broken windows theory (http://en.wikipedia.org/wiki/Broken_windows_theory)* implies that keeping neighbourhoods in good condition prevents vandalism and crime.

Go for a walk to force you to step away from the keyboard. (How many times have you had those "eureka" moments in the shower? Or in the bathroom?! It happens to me all the time.)

Explain it to someone else

Describe the problem to someone else. Often when describing any problem (including a bug hunt) to another person, you instantly explain it to yourself and solve it.

Failing another actual, live person, you can follow the *rubber duck strategy* described by Andrew Hunt and David Thomas.[5] Talk to an inanimate object on your desk to explain the problem to yourself. It's only a problem if the rubber duck starts to talk back.

Don't Rush Away

Once you find and fix a bug, don't rush mindlessly on. Stop for a moment and consider if there are other related problems lurking in that section of code. Perhaps the problem you've fixed is a pattern that repeats in other sections of the code. Is there further work that you could do to shore up the system with the knowledge you just gained?

Keep notes on which parts of the code harbour more faults. There are always hotspots. These hotspots are either the 20% of the code that 80% of users actually run, or a sign of ropey, badly written software. When you have spent enough time gathering notes, it may be worth devoting time to those problem areas: perhaps a rewrite, a deep code review, or an extra unit test harness.

Non-Reproducible Bugs

Sometimes you discover a bug for which you can't easily form a set of reproduction steps. The bug defies logic and reason; it's not possible to determine the cause-and-effect. These nasty, intermittent bugs seem to be caused by *cosmic rays* rather than any direct user interaction. They take ages to track down, often because we never get a chance to see them on a development machine, or when running in a debugger.

How do we go about finding, and fixing, these fiends?

- Keep records of the factors that contribute to the fault. Over time you may spot a pattern that will help you identify the common causes.

- As you get more information, start to draw conclusions. Perhaps you can identify more data points to keep in the record.

---

5. Andrew Hunt and David Thomas, *The Pragmatic Programmer* (Boston: Addison Wesley, 1999).

- Consider adding more logging and assertions in beta or release builds to help gather information from the field.

- If it's a really pressing problem, set up a test farm to run long-running soak tests. If you can automate driving the system in a representative manner, then you can accelerate the hunting season.

There are a few things that are known to contribute to such unreliable bugs. You may find they provide hints for where to start investigating:

Threaded code

As threads entwine and interact in nondeterministic and hard-to-reproduce ways, they often contribute to freaky intermittent failure.

Often this behaviour is very different when you pause the code in a debugger, so it is hard to observe forensically. Logging can also change the interaction of the threads and mask the problem. And non-optimised, "debug," builds of your software can perform rather differently from the "release" builds.

These are affectionately known as *Heisenbugs*, after the physicist Werner Heisenberg's "observer effect" in quantum mechanics. The act of observing a system can alter its state.

Network interaction

Networks are, by definition, laggy and may drop or stall at any point in time. Most code presumes that all access to *local* storage works (because, most often, it does). This is careless, and will not scale to storage over a network, where failures and intermittent long load times are common.

The variable speed of storage

It's not just network latency that can cause this. Slow spinny disks, or database operations, may change the behaviour of your program, especially if you are balanced precariously on the edge of timeout thresholds.

Memory corruption

Oh, the humanity! When your aberrant code overwrites part of the stack or the heap, you can see a myriad of unreproducible strangenesses that are *very* hard to detect. Software archaeology is often the easiest route to diagnose these errors.

Global variables/singletons

Hardcoded communication points can be a clearinghouse for unpredictable behaviour. It can be impossible to reason about the correctness of your code, or predict what will happen, when anyone at any time can reach into a piece of global state and adjust it under your feet.

Conclusion

Debugging isn't easy. But it's our own fault. We wrote the bugs.

Effective debugging is an essential skill for any programmer.

Questions

1. Assess how much of your time you think you spend debugging. Consider every activity that isn't writing a fresh line of code in a system.

2. Do you spend more time debugging new lines of code you have written, or on adjustments to existing code?

3. Does the existence of a suite of unit tests for existent code change the amount of time you spend debugging, or the way you debug?

4. Is it realistic to aim for bug-free software? Is this achievable? When is it appropriate to genuinely aim for bug-free software? What determines the optimal amount of "bugginess" in a product?

See also

- *Expected the Unexpected* Most bugs are caused by failing to account for all possible conditions in the code's control flow.

- *The Ghost of a Codebase Past* Discovering bugs in your old code forces you to visit and appraise your old work.

- *Testing Times* Use unit tests to document and help fix the bugs you find, and to prevent future regressions in the code.

> Try this....
>
> Next time you face a bug, attempt a more methodical approach to finding the cause. How can you employ trap laying, binary chop, and sharp tools to more effectively track it?

CHAPTER 11

Testing Times

Quality is free, but only to those who are willing to pay heavily for it.

— Tom DeMarco and Timothy Lister
Peopleware: Productive Projects and Teams

Test-driven development (TDD): to some it's a religion. To some, it's the only sane way to develop code. To some, it's a nice idea that they can't quite make work. And to others, it's a pure waste of effort.

What is it, really?

TDD is an important technique for building better software, although there is still confusion over what it means to be *test driven*, and over what a *unit test* really is. Let's break through this and discover a healthy approach to developer testing, so we can write better code.

Why Test?

It's a no-brainer: we *have* to test our code.

Of course you run your new program to see whether it works. Few programmers are confident enough, or arrogant enough, to write code and release it without trying it out *somehow*. When you do see corners cut, the code rarely works the first time: problems are found, either by QA, or—worse—when a customer uses it.

Shortening the Feedback Loop

To develop great software, and develop it well, programmers need *feedback*. We need to receive feedback as frequently and as quickly as possible. Good testing strategies shorten the feedback loop, so we can work most effectively:

- We know that our code works when it's used in the field and returns accurate results to users. If it doesn't, they complain. If that was our only feedback loop, software development would be very slow and very expensive. We can do better.

- To ensure correctness *before* we ship, the QA team tests candidate releases. This pulls in the feedback loop; the answers come back more quickly, and we avoid making expensive (and embarrassing) mistakes in the field. But we can still do better.

- We want to check that our new subsystems work before integrating them into the project. Typically, a developer will spin up the application and execute their new code as best they can. Some code can be rather inconvenient to test like this, so it's possible to create a small separate test harness application that exercises the code. These *development tests* again reduce the feedback loop; now we find out whether our code is functioning correctly *as we work on it*, not later on. But we can still do better.

- The subsystems are comprised of smaller units: classes and functions. If we can easily get feedback on correctness and quality of code at this level, then we reduce the feedback loop again. Tests at the smallest level give the fastest feedback.

The shorter the feedback loop, the faster we can iterate over design changes, and the more confident we can feel about our code. The sooner we learn that there's a problem, the easier and less expensive the fix is, because our brain is still engaged with the problem and we recall the shape of the code.

> KEY ➤ To improve our software development we need rapid feedback, to learn of problems as soon as they appear. Good testing strategies provide short feedback loops.

Manual tests (either performed by a QA team, or by the programmers inspecting their own handiwork) are laborious and slow. To be at all comprehensive, it requires many individual steps that need repeating each time you make a minor adjustment to the code.

But hang on, isn't repeated laborious work something that computers are good at? Surely we can use the computer to run the tests for us automatically. That speeds up the running of the tests, and helps to close the feedback loop further.

Automated tests with a short feedback loop don't just help you to develop the code. Once you have a selection of tests, you needn't throw them away. Stash them in a test pool, and keep running them. In this way your test code works like a canary in a mine —signalling any problem before it becomes fatal. If in the future someone (even you on a bad day) modifies the code to introduce errant behaviour (a functional *regression*), the test will point this out immediately.

Code That Tests Code

So the ideal is to automate our development testing as much as possible: *work smarter, not harder*. Your IDE can highlight syntax errors as you type—wouldn't it be great if it could show you test breakages at the same speed?

Computers can run tests rapidly and repeatedly, reducing the feedback loop. Although you can automate desktop applications with UI testing tools, or use browser-based technology, most often development tests see the coder writing a programmatic test scaffold that invokes their production code (the SUT: *System Under Test*), prodding it in particular ways to check that it responds as expected.

We write code to test code. Very meta.

Yes, writing these tests takes up the programmer's precious time. And yes, your confidence in the code is only as good as the quality of the tests that you write. But it's not hard to adopt a test strategy that improves the quality of your code and makes it safer to write. This helps *reduce* the time it takes you to develop code: *more haste, less speed*. Studies have shown that a sound testing strategy substantially reduces the incidence of defects.[1]

It is true that a test suite can slow you down if you write brittle, hard to understand tests, and if your code is so rigid that a change in one method forces a million tests to be rewritten. That is an argument against *bad* test suites, not against testing in general (in the same way that bad code is not an argument against programming in general).

Who Writes the Tests?

In the past some have argued for the role of a dedicated "unit-test engineer" who specialises in verifying the code of an upstream programmer. But the most effective approach is for the programmers themselves to write their own development tests.

After all, you'd be testing your code as you write it, anyway.

> KEY ➤ We need tests at all levels of the software stack and development process. However, programmers particularly require tests at the smallest scope possible, to reduce the feedback loop and help develop high-quality software as quickly and easily as possible.

---

1. David Janzen and Hossein Saiedian, "Test-Driven Development Concepts, Taxonomy, and Future Direction," *Computer* 38:9 (2005).

Types of Tests

There are many kinds of tests, and often when you hear someone talk about a "unit test" they may very likely mean some other kind of code test. We employ:

Unit tests

Unit tests specifically exercise the smallest "units" of functionality *in isolation*, to ensure that they each function correctly. If it's not driving a single unit of code (which *could* be one class or one function) in isolation (i.e., without involving any other "units" from the production code), then it's not a unit test.

This isolation specifically means that a unit test will not involve any external access: no database, network, or filesystem operations will be run.

Unit-test code is usually written using an off-the-shelf "xUnit" style framework. Every language and environment has a selection of these, and some have a de facto standard. There's nothing magical about a testing framework, and you can get a long way writing unit tests with just the humble `assert`. We'll look at frameworks later.

Integration tests

These tests inspect how individual units integrate into larger cohesive sets of co-operating functionality. We check that the integrated components glue together and interoperate correctly.

Integration tests are often written in the same unit test frameworks; the difference is simply the scope of the system under test. Many people's "unit tests" are really integration-level tests, dealing with more than one object in the SUT. In truth, what we call this test is nowhere near as important as the fact that the test exists!

System tests

Otherwise known as *end-to-end* tests, these can be seen as a specification of the required functionality of the entire system. They run against the fully integrated software stack, and can be used as acceptance criteria for the project.

System tests can be implemented as code that exercises the public APIs and entry points to the system, or they may drive the system from outside using a tool like Selenium, a web browser automator. It can be hard to realistically test all of an application's functionality through its UI layer, in which case we employ *subcutaneous tests* that drive the code from the layer just below the interface logic.

Because of the larger scope of system tests, the full suite of tests can take considerable time to execute. There may be much network traffic involved or slow database access to account for. The set-up and tear-down costs can be huge to get the SUT ready to run each system test.

Each level of developer tests establishes a number of facts about the SUT, and constructs a series of *test cases* that prove that these facts hold.

There are different styles of test-driven development. A project can be driven by a unit-test mentality: where you would expect to see more unit tests than integration tests, and more integration tests than system tests. Or it may be driven by a system-test mentality: the reverse, with far fewer unit tests. Each kind of test is important in its own right, and all should be present in a mature software project.

When to Write Tests

The term TDD (that is, *test-driven development*) is conflated with *test-first* development, although there really are two separate themes here. You can "drive" your design from the feedback given by tests without religiously writing those tests first.

However, the longer you leave it to write your tests, the less effective those tests will be: you'll forget how the code is supposed to work, fail to handle edge cases, or perhaps even forget to write tests at all. The longer you leave it to write your tests, the slower and less effective your feedback loop will be.

The test-first "TDD" approach is commonly seen in XP circles. The mantra is: *don't write any production code unless you have a failing test.* The test-first TDD cycle is:

1. Determine the next piece of functionality you need. Write a test for your new functionality. Of course, it will fail.

2. Only then implement that functionality, in the simplest way possible. You know that your functionally is in place when the test passes. As you code, you may run the test suite many times. Because each step adds a small new part of functionality, and therefore a small test, these tests should run rapidly.

3. *This is the important part that's often overlooked:* now tidy up the code. Refactor unpleasant commonality. Restructure the SUT to have a better internal structure. You can do all this with full confidence that you won't break anything, as you have a suite of tests to validate against.

4. Go back to step 1 and repeat until you have written passing test cases for all of the required functionality.

This is a great example of a powerful, and gloriously short, feedback loop. It's often referred to as the *red-green-refactor* cycle in honour of unit-test tools that show failing tests as a red progress bar, and passing tests as a green bar.

Even if you don't honour the test-first mantra, keep your feedback loop short and write unit tests during, or very shortly after, a section of code. Unit tests really do help "drive" our design: not only does it ensure that everything is functionally correct and prevent regressions, it's also a great way to explore how a class API will be used in production

—how easy and neat it is. This is invaluable feedback. The tests also stand as useful documentation of how to use a class once it's complete.

> **KEY ➤** Write tests *as you write* the code under test. Do not postpone test writing, or your tests will not be as effective.

This test-early, test-often approach can be applied at the unit, integration, and system level. Even if your project has no infrastructure for automated system tests, you can still take responsibility and verify the lines of code you write with unit tests. It's cheap and, given good code structure, it's easy.[2]

Another essential time to write a test is when you have to fix a bug in the production code. Rather than rush out a code fix, first write a failing unit test that illustrates the cause of the bug. Sometimes the act of writing this test serves to show other related flaws in the code. Then apply your bugfix, and make the test pass. The test enters your test pool, and will serve to ensure that the bug doesn't reappear in the future.

When to Run Tests

You can see a lot by just looking.

— Yogi Berra

Clearly, if you develop using TDD, you will be running your tests *as* you develop each feature to prove that your implementation is correct and sufficient.

But that is not the only life of your test code.

Add both the production code *and* its tests to version control. Your test is not thrown away, but joins the suite of existent tests. It lives on to ensure that your software continues to work as you expect. If someone later modifies the code badly, they'll be alerted to the fact before they get very far.

All tests should run on your build server as part of a *continuous integration* toolchain. Unit tests should be run by developers frequently on their development machines. Some development environments provide shortcuts to launch the unit tests easily; some systems scan your filesystem and run the unit tests when files change. However, I prefer to bake tests right into the build/compile/run process. If my unit-test suite fails, the code compilation is considered to have *failed* and the software cannot be run. This way, the tests are not ignorable. They run *every* time the code is built. When invoked manually, developers can forget to run tests, or will "avoid the inconvenience" whilst working.

Injecting the tests directly into the build process also encourages tests to be kept small, and to run fast.

---

2. Without good code structure, an attempt to write a test will help drive you towards better code structure.

Integration and system tests may take too long to run on a developer's machine every compilation. In this case, they may justifiably run only on the CI build server.

Remember that code-level, automated testing doesn't remove the need for a human QA review before your software release. Exploratory testing by real testing experts is invaluable, no matter how many unit, integration, and system tests you have in place. An automated suite of tests avoids introducing those easily fixable, easily preventable mistakes that would waste QA's time. It means that the things the QA guys do find will be *really* nasty bugs, not just simple ones. Hurrah!

What to Test

Test whatever is important in your application. What are your requirements?

Your tests must, naturally, test that each code unit behaves as required, returning accurate results. However, if performance is an important requirement for your application, then you should have tests in place to monitor the code's performance. If your server must answer queries within a certain time frame, include tests for this condition.

You may want to consider the *coverage* of your production code that the test cases execute. You can run tools to determine this. However, this tends to be an awful metric to chase after. It can be a huge distraction to write test code that tries to laboriously cover every production line; it's more important to focus on the most important behaviours and system characteristics.

Good Tests

Writing good tests requires practice and experience; it is perfectly possible to write bad tests. Don't be overly worried about this at first—it's most important to actually *start* writing tests than to be paralysed by fear that your tests are rubbish. Start writing tests and you'll start to learn.

Bad tests become baggage: a liability rather than an asset. They can slow down code development if they take ages to run. They can make code modification difficult if a simple code change breaks many hard-to-read tests.

The longer your tests take to run, the less frequently you'll run them, the less you'll use them, the less feedback you'll get from them. The less value they provide.

I once inherited a codebase that had a large suite of unit tests; this seemed a great sign. Sadly, those tests were effectively worse *legacy code* than the production code. Any code modification we made caused several test failures in hundreds-of-lines-long test methods that were intractable, dense, and hard to understand. Thankfully, this is not a common experience.

> **KEY** ➤ Bad tests can be a liability. They can impede effective development.

These are the characteristics of a good test:

- Short, clear name, so when it fails you can easily determine what the problem is (e.g., *new list is empty*)
- Maintainable: it is easy to write, easy to read, and easy to modify
- Runs quickly
- Up-to-date
- Runs without any prior machine configuration (e.g., you don't have to prepare your filesystem paths or configure a database before running it)
- Does not depend on any other tests that have run before or after it; there is no reliance on external state, or on any shared variables in the code
- Tests the *actual* production code (I've seen "unit tests" that worked on a *copy* of the production code—a copy that was out of date. Not useful. I've also seen special "testing" behaviour added to the SUT in test builds; this, too, is not a test of the real production code.)

These are some common descriptions of badly constructed tests:

- Tests that sometimes run, sometimes fail (often this is caused by the use of threads, or racy code that relies on specific timing, by reliance on external dependencies, the order of tests being run in the test suite, or on shared state)
- Tests that look awful and are hard to read or modify
- Tests that are too large (large tests are hard to understand, and the SUT clearly isn't very isolatable if it takes hundreds of lines to set up)
- Tests that exercise more than one thing in a single test case (a "test case" is a *singular* thing)
- Tests that attack a class API function by function, rather than addressing individual behaviours
- Tests for third-party code that you didn't write (there is no need to do that unless you have a good reason to distrust it)

- Tests that don't actually cover the main functionality or behaviour of a class, but that hide this behind a raft of tests for less important things (if you can do this, your class is probably too large)
- Tests that cover pointless things in excruciating detail (e.g., property getters and setters)
- Tests that rely on "white-box" knowledge of the internal implementation details of the SUT (this means you can't change the implementation without changing all the tests)
- Tests that work on only one machine

Sometimes a bad test smell indicates not (only) a bad test, but also bad code under test. These smells should be observed, and used to drive the design of your code.

What Does a Test Look Like?

The test framework you use will determine the shape of your test code. It may provide a structured set-up, and tear-down facility, and a way to group individual tests into larger *fixtures*.

Conventionally, in each test there will be some preparation, you then perform an operation, and finally validate the result of that operation. This is commonly known as the *arrange-act-assert* pattern. For unit tests, at the assert stage we typically aim for a single check—if you need to write multiple assertions then your test may not be performing a single test case.

Here's an example Java unit test method that follows this pattern:

```java
@Test
public void stringsCanBeCapitalised()
{
    String input    = "This string should be uppercase.";   ❶
    String expected = "THIS STRING SHOULD BE UPPERCASE.";

    String result = input.toUpperCase();                     ❷

    assertEquals(result, expected);                          ❸
}
```

❶ Arrange: we prepare the input

❷ Act: we perform the operation

❸ Assert: we validate the results of that operation

Maintaining this pattern helps keep tests focused and readable.

Of course, this test alone does not cover all of the potential ways to use and abuse String capitalisation. We need more tests to cover other inputs and expectations. Each test should be added as a new test method, not placed into this one.

Test Names

Focused tests have very clear names that read as simple sentences. If you can't easily name a test case, then your requirement is probably ambiguous, or you are attempting to test multiple things.

The fact that the test method *is* a test is usually implicit (because of an attribute like the `@Test` we saw earlier), so you needn't add the word `test` to the name. The preceding example need not be called `testThatStringsCanBeCapitalised`.

Imagine that your tests are read as specifications for your code; each test name is a statement about what the SUT does, a single fact. Avoid ambiguous words like "should," or words that don't add value like "must." Just as when we create names in our production code, avoid redundancy and unnecessary length.

Test names need not follow the same style conventions as production code; they effectively form their own domain-specific language. It's common to see much longer method names and the liberal use of underscores, even in languages like C# and Java where they are not idiomatic (the argument being `strings_can_be_capitalised` requires less squinting to read).

The Structure of Tests

Ensure that your test suite covers the important functionality of your code. Consider the "normal" input cases. Consider also the common "failure cases." Consider what happens at boundary values, including the empty or zero state. It's a laudable goal to aim to cover all requirements and all the functionality of your entire system with system and integration tests, and cover all code with unit tests. However, that can require some serious effort.

Do not duplicate tests: it adds effort, confusion, and maintenance cost. Each test case you write verifies one fact; that fact does not need to be verified again, either in a second test, or as part of the test for something else. If your first test case checks a precondition after constructing an object, then you can assume that this precondition holds in every other test case you write—there is no need to reproduce the check every time you construct an object.

A common mistake is to see a class with five methods, and think that you need five tests, one to exercise each method. This is an understandable (but naïve) approach. Function-based tests are rarely useful, as you cannot generally test a single method in isolation. After calling it, you'll need to use other methods to inspect the object's state.

Instead, write tests that go through the specific behaviours of the code. This leads to a far more cohesive and clear set of tests.

Maintain the Tests

Your test code is as important as the production code, so consider its shape and structure. If things get messy, clean it, and refactor it.

If you change the behaviour of a class so its tests fail, don't just comment out the tests and run away. Maintain the tests. It can be tempting to "save time" near deadlines by skipping test cleanliness. But rushed carelessness here *will* come back to bite you.

On one project, I received an email from a colleague: *I was working on your XYZ class, and the unit tests stopped working, so I had to remove them all.* I was rather surprised by this, and looked at what tests had been removed. Sadly, these were important test cases that were clearly pointing out a fundamental problem with the new code. So I restored the test code and "fixed" the bug by backing out the change. We then worked together to craft a new test case for the required functionality, and then reimplemented a version that satisfied the old tests and the new.

> **KEY** ➤ Maintain your test suite, and listen to it when it talks to you.

Picking a Test Framework

The unit or integration test framework you use shapes your tests, dictating the style of assertions and checks you can use, and the structure of your test code (e.g., are the test cases written in free functions, or as methods within a test fixture class?).

So it's important to pick a good unit test framework. It doesn't need to be complex or heavyweight. Indeed, it's preferable to not choose an unwieldy tool. Remember, you can get very very far with the humble `assert`. I often start testing new prototype code with just a `main` method and a series of `assert`s.

Most test frameworks follow the "xUnit" model which came from Kent Beck's original Smalltalk SUnit. This model was ported and popularised with JUnit (for Java) although there are broadly equivalent implementations in most every language—for example, NUnit (C#) and CppUnit (C++). This kind of framework is not always ideal; xUnit style testing leads to non-idiomatic code in some languages (in C++, for example, it's rather clumsy and anachronistic; other test frameworks can work better—check out *Catch* as a great alternative[3]).

Some frameworks provide pretty GUIs with red and green bars to clearly indicate success or failure. That might make you happy, but I'm not a big fan. I think you shouldn't

---

3. The Catch unit test framework (available from GitHub (*http://github.com/philsquared/Catch*)).

need a separate UI or a different execution step for development tests. They should ideally be baked right into your build system. The feedback should be reported instantly like any other code error.

System tests tend to use a different form of framework, where we see the use of tools like Fit (*http://fit.c2.com/*) and Cucumber (*http://cukes.info*). These tools attempt to define tests in a more humane, less programmatic manner, allowing nonprogrammers to participate in the test/specification-wring process.

No Code Is an Island

When writing unit tests, we aim to place truly *isolated* units of code into the "system under test." These units can be instantiated without the rest of the system being present.

A unit's interaction with the outside world is expressed through two contracts: the interface it provides, and the interfaces it expects. The unit must not depend on anything else—specifically not on any shared global state or singleton objects.

> KEY ➤ Global variables and singleton objects are anathema to reliable testing. You can't easily test a unit with hidden dependencies.

The interface that a unit of code *provides* is simply the methods, functions, events, and properties in its API. Perhaps it also provides some kind of callback interface.

The interfaces it *expects* are determined by the objects it collaborates with through its API. These are the parameter types in its public methods or any messages it subscribes to. For example, an `Invoice` class that requires a `Date` parameter relies on the date's interface.

The objects that a class collaborates with should be passed in as constructor parameters, a practice known as *parameterise from above*. This allows your class to eschew hardwired internal dependencies on other code, instead having the link configured by its owner. If the collaborators are described by an *interface* rather than a concrete type, then we have a seam through which we can perform our tests; we have the ability to provide alternative test implementations.

This is an example of how tests tend to lead to better factored code. It forces your code to have fewer hardwired connections and internal assumptions. It's also good practice to rely on a minimal interface that describes a specific collaboration, rather than on an entire class that may provide much more than the simple interface required.

> KEY ➤ Factoring your code to make it "testable" leads to better code design.

When you test an object that relies on an external interface, you can provide a "dummy" version of that interface in the test case. Terms vary in testing circles, but often these are called *test doubles*. There are various forms of doubles, but we most commonly use:

Dummies

Dummy objects are usually empty husks—the test will not invoke them, but they exist to satisfy parameter lists.

Stubs

Stub objects are simplistic implementations of an interface, usually returning a canned answer, perhaps also recording information about the calls into it.

Mocks

Mock objects are the kings of test double land, a facility provided by a number of different mocking libraries. A mock object can be created automatically from a named interface, and then told up-front about how the SUT will use it. A SUT test operation is performed, and then you can inspect the mock object to verify the behaviour was as expected.

Different languages have different support for mocking frameworks. It's easiest to synthesize mocks in languages with reflection.

Sensible use of mock objects can make tests simpler and clearer. But, of course, you can have too much of a good thing. Tests that are encumbered by complex use of many mock objects can become very tricky to reason about, and hard to maintain. *Mock mania* is another common smell of bad test code, and may highlight that the structure of the SUT is not correct.

Conclusion

> *If you don't care about quality, you can meet any other requirement.*
>
> — Gerald M. Weinberg

Tests help us to write our code. They help us to write *good* code. They help maintain the *quality* of our code. They can *drive* the code design, and serve to document how to use it. But tests don't solve all problems with software development. Edsger Dijkstra said: *Program testing can be used to show the presence of bugs, but never to show their absence.*

No test is perfect, but the existence of tests serves to increase confidence in the code you write, and in the code you maintain. The effort you put into developer testing is a trade-off; how much effort do you want to invest in writing tests to gain confidence? Remember that your test suite is only as good as the tests you have in it. It is perfectly possible to miss an important case; you can deploy into production and still let a problem slip through. For this reason, test code should be reviewed as carefully as production code.

Nonetheless, the punchline is simple: if code is important enough to be written, it is important enough to be tested. So write development tests for your production code. Use them to *drive* the design of your code. Write the tests *as* you write the production code. And automate the running of those tests.

Shorten the feedback loop.

Testing is fundamental and important. This chapter can only really scratch the surface, encourage you to test, and prompt you to find out more about good testing techniques.

Questions

1. How many styles of testing have you been exposed to?

2. Which is the best development test technique: test-first, or test (very shortly) after coding? Why? How has your experience shaped this answer?

3. Is it a good idea to employ a specialist unit-test writing engineer to help craft a high-quality test suite?

4. Why do QA departments traditionally not write much test code, and generally focus on running through test scripts and performing exploratory testing?

5. How can you best introduce test-driven development into a codebase that has never received automated testing? What kind of problems would you encounter?

6. Investigate *behaviour-driven development*. How does it differ from "traditional" TDD? What problems does it solve? Does it complement or replace TDD? Is this a direction you should move your testing in?

See also

- *Getting One Past the Goalpost* Programmer testing improves confidence in the releases we give to the QA team for their testing purposes.

- *Keeping Up Appearances* Good code layout and presentation is as essential in test code as it is in production code.

- *Expect the Unexpected* It is sensible to include test cases for the "less likely" scenarios that your code may not be expecting.

- *Bug Hunting* Use tests to guide your debugging process.

- *A Tale of Two Systems* An example of how unit tests help to improve code quality.

Try this....

If you don't already, start to write unit tests for your code today. If you already use tests, pay attention to how they inform and drive your code design.

10,000 MONKEYS
(OR THEREABOUTS)

DEVELOPER

THERE IS NO "I" IN TEAM

TESTERS

BUT WE CANNOT SPELL
BUG WITHOUT "U"

CHAPTER 12

Coping with Complexity

Simplicity is a great virtue but it requires hard work to achieve it and education to appreciate it. And to make matters worse: complexity sells better.

— Edsger Dijkstra

Code is complex. Complexity is a battle that we all have to fight daily.

Of course, your code is great, isn't it? It's other people's code that is complex.

Well, no. Not always. Admit it. It's all too easy to write something complicated. It happens when you're not paying attention. It happens when you don't plan ahead sufficiently. It happens when you start working on a "simple" problem, but soon you've discovered so many corner cases that your simple algorithm has grown to reflect a labyrinth, ready to entrap an unwary programmer.

My observation is that software complexity stems from three main sources. Blobs. And lines.

And what you get when you combine them: people.

In this chapter, we'll take a look at each of these and see what we can learn about writing better software.

Blobs

The first part of software complexity we should consider relates to *blobs*: that is, the components we write. The size and number of those blobs determine complexity.

Some software complexity is a natural consequence of size; the larger a project becomes, the more blobs we need, the harder it is to comprehend, and the harder it is to work with. This is *necessary* complexity.

But there is plenty of unnecessary complexity that causes hassle. I've lost count of the times I have opened a C++ header file, and balked at thousands of lines in a single class declaration. How is a mere mortal supposed to be able to understand what such a beast does? This is surely *unnecessary* complexity.

Sometimes these large monsters are autogenerated by code "wizards" (notable examples are GUI construction tools). However, it's not just tools that are to blame. Serious code hooligans can produce these code monsters without a second thought. (In fact, the lack of thought is often the cause of such abominations.)

So we need to manage our *necessary* complexity. And educate—or shoot—our unnecessary programmers.

It's important to realise that size itself *is not* the enemy. If you have a software system that has to do three things, then you need to put code in there to do those three things. If you remove some of that code in order to reduce complexity, then you'll have different problems. (That's being *simplistic* rather than simple, and it's not a good thing.)

No, size itself is not the problem. We need enough code to meet requirements. The problem is how we structure that code. It's how that size is distributed.

Imagine you start working on a *vast* system. And you discover that the class structure of the beast is like the image shown here:

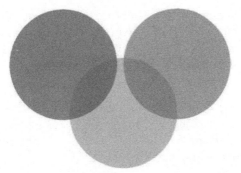

Three whole classes! Now, is that a complex system or not?

On one level, it doesn't seem complicated at all. There are only three parts! How could that be hard to understand? And the software design has the added benefit of looking like Mickey Mouse, so it must be good.

In fact, this appears to be a beautifully simple design. You could describe it to someone in seconds.

But, of course, each of those parts will be so large and dense, presumably with so much interconnection and spaghetti logic that they are likely to be practically impossible to work with. So this is almost certainly a *very* complex system, hidden behind a *simplistic* design.

Clearly, a better structure—one that is simpler to understand, and simpler to maintain —would consider those three sections as "modules" and further subdivide them into other parts: packages, components, classes, or whatever abstraction makes sense. Something more like the following image:

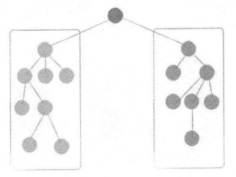

Immediately, this feels better. It looks like a lot of small (so understandable, and likely simpler) components connected into a larger whole. Our brains are suited to dividing problems into hierarchies like this and reasoning about the problems when thus abstracted.

The consequences of such a design are increased comprehension and greater modifiability (you can work on a part of the system's functionality by identifying the smaller part that relates to it, rather than having to roll your sleeves up and dive into a single behemoth class). We prefer classes with better *cohesion* that do a small number of things well—preferably just *one* thing.

Of course, the trick to making this work—the trick that enables a design like this to actually *be* simple rather than just *look* simple—is to ensure that each of the blobs has the correct *roles and responsibilities*. That is, a single responsibility resides in a single part of the system rather than smeared across it.

Case Study: Reducing Blob Complexity

One of my favourite recent reductions in software complexity was a section of code with two very large objects that were so interrelated they were practically one and the same class.

I started chipping away at one of the objects, realising that it contained hundreds of unused "helper" methods. I mercilessly removed them; an enjoyable experience not unlike deflating a helium balloon. And so for effect, I started speaking in an excitable high voice. This was code becoming simpler.

Now that I could see the remainder of the object, it was clear that the majority of its methods simply forwarded to the partner. So I removed those methods and made all calling code just use the other object. There were just two remaining methods, one of which belonged on the partner anyway, and one which should have been a simple non-member function.

The result?

A far simpler class design, I think you'll agree.

Of course, the next step was to decompose the remaining blob. But that's another story. (And nowhere near as interesting.)

Lines

We've considered blobs: the components and objects that we create. To paraphrase John Donne: *No code is an island.* Complexity is not borne solely from the blobs, but from the way they connect.

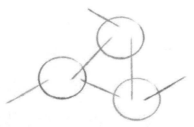

In general, software designs are simpler when there are fewer lines. The more connections between blobs (this is known as greater *coupling* if you're talking like a proper grown-up), the more rigid a design is, and the more interoperation you have to comprehend (and fight) as you work on a system.

At the most basic level, a system comprised of many objects, none of which are connected at all, would appear the simplest. But it is not a single system at all. It's a number of separate systems.

As we add connections, we create actual software systems. As we add more blobs and, crucially, lines between them, the more complex our systems become.

The structure of our software interconnections dramatically affects our ease of working with it. Consider the following structures, which are based on real examples I have been working on.

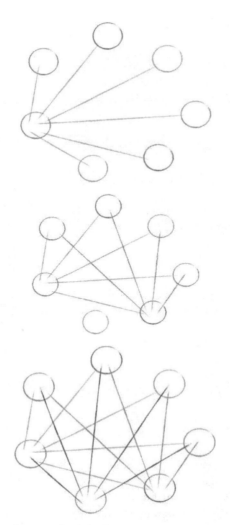

What's your reaction to them? Which looks simpler? I'll admit that working on the last one almost caused my head to explode.

When we map out connections, we see that complexity often springs from cycles in our graph. Cyclical dependencies are generally the most complex relationships to consider. When objects are codependent, their structure is rigid, not easy to change, and often very hard to work with. A change to one object usually requires a change to the other. The objects effectively become one entity; one that's harder to maintain.

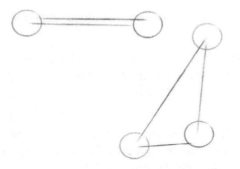

These kinds of relationships can be simplified by breaking one of the links. Perhaps by introducing new abstract interfaces to reduce the coupling between objects.

This kind of structure enhances composability, introduces flexibility, and fosters testability (you can write testing versions of components behind those abstract interfaces). We can use well-named interfaces to make those relationships descriptive.

One of the nastiest systems I've had to work with in a long time looked like this:

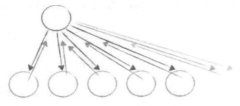

It seems a superficially simple model: one parent object represents "the system" and creates all of the child objects. However, each of those objects was given a back-reference to the parent, so they could access each other. This design effectively allowed every child-object to rely on (and become closely coupled with) every sibling, locking the entire system down into one rigid shape.

Michael Feathers described this to me as the known anti-pattern *distributed self*. I had another name for it, but it's not polite enough to print.

And Finally: People

So software complexity depends on the structure of our blobs and lines.

But it's important to observe that blobs and lines don't create themselves. Those structures are not intrinsically to blame. It is the *people writing the code* who are responsible (yes, that's you, gentle reader). It is the programmer who has the power to introduce incredible complexity, or to reduce a nasty problem down to an elegant and simple solution.

How often do people set out to write nasty, complex code? You may think that your corrupt coworkers are planning to introduce more stress in your life with their Machiavellian code. But complexity is generally accidental, *rarely* something someone adds wilfully.

It's often the product of history: programmers extend and extend and extend the system, with no time allowed for refactoring. Or the "prototype to throw away" turns into a production system. By the time it's being used, there's no chance to take it apart and start again.

Software complexity is caused by humans working in real-world situations. The only way we can reduce complexity is by taking charge of it, and trying to prevent work pressures from forcing our code into unworkable structures.

Conclusion

In this little saunter through software complexity territory, we've seen that complexity arises from blobs (our software components), lines (the connections between those components), but mostly from the people who construct these software monstrosities.

Oh, and of course, it comes from the Singleton design pattern. But no one uses that anymore, do they?

Questions
1. Why is simplicity in code design better? Is there a difference between simplicity in *design* and in code *implementation*?
2. How do you strive for simplicity in your code? How do you know you've achieved it?
3. Does the *nature* of connections matter as much as the number of connections? What connections are "better" than others?
4. If software complexity stems from social problems, how can we address it?
5. How can you tell the difference between *necessary* and *unnecessary* complexity?
6. If it's true that many programmers *do* know that their software designs should be simpler, how can we encourage them to craft simpler code?

See also
- *Keep It Simple* The flip side of complexity: *simplicity*. This chapter covers some ideas for constructing simple designs.
- *People Power* It's *people* who create complexity. Aim to work with the kind of people who reduce, not promote, disorder.

- *Wallowing in Filth* Unnecessary complexity leads to messy code that is hard to understand.

- *A Case for Code Reuse* Employing the right *code reuse* strategy can help reduce complexity. The wrong strategy makes a complex ball of mud.

- *A Tale of Two Systems* An example of a complex design contrasted with a simpler one, showing the consequences of each design.

Try this....

Identify the ways that you have introduced unnecessary complexity into your recent code. How can you address this?

CHAPTER 13

A Tale of Two Systems

> *Architecture is the art of how to waste space.*
>
> — Philip Johnson

A software system is like a city—an intricate network of highways and hostelries, of backroads and buildings. There's a lot going on in a busy city; flows of control are continually being born, weaving their life through it, and dying. A wealth of data is amassed, stored, and destroyed. There are a range of buildings: some tall and beautiful, some squat and functional, others dilapidated, falling into disrepair. As data flows around them, there are traffic jams and tailbacks, rush hours, and road works. The quality of your software city is directly related to how much town planning went into it.

Some software systems are lucky; they have had thoughtful design from experienced architects. They are structured with a sense of elegance and balance. They are well-mapped and easy to navigate. Others are not so lucky—a software settlement that grew up around the accidental gathering of some code. The transport infrastructure is inadequate and the buildings are drab and uninspiring. Placed in the middle of it, you'd get completely lost trying to find a route out.

Where would your code rather live? What kind of software city would you rather construct?

In this chapter I will tell the story of two such software cities. It's a true story and, like all good stories, this one has a moral at the end. They say *experience is a great teacher*, but other people's experience is even better; if you can learn from these projects' mistakes and successes then you might save yourself—and your software—a lot of pain.

These two systems are particularly interesting because they turned out very differently, despite being superficially very similar, having similar code size, product domain, and experience level of engineers.

In this story, names have been changed to protect the innocent. And the guilty.

The Messy Metropolis

Build up, build up, prepare the road! Remove the obstacles out of the way of my people.

— Isaiah 57:14

The first software system we'll look at is known as The Messy Metropolis. It's one I look back on fondly—not because it was good, or because it was enjoyable to work with, but because it taught me a valuable lesson about software development when I first came across it.

I joined the Metropolis project when it was "mature." It was a complex codebase that took a fantastically long time to learn. At the micro level, lines of code were messy and inconsistent. At the macro level, the design was messy and inconsistent.

No one on the team really knew how all of the code worked. The code had grown "organically" over a period of years (which is a polite way to say that no one had performed any architectural design of note, and that various bits had been bolted on over time without much thought). No one had ever stopped to impose a sane structure on the code. It had grown by acretion; this was a classic example of a system that had received absolutely no architectural design. But a codebase never has *no* architecture. It just has a very poor one.

The Metropolis' state of affairs was understandable (but not condonable) when you looked at the history of the company that built it: it was a start-up with heavy pressure to get many new releases out rapidly. Delays were not tolerable—they would spell financial ruin. The software engineers were driven to get code shipping as quickly as humanly possible (if not sooner). And so the code had been thrown together in a series of mad dashes.

> KEY ➤ Poor company structure and unhealthy development processes will be reflected by a poor software architecture.

The Metropolis' lack of town planning had many consequences, which we'll see here. These ramifications were severe and went far beyond what you might naïvely expect of a bad design.

Incomprehensiblity

The Metropolis' architecture, with its lack of imposed structure, had led to a software system that was remarkably tricky to comprehend, and practically impossible to modify. New recruits coming into the project (like myself) were stunned by the complexity and unable to get to grips with what was going on.

The bad design encouraged further bad design to be bolted onto it—in fact, it literally forced you to do so—as there was no way to extend the design in a sane way. The path of least resistance for the job in hand was always taken; there was no obvious way to fix the structural problems and so new functionality was thrown in wherever it would cause less hassle.

> KEY ➤ Maintain the quality of a software design. Bad design leads to further bad design.

Lack of Cohesion

The system's components were not at all cohesive. Where each one should have had a single, well-defined role, they each contained a grab bag of functionality that wasn't necessarily related. This made it hard to determine why a component existed at all, and hard to work out where a particular piece of functionality had been implemented in the system.

Naturally, this made bug fixing a nightmare. It seriously affected the quality and reliability of the software.

Both functionality and data were located in the wrong place in the system. Many things you'd consider "core services" were not implemented in the hub of the system, but were simulated by the outlying modules (at great pain and expense).

Further software archaeology showed why: there had been personality struggles in the original team, and so a few key programmers had begun to build their own little software empires. They'd grab the functionality they thought was cool and plonk it into their module, even if it didn't belong there. To deal with this they would then make ever-more baroque communication mechanisms to stitch the control back to the correct place.

> KEY ➤ The health of the working relationships in your development team will feed directly into the software design. Unhealthy relationships and inflated egos lead to unhealthy software.

Cohesion and Coupling

Key qualities of software design are *cohesion* and *coupling*. This is not a newfangled "OO" concept; developers have been talking about this for many years (since the emergence of structured design in the early 1970s). We aim to design systems with components that have:

Strong cohesion
  Cohesion is a measure of how related functionality is gathered together and how well the parts *inside* a module work as a whole. Cohesion is the glue holding a module together.

Weakly cohesive modules are a sign of bad decomposition. Each module must have a clearly defined role, and not be a grab bag of unrelated functionality.

Loose coupling

Coupling is a measure of the interdependency *between* modules; the amount of wiring to and from them. In the simplest designs, modules have little coupling and so are less reliant on one another. Obviously, modules can't be totally decoupled, or they wouldn't be working together at all!

Modules interconnect in many ways, some direct, some indirect. A module can call functions on other modules or be called by other modules. It may use web services or facilities published by another module. It may use another module's data types or share some data (perhaps variables or files).

Good software design limits the lines of communication to only those that are absolutely necessary. These communication lines are part of what determines the architecture.

Unnecessary Coupling

The Metropolis had no clear layering. Dependencies between modules were not unidirectional; coupling was often bidirectional. Component A would hackily reach into the innards of component B to get its work done for one task. Elsewhere component B had hardcoded calls onto component A. There was no bottom layer, or central hub to the system. It was one monolithic blob of software.

This meant that the individual parts of the system were so tightly coupled that you couldn't bring up a skeletal system without creating every single component. Any change in a single component rippled out, requiring changes in many dependent components. The code components did not make sense in isolation.

This made low-level testing impossible. Not only were code-level unit tests impossible to write, but component-level integration tests could not be constructed as every component depended on almost every other component. Of course, testing had never been a particularly high priority in the company (we don't have anywhere near enough time to do that), so this "wasn't a problem." Needless to say, the software was not very reliable.

> KEY ➤ Good design takes into account connection mechanisms and the number (and nature) of inter-component connections. The individual parts of a system should be able to stand alone. Tight coupling leads to untestable code.

Code Problems

The problems with bad top-level design had wormed their way down to the code level. Problems beget problems. Because there was no common design and no overall project "style," no one bothered with common coding standards, the use of common libraries, or employing common idioms. There were no naming conventions for components, classes, or files. There was not even a common build system; duct tape, shell scripts, and Perl glue nestled alongside makefiles and Visual Studio project files. Compiling this monster was considered a rite of passage!

One of the most subtle, but serious, Metropolis problems was duplication. Without a clear design, and a clear place for functionality to live, wheels had been reinvented across the entire codebase. Simple things like common algorithms and data structures were repeated across many modules, each implementation with its own set of obscure bugs and quirky behavioural traits. Larger-scale concerns like external communication and data caching were also implemented multiple times.

More software archaeology showed why: the Metropolis started out as a series of separate prototypes that got tacked together when they should have been thrown away. The Metropolis was actually an accidental conurbation. When stitched together, the code components had never really fitted together properly. Over time, the careless stitches began to tear, so the components pulled against one another and caused friction in the codebase, rather than working in harmony.

> KEY ➤ A lax and fuzzy architecture leads to individual code components that are badly written and don't fit well together. It also leads to duplication of code and effort.

Problems Outside the Code

The problems within the Metropolis spilled out from the codebase to cause havoc elsewhere in the company. There were problems in the development team, but the architectural rot also affected the people supporting and using the product:

The development team
New recruits coming into the project (like myself) were stunned by the complexity and unable to get to grips with what was going on. This partially explains why very few new recruits stayed at the company for any length of time—staff turnover was very high.

Those who remained had to work very hard—stress levels on the project were high. Planning new features instilled a dread fear.

Slow development cycle
Maintaining the Metropolis was a frightful task, so even simple changes or *small* bugfixes took an unpredictable length of time. Managing the software development cycle was difficult, timescales were hard to plan, and the release cycle was cumbersome and slow. Customers were left waiting for important features, and manage-

ment got increasingly frustrated at the development team's inability to meet business requirements.

Support engineers
The product support engineers had an awful time trying to support a flaky product, whilst working out the intricate behavioural differences between relatively minor software releases.

Third-party support
An external control protocol has been developed, enabling other devices to control the Metropolis remotely. Because it was a thin veneer over the guts of the software, it reflected the Metropolis' architecture, which means that it was baroque, hard to understand, prone to fail randomly, and impossible to use. Third-party engineers' lives were also made miserable by the poor structure of the Metropolis.

Intra-company politics
The development problems led to friction between different tribes in the company. The development team had strained relations with the marketing and sales guys, and the manufacturing department was permanently stressed every time a release loomed on the horizon. The managers despaired.

> KEY ➤ The consequences of a bad architecture are not constrained within the code. They spill outside to affect people, teams, processes, and timescales.

A Postcard from the Metropolis

The Metropolis' design was almost completely irredeemable—believe me we tried to fix it. The amount of effort required to rework, refactor, and correct the problems with the code structure had become prohibitive. A rewrite wasn't a cheap option.

The consequence of the Metropolis' "design" was a diabolical situation that was inexorably getting worse. It was so hard to add new features that people were just applying more bodges, sticking plasters, and calculated fudges. No one enjoyed working with the code, and the project was heading in a downward spiral. The lack of design had led to bad code, which led to bad team morale and increasingly lengthy development cycles. This eventually led to severe financial problems for the company.

Bad architecture has a profound effect and severe repercussions. The lack of foresight and design in the Messy Metropolis led to:

- A low-quality product with infrequent releases
- An inflexible system which couldn't accommodate change or the addition of new functionality
- Pervasive code problems

- Staffing problems (stress, morale, turnover)
- A lot of messy internal company politics
- Lack of success for the company
- Many painful headaches and late nights working on the code

Design Town

> *Form ever follows function.*
>
> — Louis Henry Sullivan

The Design Town software project was superficially very similar to the Messy Metropolis. It was a similar product implemented in the same technologies. However, it was built in a very different way and so the internal structure worked out very differently.

The Design Town project was written from scratch by a small number of programmers. Like the Metropolis, the team structure was flat. Fortunately, there was no interpersonal rivalry, or any vying for positions of power in the team. From the outset there was a clear vision and set of requirements for the initial product.

An initial design direction was decided (not a big up-front design, but *just enough* design to work). The major functional areas were demarked, and some core architectural concerns like threading models sketched. The most important functional areas received some initial design attention.

Decisions about some of the basic housekeeping concerns were made early to ensure that the code would grow easily and cohesively: the top-level file structure, how we'd name things, a "house" presentation style with common coding idioms, the choice of unit test framework, and the supporting infrastructure. These *fine detail* factors were very important, they influenced many later design decisions.

Design and code construction was either done in pairs or carefully reviewed to ensure that work was correct. The design and the code developed and matured over time, and as the story of Design Town unfolded, there were consequences.

Locating Functionality

With a clear overview of the system structure in place from the very beginning, new units of functionality were consistently added to the correct functional areas of the codebase. There was never a question about where code belonged. It was also easy to find the implementation of existing functionality in order to extend it, or to fix problems.

Now, sometimes putting new code in the *right* place was harder than simply bodging it into a more convenient, but less tasteful, place. So the existence of an architectural plan sometimes made the developers work harder. The payoff for this extra effort was a *much* easier life later on, when maintaining or extending the system—there was very little cruft to trip over.

An architecture helps you to locate functionality: to add it, to modify it, or to fix it. It provides a template for you to slot work into and a map to navigate the system.

Consistency

The entire system was consistent. Every decision at every level was taken in the context of the whole design. The developers did this intentionally from the outset so all the code produced matched the design fully, and matched all the other code written.

Over the project's history, despite many changes ranging across the entire scope of the codebase—from individual lines of code to the system structure—everything followed the original design template.

> KEY ➤ A clear architectural design leads to a consistent system. All decisions should be taken in the context of the architectural design.

The good taste and elegance of the top-level design naturally fed down to the lower levels. Even at the lowest levels, the code was uniform and neat. A clearly defined software design ensured that there was no duplication, that familiar design patterns were used throughout, familiar interface idioms were adopted, and that there were no unusual object lifetimes or odd resource management issues. Lines of code were written in the context of the town plan.

> KEY ➤ Clear architecture helps reduce duplication of functionality.

Growing the Architecture

Some entirely new functional areas appeared in the "big picture" design—storage management and an external control facility, for example. In the Metropolis project, this was a crushing blow and incredibly hard to do. But in Design Town things worked differently.

The system design, like the code, was considered malleable and refactorable. One of the development team's core principles was to stay nimble—that nothing should be set in stone—and so the architecture should be changed when necessary. This encouraged us to keep our designs simple and easy to change. Consequently the code could grow rapidly and maintain a good internal structure. Accommodating new functional blocks was not a problem.

> KEY ➤ Software architecture is not set in stone. Change it if you need to. To be changeable, the architecture must remain simple. Resist changes that compromise simplicity.

Deferring Design Decisions

An XP principle that enhanced the quality of Design Town was YAGNI (don't do anything if *you aren't going to need it*). It encouraged us to design only the important stuff early on, and to defer all remaining decisions until later—when we had a clearer picture of the actual requirements and how best to fit them into the system. This is an immensely powerful design approach, and quite liberating:

- One of the worst things you can do is design something you don't yet understand. YAGNI forces you to wait until you know what the problem really is and how it should be accommodated by the design. It eliminates guesswork, and ensures that the design will be correct.

- It is dangerous to add everything you *might* need (including the kitchen sink) to a software design when you first create it. Most of your design work will be wasted effort, extra baggage that you'll need to support over the entire changing life of the software. It costs more at first, and continues to cost over the life of the project.

> KEY ➤ Defer design decisions until you *have* to take them. Don't make architectural decisions when you don't know the requirements yet. Don't guess.

Maintaining Quality

From the outset, the Design Town project put a number of quality control processes in place:

- Pair programming
- Code/design reviews for anything not pair programmed
- Unit tests for every piece of code

These ensured that the system never had an incorrect, badly fitting change applied. Anything that didn't mesh with the software design was rejected. This might sound draconian, but these were processes that the developers bought into.

This buy-in highlights an important attitude: the developers believed in the design, and considered it important enough to protect. They took ownership of, and personal responsibility for, the design.

> KEY ➤ Design quality must be maintained. This can only happen when the developers are given responsibility and take it seriously.

Managing Technical Debt

Despite these quality control measures, Design Town development was fairly pragmatic. As deadlines approached, a number of corners were cut to allow projects to ship on time. Small code *sins* or design warts were allowed to enter the codebase, either to get functionality working quickly or to avoid high-risk changes near a release.

However, unlike the Messy Metropolis project, these fudges were marked as *technical debt* and scheduled for later revision. These warts stood out clearly and the developers were not happy about them until they were dealt with. Again, we see the developers taking responsibility for the quality of the design.

Technical Debt

Technical debt is a term coined by Ward Cunningham that's widely used in the software industry today. The metaphor leans on the financial world: making a decision to help ship software quickly is like taking on a loan. It can enable you to do something *now* that you would not otherwise be able to do.

But you can't ignore that loan—you always have to pay it back. The longer it takes to pay back, the more it costs you. If you fail to make timely repayments, you'll be stuck paying off interest on the loan, and your purchase power diminishes.

In the software world, that means return to your code to update it, or else your progress will slow as the code bogs down in accrued debt. This is important: in the long run, lower code quality means longer development times, but a responsible short-term loan *can* speed things up.

Technical debt might be deferred refactoring, design adjustments that reflect what you've discovered, waiting to update libraries or toolchains until after the next major release, or rationalising the logging/debugging scaffolding.

This is a colourful metaphor that can be misused: technical debt does *not* just mean doing something badly. Sometimes writing bad code is justified as being "pragmatic"; there is a difference between a pragmatic choice and a sloppy one.

Consciously managing technical debt is a powerful weapon in your development arsenal. Don't let debt build up, and keep it visible. Like a real loan, pay back debt as early as possible to avoid suffering excessive interest and charges.

Tests Shape Design

One of our core decisions was that the code should be unit tested and the system covered with integration and acceptance tests. Unit testing brings many advantages, one of which is the ability to change sections of the software without worrying about destroying everything else in the process.

Some areas of the Design Town internal structure received quite radical rework whilst the unit tests gave us confidence that the rest of the system had not been broken. For example, the thread model and interconnection interface of the data pipeline was changed fundamentally. This was a serious design change relatively late in the development of that subsystem, but the rest of the code interfacing with that pipeline continued executing perfectly. The tests gave us capability to change the design.

This kind of "major" design change slowed down as Design Town matured. After an amount of design rework, things settled down, and subsequently there were only minor design changes. The system developed quickly, in an iterative manner, with each step improving the design, until it reached a relatively stable plateau.

> KEY ➤ Having a good set of automated tests for your system allows you to make fundamental architectural changes with minimal risk. It gives you space to work in.

Another major benefit of the unit tests was their remarkable shaping of the code design; they practically enforced good structure. Each small code component was crafted as a well-defined entity that could stand alone—as it had to be constructible in a unit test without requiring the rest of the system to be built up around it. Writing unit tests ensured that each module of code was internally cohesive and loosely coupled from the rest of the system. The unit tests forced careful thought about each unit's interface, and ensured that its API was meaningful and internally consistent.

> KEY ➤ Unit testing your code leads to better software designs, so design for testability.

Time for Design

One of the contributing factors to Design Town's success was the allotted development timescale, which was neither too long nor too short (as Goldilocks would say, it was "just right"). A project needs a conducive environment in which to thrive.

Given too much time, programmers often want to create their magnum opus (the kind of thing which will always be *almost* ready, but never quite materialises). A little pressure is a wonderful thing, and a sense of urgency helps to get things done. However, given too little time, it simply isn't possible to achieve any worthwhile design, and you'll only get a half-baked solution rushed out—just like the Metropolis.

> KEY ➤ Good project planning leads to superior designs. Allot sufficient time to create an architectural masterpiece—they don't appear instantly.

Working with the Design

Whilst the codebase was large, it was coherent and easily understood. New programmers could pick it up and work with it relatively easily. There were no unnecessarily complex interconnections to understand, or weird legacy code to work around.

Because the code has generated relatively few problems, and is still enjoyable to work with, there has been a very, very low turnover of team members. This is due, in part, to the developers taking ownership of the design and continually wanting to improve it.

It was interesting to observe how the development team dynamics followed the architecture. Design Town project principles mandated that no one *owned* any area of the design, that any developer could work anywhere in the system. Everyone was expected to write high-quality code. Whereas the Metropolis was a sprawling mess created by many uncoordinated, fighting programmers, Design Town was clean and cohesive, closely cooperating software components created by closely cooperating colleagues. In many ways, Conway's law worked in reverse and the team gelled together as the software did.[1]

> KEY ➤ A team's organisation has an inevitable effect on the code it produces. Over time, the architecture also affects how well the team works together. When teams separate, the code interacts clumsily. When they work together, the architecture integrates well.

So What?

This simple story about two software systems is certainly not an exhaustive treatise on software architecture, but I have shown how architecture profoundly affects a software project. An architecture influences almost everything that comes into contact with it, determining the health of the codebase and also the health of the surrounding areas. Just as a thriving city can bring prosperity and renown to its local area, a good software architecture will help its project flourish and bring success to those depending on it.

Good architecture is the product of many factors, including (but not limited to):

- Actually doing intentional up-front design before ploughing into code. Many projects fail in this way before they even start. There is a tension here: to not under-design, but likewise to not over-design.

- The quality and experience of the designers. (It helps to have made a few mistakes beforehand to point you in the right direction next time! The Metropolis project certainly taught me a thing or two.)

---

1. Conway's law states that code structure follows team structure. Simply stated, it says, *If you have four groups working on a compiler, you'll get a four-pass compiler.*

- Keeping the design clearly in view as development progresses.
- The team being given, and taking responsibility for the overall design of the software.
- Never being afraid of changing the design: nothing is set in stone.
- Having the right people on the team: including designers, programmers, and managers. Ensure that the development team is the right size. Ensure that they have healthy working relationships, as these relationships will inevitably feed into the structure of the code.
- Making design decisions at the appropriate time, when you know all the information to be able to make them. Deferring design decisions you cannot yet make.
- Good project management, with the right kind of deadlines.

Questions

1. What's the best system architecture you've ever seen?

    - How did you recognise it as good?
    - What were the consequences of this architecture, both inside the codebase and outside?
    - What led to it being so well-designed?
    - What have you learnt from it?

2. What's the worst architecture system you've ever seen?

    - How did you recognise it as bad?
    - What were the consequences of this architecture, both inside the codebase and outside?
    - How did it get into that state?
    - What have you learnt from it?
    - How would you resolve its problems?

3. Where does your current project sit between the two? Which of your prior experiences can you build on now to improve the code, or the processes with which you build it?

See also

- *Coping With Complexity* How to cope with (and avoid) complex designs.
- *Keep It Simple* The shape of simple code.
- *The Ghost of a Codebase Past* About learning from existing code. No matter how good a system, you can learn from it and improve on it in your next design.

- *Testing Times* Unit tests helped Design Town develop in a well-factored and reliable manner.

Try this....

Consider how you'd describe your current project to an outsider. What are you proud of, and what could be improved? How can your team celebrate the good things you're doing? Determine what you can do now to strengthen your weak areas.

PART II

Practice Makes Perfect

Now we step back from the codeface, and take a broader view. We'll inspect the important *practices* that comprise better programming.

These chapters cover important techniques, practices, and approaches to writing good code. I'll introduce rules of engagement with the software development process, ways of approaching the coding task, and sound techniques that will help you collaborate with other development team members.

CHAPTER 14

Software Development Is...

And this, our life, exempt from public haunt, finds tongues in trees,
books in the running brooks, sermons in stones, and good in everything.

— William Shakespeare
As You Like It

It's a sad fact that I won't be able to rely on my sharply honed intellect forever. Some time in the future my wits will fade, and I'll no longer be the sharp, erudite, humble genius I am now. So I need a pension plan, a way to make my millions so that I can live in luxury in my old age.

My original plan for world domination seemed so simple it couldn't fail: *fizzy milk!* However, before I got a chance to work out the finer details of the recipe, I received devastating news: fizzy milk had already been invented. Gutted, and with the patent rights slipping through my fingers, I went back to the drawing board to come up with a new pension plan. And this time it was a good one.

This piece of genius goes back to the classic foods of my youth: custard and Alphabetti Spaghetti. I'm sure you can see where I'm going: *Alphabetti custard!* My initial experiments have proved promising. And almost palatable: it's a bit like rice pudding, but wheatier. Admittedly, it's an acquired taste, but I think it could catch on.

This Software (Food)stuff

Too much modern software is like my Alphabetti custard: it's *the wrong thing*, written *the wrong way*.

To make Alphabetti custard the "right" way you'd make the pasta first by hand, and hand-mix a custard. The cheating, wrong way would be to buy tins of pasta, wash the sauce off, and then pour instant custard over the top.

One is a recipe, a method for reliable construction. The other is, at best, an adequate way to prototype, but not a large-scale fabrication technique.

As conscientious software developers, we should all aspire to write *the right thing* in the *right way*. One of the key characteristics of truly excellent programmers is actually caring about the software that we write, and how we write it. We need more lovingly baked artisanal code, no more of this tinned spaghetti nonsense.

In this chapter, we'll peer into the saucepan to investigate the nature of the software we write, and how we can avoid writing alphanumeric spaghetti ourselves. I'll pose a series of questions along the way to apply the lessons we learn. The first being: *Do you want to improve as a programmer? Do you actually want to write the right thing in the right way?*

If your answer is "no" then give up and stop reading now.

So, what *is* software development? To be sure, it's complex, with many interweaving aspects. Whilst this chapter can't be a comprehensive intellectual treaty on software development, we can investigate some of its nuances: that it is part science, art, game, sport, chore, and more.

Software Development Is…an Art

A great programmer needs to be, in part, a great artist. But is programming *really* an art? This is a debate that has long been held in software development circles. Some people think that programming is an engineering discipline, some an art form, some sit in-between, considering it a craft (I did call my first book *Code Craft*, after all).

Knuth is probably the most famous proponent of software as art, naming his famous series of books *The Art of Computer Programming*. He said this: *Some programs are elegant, some are exquisite, some are sparkling. My claim is that is it possible to write grand programs, noble programs, truly magnificent ones!* Stirring stuff.

There's more to code than bits and bytes, more than brackets and braces. There's structure and elegance. There's poise and balance. There is a sense of taste and aesthetics.

> KEY ➤ A programmer needs good taste and a sense of aesthetics to write exceptional code.

There are many parts of the software development process akin to the creation of a work of art. The process is:

Creative
> It requires imagination. The software must be skilfully constructed and precisely designed. Programmers must have a vision for the code they are about to create, and a plan of how they will make it. Sometimes that involves a great deal of ingenuity.

Aesthetic

Good code is hallmarked by elegance, beauty, and balance. It stands within the framework of certain cultural idioms. We consider the code's form alongside its function.

Mechanical

As any artist, we work in our particular medium with our particular tools, processes, and techniques. We work under commission for generous benefactors.

Team-based

Many forms of art are not single-person endeavours. Not every art form sees an artist sitting alone in their studio slaving day and night until their masterpiece is complete. Consider master sculptors with their apprentices. Consider the orchestra, each member held together by the conductor. Consider a musical composer, writing a piece which will then be interpreted by the performer(s). Or the architect designing a building that will be erected by a team of builders.

In many respects, the skill set of an artist is similar to that of a programmer.

Michelangelo was the archetypal renaissance man: a painter, sculptor, architect, poet, and engineer. Perhaps he would have made an incredible programmer. When asked about how he created one of his most famous works, the statue of David, he said: *I looked into the stone and saw him there, and just chipped away everything else.*

Is that what you do? Do you reduce and remove the complexities of the problem space, chipping them all away until you reach the beautiful code you were aiming for?

Here are a few questions to ask yourself on the theme of software as art:

- Do I consider the creative aspects of software development, or do I treat it as a mechanistic activity?

- Should I develop a keener sense of elegance and aesthetics in my code? Should I look beyond what's functional and solves the immediate problem?

- Do I think that my idea of "beautiful" code is the One True Opinion? Should I consider artistry as a team pursuit?

Software Development Is…a Science

We talk about *computer science*. So there must be something vaguely scientific going on somewhere, mustn't there? It's probably fair to say that in most development organisations there is much less science and far more plumbing happening.

The archetypal scientist is, of course, Albert Einstein. He was not only a genius, but also one of the most quotable people there has ever been (which helps authors considerably).

He said this: *Any intelligent fool can make things bigger, more complex, and more violent. It takes a touch of genius—and a lot of courage—to move in the opposite direction.*

That is really profound; inappropriate complexity is a real killer in most software projects.

Einstein was also an aesthete. He appreciated elegance and beauty in his theories, and aimed to reduce things to a coherent whole. He said: *I am enough of an artist to draw freely upon my imagination. Imagination is more important than knowledge. Knowledge is limited. Imagination encircles the world.*

See, I told you he was quotable.

So if software development is like a science, what does that mean? It is (or, rather, should be):

Rigourous

We look for bug-free code that works, all the time, every time. It must work with all sets of valid input, and respond appropriately to invalid input. Good software must be accurate, proven, measured, tested, and verified.

How do we achieve this? Good testing is key. We look for unit tests, integration tests, and system tests. Preferably automated to remove the risk of human error. We also look for experiential testing.

Systematic

Software development is not a hit-and-miss affair. You can't aim to create a well-structured large computer system by randomly accreting blobs of code until it appears to work. You need to plan, design, budget, and systematically construct.

It is an intellectual, logical, rational process; bringing order and understanding out of the chaos of the problem space and the design alternatives.

Insightful

Software development requires intellectual effort and astute analytical powers. This is especially apparent when tracking down tricky bugs. Like scientists, we form hypotheses, and apply something akin to scientific method (form a hypothesis, work out experiments, run experiments, and validate the theory).

> KEY ➤ Good software development is not *cowboy coding*, throwing down the first code you can think of. It is a deliberate, considered, accurate endeavour.

Based on that, ask yourself:

- Is my software always totally correct and completely accurate? How do I prove this? How can I make this explicit, now and in the future?

- Do I strive to bring order out of chaos? Do I collapse complexity in my code until there are a few, small, unified parts?
- Do I approach problems methodically and thoughtfully, or do I rush headlong into them in an unstructured way?

Software Development Is...a Sport

Most sports require great skill and effort: tenacity, training, discipline, teamwork, coaching, and self-consciousness. Likewise, software development involves:

Teamwork
> It requires the concert of many people, with different skills, working in harmony.

Discipline
> Each team member must be committed to the team, and willing give their best. This requires dedication, hard work, and a lot of training.

> You can't get good at soccer by sitting on a couch and watching soccer training videos. In fact, if you do it with a few beers and a tub of popcorn, you're likely to get worse at soccer! You have to actually do it, get out there on the pitch with people, practise your skills, and then you'll improve. You must train—have someone tell you how to improve.

> The team must practise together, and work out how to function as a whole.

Rules
> We're playing to (developing to) a set of rules, and a particular team culture. This is embodied in our development processes and procedures, as well as the rites and rituals of the software team and their tool workflows (consider how you collaborate around things like the source control system).

The teamwork analogy is clearest with a sport like soccer. You work in a group of closely functioning people, playing a game by a set of well-defined rules.

Have you seen a team of seven-year-olds playing soccer? There's one small guy left back standing in the goal mouth, and every other kid is running around the pitch maniacally chasing the ball. There's no passing. There's no communication. There's no awareness of the other team members. Just a pack of children converging on a small moving sphere.

Contrast that to a high-quality premier league team. They operate in a much more cohesive way. Everyone knows their responsibility, and the team works cohesively together. There is a shared vision that they work towards, and they form a high-functioning, well-coordinated whole:

- Do I have all of these skills? Do I work well in a team, or could I improve in some areas?

- Am I committed to my team, willing to work for the good of everyone?

- Am I still learning about software development? Do I learn from others, and am I perfecting my team skills?

Software Development Is…Child's Play

For me, this observation seems particularly appropriate; I'm really just a child at heart. Aren't we all?

It's fascinating to see how children grow and learn, how their world view changes and is shaped by each new experience. We can glean a lot from the way a child learns and reacts to the world.

Consider how this applies to our software development:

Learning

A child is aware that they are learning, that they don't know everything. This requires a simple characteristic: *humility*. Some of the programmers I have found hardest to work with think that they know it all. If there's something new they need to know, they read a book and then presume that they're an expert. A total humility bypass.

A child is constantly assimilating new knowledge. We must recognise that if we want to improve, we must learn. And we must be realistic about what we do, and do not, know.

Enjoy learning, savour finding out new things. Practise and improve your craft.

> KEY ▶ Good programmers work with humility. They admit that they don't know it all.

Simplicity

Do you write the simplest code possible? Do you reduce everything to the least complex form to make it easier to understand and easier to code?

I love the way kids try to get to the bottom of things, to understand things from their own limited perspective. They're always asking *why*. Take, for example, a conversation I had with my daughter when she was six: *Daddy, why is Millie my sister?* Because you're in the same family as her, Alice. *Why?* Well, because you have the same mummy and daddy. *Why?* Because, well, you see, there are the birds and the bees… Oh go and get a book! … *(thinking)* … *Why?*…

We should be constantly asking *why*—questioning what we are doing and the reasons for it. Seeking a better understanding of the problem and the best solution. And we should strive for simplicity in our handiwork. That is not the most *simplistic* "dumb" code possible, but the appropriately non-complex code.

Having fun
> If all else fails, there's nothing wrong with this. All good developers enjoy a little playtime. My office currently houses a unicycle and a makeshift cricket pitch.

With that in mind, we can ask ourselves:

- Do I strive to write the simplest code possible? Or do I type what comes to mind, and not think about commonality, refactoring, or code design?
- Am I still learning? What can I learn about? What do I need to learn about?
- Am I a humble programmer?

Software Development Is...a Chore

A lot of our software development work is not pleasant. It's not glamourous. It's not plain sailing. It's just donkeywork that has to be done to get a project completed.

To be an effective programmer, you mustn't be afraid of the chores. Recognise that programming *is* hard work. Yes, it's great to do a cool design on the newest product version, but sometimes you need to do the tedious bug fixing and grubbing around the old awful messy code to get a product shipping and make some money.

From time to time we must become software janitors. This requires us to:

Clean up
> We must spot problems and address them; work out where breakages are and what the appropriate fixes are. These fixes must be made in a timely and nondisruptive manner. A janitor does not leave the unpleasant tasks to someone else, but takes responsibility for them.

Work in the background
> Janitors do not work in the limelight. They probably receive little recognition for their heroic efforts. This is very much a supporting, not a lead role.

Maintenance
> A software janitor will remove dead code, fix broken code, refactor and rebuild inappropriate workmanship, and tidy and clean the code to ensure that it doesn't fall into disrepair.

Ask yourself:

- Am I happy to do code *chores*? Or do I only want the glamourous work?
- Do I take responsibility for messy code and clean it up?

Metaphor Overload

We often construct metaphors for the act of software development. Many of the insights we glean can be informative. However, no metaphor is perfect. Software development is its own special thing, and the act of creating it is not entirely like any other discipline. It's still a field we're exploring and refining. Beware of making wonky deductions from bad comparisons.

Good code and good coders are born from a desire to write the right thing in the right way, not from the software equivalent of Alphabetti custard.

Questions

1. Which of the metaphors outlined here do you relate most clearly with? Which most accurately reflects your work at the moment?

2. What other metaphors can you construct for the software pursuit? (Perhaps gardening or shepherding.) What new insights do these reveal?

3. How would *you* make Alphabetti custard?

See also

- *Care About the Code* We must care about crafting the *right software*, the *right way*.

- *People Power* Here we've seen a couple of metaphors that speak of our software development teamwork. Programming is a people pursuit.

Try this....

Revisit the preceding questions. Which area should you focus on most right now?

SAUCE CODE

WHAT YOU USE
TO COVER UP
SPAGHETTI CODE

CHAPTER 15

Playing by the Rules

If I'd observed all the rules, I'd never have got anywhere.

— Marilyn Monroe

We live our lives by many rules. This could be a dystopian Orwellian nightmare, but it's not. Some rules are imposed on us. But some we set ourselves. These rules oil the cogs of our lives.

Rules facilitate our play, describing how a game works: saying who has won and how. They make our sports fair and enjoyable, and provide plenty of opportunity for (mis)interpretation (see soccer's off-side rule).

They impinge on our travel, where security rules dictate you can only carry so much liquid, and no sharp objects, on airplanes. They describe traffic speed limits, and how to safely navigate a path on the road. Such rules ensure the safety of all.

Rules bound our social norms, stating that it's not appropriate to lick a stranger's ear when you first meet them, no matter how tasty it looks.

Yes, we live our lives continually observing a set of rules. We're so used to this that we often don't think about them.

Unsurprisingly, the same holds in our development work. There are a wide range of rules we follow at the codeface. Development process norms. Mandated toolchains and workflows. Office etiquette. Language syntax. Design patterns. These are the things that define what it is to be a professional programmer, and the way we play the development game with other people.

If you join a new project, there are various rules that you'd expect to be in place. Rules governing the responsible creation of high-quality code. Rules governing working processes and practices. And specific rules about the project and problem domain: perhaps legal regulations in force for financial trading, or safety guidelines for health markets.

These rules they help us work well together. They help orchestrate and harmonise our efforts.

We Need More Rules!

But sometimes all of these rules, good as they are, aren't enough. Sometimes the poor programmers need *more* rules. Really, we do.

We need rules that we've *made ourselves*. Rules that we can take ownership of. Rules that define the culture and working methods of development in our particular team. These needn't be large unwieldy draconian edicts. Just something simple you can give new team members so that they can immediately play the game with you. These are rules that describe something more than mere methods and processes; they are rules that describe a coding culture—how to be a good player in the team.

> KEY ➤ Programming teams have a set of rules. These rules define *what* we do and *how* we do it. But they also describe a *coding culture*.

Sound sane? Well, we think so. Our team's Tao of development is summed up in three short complementary statements. From these all other practices follow. These statements are now enshrined in our team folklore, have been printed out in large, friendly letters, and emblazon our communal work area. They reign over all we do; whenever we face a choice, a tricky decision, or a heated discussion, they help to guide us to the right answer.

Are you ready to receive our wisdom? Brace yourself. Our three earth-shattering rules for writing good code are:

- Keep it simple
- Use your brain
- Nothing is set in stone

That's it. Aren't they great?

We set these rules because we think they lead to better software, and have helped us become better programmers. I'll describe what they mean in the following chapters.

They perfectly describe the attitude, the sense of community, and the culture of our team. Our rules are purposefully short and pithy; we don't like lengthy bureaucratic dictats or unnecessary complication. They require developer responsibility to interpret and follow; we trust our team, and these rules empower the team. They are always new ways to apply them in our codebase; we are always learning and seeking to improve.

Set the Rules

These rules make sense to us, in our project, in our company, and in our industry. They may not have the same import for you.

What rules are you currently working to? That is, apart from the ban on licking your colleagues' ears. Do you have a coding standard (either formal, or informal) in place? Do you have development process rules (perhaps the likes of: *Be in for 10 a.m. because we have a stand-up meeting. All code must be reviewed before check-in. All bug reports must have clear repro steps before being handed to a developer*)?

What rules govern your team culture? What informal, unwritten ways of collaborating, or approaches to the code, are particular to your team?

Consider formulating a small, simple set of rules that you can define your coding culture with. Can you distill it to something pithy like our three rules?

> KEY ➤ Don't rely on vague unwritten team "rules." Make the implicit rules explicit, and take control of your coding culture.

In the spirit of our third rule, don't forget that *nothing is set in stone*—including your rules. Rules are there to be broken, after all. Or rather, rules are there to be *remade*. Your rules may justifiably change over time as your team learns and grows. What is pertinent now may not be in the future.

Questions

1. List the software development process rules currently in place in your project. How well are these enforced and followed?

2. How does this project's culture differ from your previous projects? Is it a better or worse project to work in? Can the difference be captured or improved in a rule?

3. Do you think your team would rally around an agreed set of rules?

4. Does the shape, style, and quality of your code have any effect on a projects' coding culture? Does the team shape the code, or does the code shape the team?

See also

- *Keep It Simple, Use Your Brain, Nothing Is Set in Stone* Exposition of my team's three earth shattering rules for effective software development.

- *Many-festos* The militant side of rule creation: manifestos.

- *It's the Thought That Accounts* You must be in agreement with, and accountable to, others when following team rules.

Formulate your own team "rules" for software development. Print them out and stick them in a wall over your development office.

CHAPTER 16

Keep It Simple

Simplicity is the ultimate sophistication.

— Leonardo da Vinci

You've heard the advice before: "KISS." *Keep it simple, stupid.* Exactly how stupid do you have to be to get *that* wrong? Simplicity is an undoubtedly excellent objective; you should certainly strive for it in your code. No programmer yearns to work with overly complex code. Simple code is transparent; its structure is clear, it does not hide bugs, it is easy to learn, and easy to work with.

So why isn't all code like that?

In the developer world, there are two kinds of simplicity: the *wrong* sort and the *right* sort. The "simplicity" we are looking for specifically does *not* mean: write your code the easiest way you can, cut corners, ignore all the nasty complicated stuff (brush it all under the rug and hope it goes away), and generally be a programming simpleton.

Oh, if only it were that easy. Too many programmers in the real world *do* write "simple" code like this. Their brain does not engage. Some of them don't even realise that they're doing anything wrong; they just don't think enough about the code they're writing, and fail to appreciate all of the inherent subtle complexities.

Such a mindless approach leads not to simple code, but to *simplistic* code. Simplistic code is incorrect code. Because it is ill-thought through, it doesn't perform exactly as required—often it only covers the obvious "main case," ignoring error conditions, or it does not correctly handle the less likely inputs. For this reason, simplistic code harbours faults. These are cracks that (in the typical simplistic-coder way) tend to get papered over with more ill-applied simplistic code. These fixes begin to pile on top of one another until the code becomes a monstrous lumpy mess; the very opposite of well-structured, simple code.

Simplicity is never an excuse for incorrect code.

> KEY ▶ Simple code takes effort to design. It is not the same thing as overly *simplistic* code.

Instead of this wrong simple-minded "simplicity," we must strive to write the *simplest* code possible. This is very different from disengaging your brain and writing stupid, simplistic code. It is a very brain intensive pursuit—ironically, it's hard to write something simple.

Simple Designs

There is one sure sign of a simple design: the fact thatit can be quickly and clearly described, and easily understood. You can summarise it in a simple sentence, or in one clear diagram. Simple designs are easy to conceptualise.

Simple designs have a number of notable properties. Let's take a look.

Simple to Use

A simple design is, by definition, simple to use. It has a low cognitive overhead.

It is easy to pick up because there is not too much to learn at first. You can start working with the most basic facilities, and as you need to adopt the more advanced capabilities, they gradually open up like a well-crafted narrative.

Prevents Misuse

A simple design is hard to misuse and hard to abuse. It reduces burden on the code's clients by keeping interfaces clean and not putting an unnecessary burden on the user. For example, a "simple" interface design will not return dynamically allocated objects that the user has to manually delete. The user will forget. The code will leak or fail.

The secret is to place the complexity in the right places: generally hidden away behind a simple API.

> KEY ▶ Simple designs aim to prevent misuse. They may involve extra internal complexity in order to present a simpler API.

Size Matters

Simple code minimises the number of components in the design. Big projects with many moving parts may justifiably require a large number of components; it is possible to have many flying parts and be "as simple as possible."

> KEY ▶ Simple designs are as small as possible. And no smaller.

Shorter Code Paths

Remember the famous programmers' maxim: *every problem can be solved by adding an extra level of indirection*? Many complex problems can be subtly masked, and even caused by, unnecessary levels of indirection hiding the problem. If you have to follow a long chain of function calls, or trace indirected data access through many levels of "getter" functions, forwarding mechanisms, and abstraction layers, you will soon lose the will to live. It's inhuman. It's unnecessarily complex.

Simple designs reduce indirection, and ensure that functionality and data are close to where it's needed.

They also avoid unnecessary inheritance, polymorphism, or dynamic binding. These techniques are all good things, when used at the right times. But when applied blindly, they bring unnecessary complexity.

Stability

The sure sign of a simple design is that it can be enhanced and extended without massive amounts of rewriting. If you continually end up reworking a section of code as your project matures, then you either have a ludicrously volatile set of requirements (which *does* happen, but is a very different problem) or you have an indication that the design was not simple enough in the first place.

Simple interfaces tend to be stable, and don't change much. You may extend them with new services, but do not need to rework the entire API. However, this should not be a straightjacket: interfaces need not be set in stone. Don't make your code unnecessarily rigid—this itself is not simple.

Simple Lines of Code

Simple code is easy to read, and easy to understand. It is therefore easy to work with.

Personal preference and familiarity tends to determine what makes individual lines of code look simple. Some people find that certain layout idioms help clarify their code. Others find those same idioms a huge hindrance. More than anything else, *consistency* leads to simple code. Code with widely varying styles, naming conventions, design approaches, and file formats is needlessly obfuscated.

> KEY ➤ Consistency leads to clarity.

Do not write needless obscure code for any reason: not for job security (we joke about this, but some people truly do), not to impress your colleagues by your coding prowess, and not to try out a new language feature. If you can write an acceptable implementation in mundane, but clear, coding style then do so. The maintenance programmers will thank you for that.

Keeping It Simple, Not Stupid

When you encounter a bug, there are often two ways to address it:

- Take the easiest route to solve the problem. Hey, you're keeping things *simple*, right? Fix the superficial problem—that is, apply a sticking plaster—but don't worry about solving any deeper underlying issues if it will be too much work. This is the least effort for you now, but will likely lead to the kind of simplistic code mess we saw earlier.

  This doesn't make things simpler; it makes things more complex. You've added a new wart and not addressed the underlying problem.

- Or, you can rework the code so that it accommodates a fix, and remains simple. You may have to adjust APIs to be more appropriate, refactor some logic to create the correct seam for the bugfix, or even perform serious rework because you spot code assumptions that do not hold.

This latter option is the goal. It does require more effort, but boiling the code down to its simplest form pays off in the long run.

> KEY ➤ Apply bugfixes to the root cause, not where symptoms manifest. Sticking plaster symptom-fixes do not lead to simple code.

Assumptions Can Reduce Simplicity

Invalid "simplifying" assumptions are easy to make when you're coding and, whilst they can reduce the complexity in your head, they tend to build into twisted logic.

Simple code does not make unnecessary assumptions, either about the requirements or problem domain, about the reader, about the runtime environment, or about the toolchain used. Assumptions can reduce simplicity, as you implicitly require the reader to know extra information to make sense of the code.

> KEY ➤ Avoid implicit assumptions in your code.

Assumptions can, though, *increase* simplicity. The trick is to make it clear exactly what assumptions are being made; for example, the constraints and context that the code is designed for.

Avoid Premature Optimisation

Optimisation is the antithesis of simplicity. Knuth famously said: *Premature optimisation is the root of all evil (or at least most of it) in programming.*[1]

The act of code optimisation is generally that of taking a straightforward, readable, algorithmic implementation and butchering it: pulling the algorithm out of shape so that it executes faster on a given machine under particular conditions. This inevitably alters the shape to be less clear and, therefore, less simple.

Write clear code first. Make it complex only when needed.

Employ a simple, standard sort, until you know you need to make it cleverer. Write the most straightforward implementation of an algorithm and then measure to see if you need to make it faster. Again, beware of making assumptions: many programmers optimise the parts they *think* will be slow. The bottlenecks are often elsewhere.

Sufficiently Simple

Simplicity is allied with *sufficiency*. This works in a few directions:

- You should work in the simplest way possible and write the simplest code possible. But keep it sufficiently simple. If you oversimplify, you will not solve the actual problem. Our "simple" solutions *must* be "sufficient" or they are *not* solutions.

- Only write as much code as is required to solve your problem. Don't write reams of code that you *think* will be useful. Code that is not in use is just baggage. It's an extra burden. It's complexity you don't need. Write the sufficient amount of code. The less code you write, the fewer bugs you'll create.

- Don't overcomplicate solutions; excitable developers find this a very real temptation. Solve only the issue at hand. Don't invent a needlessly general solution for a whole class of problems that are not relevant. Work until you reach a splendid sufficiency.

> KEY ▶ Only write as much code as is needed. Anything extra is complexity that will become a burden.

A Simple Conclusion

We all know that beautifully simple code is better than needlessly complex code. And we've all seen our fair share of foul, ugly, complex code. Few people aim to write code

---

1. In *Computer Programming as an Art*, his 1974 Turing Award Lecture.

like that. The road to complexity is usually trodden with hurried changes and slipping standards. Just one slack change. Just one sticking plaster fix. Just one code review skipped. Just one "I don't have time to refactor." After enough of these, the code is an unholy mess, and it's hard to figure a way to restore sanity.

Sadly, simplicity is pretty hard work.

Simplicity is a banner born out by many popular developer maxims: YAGNI—*you aren't going to need it*—speaks to the theme of sufficiency. DRY—*don't repeat yourself*—speaks to the theme of code size. Our preference for high cohesion and low coupling speaks to simplicity in design.

Questions

1. What is the simplest code you've seen recently? What is the most complex code you have seen? How did they differ?

2. What sort of unnecessary assumptions can a coder make about his code that will render it too complex? What assumptions are valid to make?

3. We talk a lot about optimisation at the code level. How can you optimise at the design or architecture level?

4. Is it possible to optimise code but maintain its simplicity?

5. Does the "simplicity" of a section of code depend on the capabilities of the programmer reading it? How should an experienced coder work in order to ensure his code is of high quality, but appears "simple" to a less experienced maintenance coder?

See also

- *Playing by the Rules* "Keep it simple" is one of three complementary rules my team has converged on.

- *Coping with Complexity* The flipside of simplicity: *complexity*. Here's how to manage it.

Try this....

Check whether the code modifications you are making contribute to the simplicity of the code. Avoid adding complexity. Fight code entropy!

CHAPTER 17

Use Your Brain

"Rabbit's clever," said Pooh thoughtfully.

"Yes," said Piglet, "Rabbit's clever."

"And he has Brain."

"Yes," said Piglet, "Rabbit has Brain."

There was a long silence. "I suppose," said Pooh, "that that's why he never understands anything."

— A.A. Milne
Winnie-the-Pooh

"Use your brain" is not a derogatory injunctive to slipshod colleagues. Rather, it is a core principle for the conscientious coder. It is the second of my team's hand-picked rules for guru programming. It has a number of important applications to our daily coding regimen.

Don't Be Stupid

We've mentioned the KISS rule already: keep it simple, *stupid*. Here we take it one step further: *don't be stupid*. It sounds like obvious advice, but we programmers need repeated reminders.

It's incredible how dumb hyperintelligent people can be. Some utter geniuses suffer a chronic medical bypass of the common sense gland. Code that ninjas trip over because of their myopic vision; they miss the blindingly obvious right in front of them. Awesome architects walk into walls because their heads are stuck in the clouds.

Stereotypical geek stuff.

The desire to write an exciting new algorithm or craft a cunning data structure can consume us, obscuring the observation that a simple array will suffice. In the rush to get a release out, it's easy to dash out reams of substandard code; the pressure tempts us to think less carefully. We write *stupid* code.

The coding experts do this, and so can we mere mortals. Make sure your code doesn't miss the blindingly obvious. Don't accidentally overcomplicate designs. Don't add stupidity that is easily avoidable.

> KEY ➤ Stop and think. Don't write stupid code.

Now, we all make mistakes from time to time. No one's code is consistently perfect. So don't feel paralysed, or think that you are a failure when you realise you've written some stupid code, or conceived a dumb design.

Simply admit when you are wrong, back out the work, and take a better approach. It takes courage to admit a failure and rework the mistake. It's braver to do so than to try to save face by hobbling on with crippled code. Treat the code with respect. Clean up your messes.

> KEY ➤ Admit to your mistakes and bad coding decisions. Learn from them.

Avoid Mindlessness

Be honest, we've all done it: programming on autopilot.

It's far too easy to program without engaging your brain. Really. It's easy to just follow your fingers as they bash out lines of code. It's easy to get stuck in a rut trying to solve (what you think is) the immediate problem, without really considering the bigger picture, without thinking about the code that surrounds you, or whether what you're typing is actually correct.

This inevitably leads to stupid code. It leads to verbose, over-complex code. It leads to incorrect code that does not fulfill all requirements. It leads to buggy code that doesn't handle every case.

Whenever you face a coding task: stop, take a mental step back, and consider if there is an alternative solution. Check that you're not forging ahead with the first plan you conceived purely because you haven't tried to think of alternatives.

To paraphrase World War I propaganda: *Careless code costs lives.*

> KEY ➤ Pay attention. Don't write code without care.

The best strategies to avoid the mindlessness trap and our own stupidity involve accountability. Perform design reviews before ploughing into your editor. Pair program. Run code reviews.

You Are Allowed to Think!

"Use your brain" is, above all, an empowering rule. You are actually *allowed*, even encouraged, to use your brain.

Some programmers fail to assume enough responsibility. They function as code monkeys, filling the blanks in other people's designs, or following existing structures and idioms, rather than being empowered to think for themselves.

You are not a coding automaton. You have a brain: use it!

As you work on a section of code, make conscious decisions about its shape and structure. *Own* the code. Take responsibility for the code. Be proactive in determining any required improvements or changes.

If the existing code patterns are questionable, consider whether they should be changed. Make a judgment call as to whether now is the right time to refactor.

If you find code riddled with Band-Aid warts, don't follow suit and add another Band-Aid when a more brutal adjustment is required. Understand that it is *your responsibility* to look for this kind of problem. You are allowed to critically appraise code.

Having an opinion, and feeling able to voice it, requires you to be brave and courageous. Stand up for what will make the code better.

> KEY ➤ Have the courage to use your brain. Feel empowered to critique code and make decisions about how to improve it.

Questions

1. What is the difference between *simple* code and *stupid* code?

2. How do you ensure you don't write stupid code? Do you think you have good code "common sense"? Justify your answer.

3. What are the tell-tale signs that code was written by someone who wasn't paying attention?

4. What are the deciding factors in choosing whether to rework a section of bad code, or to "pragmatically" mark it as technical debt and chicken out?

See also

- *Playing by the Rules* "Use your brain" is one of three complementary rules my team has converged on.
- *This Time I've Got It* A case study in when to step back and employ the gray matter.

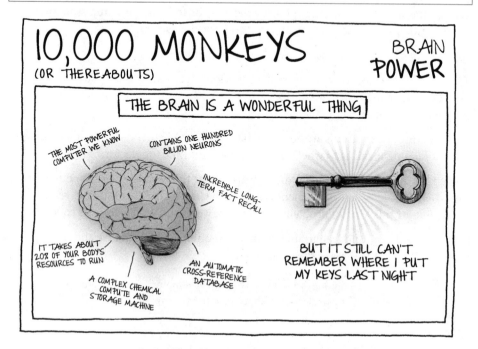

Nothing Is Set in Stone

They always say time changes things, but you actually have to change them yourself.

— Andy Warhol

There is a strange fiction prevalent in programming circles: once you've written some code then it is sacred. It should not be changed. Ever.

That goes double for anyone else's code. Don't you dare touch it.

Somewhere along the development line, perhaps at the first check-in, or perhaps just after a product release, the code gets embalmed. It changes league. It is promoted. No longer riffraff, it becomes digital royalty. The once-questionable design is suddenly considered beyond reproach and becomes unchangeable. The internal code structure is no longer to be messed with. All of the interfaces to the outside world are sacred and can never be revised.

Why *do* programmers think like this? Fear. Fear of getting it wrong. Fear of breaking things. Fear of extra work. Fear of the cost of change.

There is a very real anxiety that comes from changing code you don't know fully. If you don't understand the logic from the inside out, if you're not entirely sure what you're doing, if you don't understand every possible consequence of a change, then you *could* break the program in strange ways or alter odd corner-case behaviour and introduce very subtle bugs into the product. You don't want to do that, do you?

Software is supposed to be soft, not hard. Yet fear leads us to freeze our code solid in an attempt to avoid breaking it. This is software rigor mortis.

> KEY ➤ Do not embalm your code. If you have "unchangeable" code in your product, then your product will rot.

We see rigor mortis set when the original authors leave a project and no one left fully understands their old business-critical code. When it's hard to work with legacy code, or to even make a reliable estimate for working with it, programmers avoid the code's core. It becomes an untamed code wilderness, where wild digital beasts roam unfettered. To work in a timely and predictable way, new functionality is added as new satellite modules around the edge.

We see rigor mortis set when a product is rolled onto production servers and is used by many clients daily. The original system APIs stick because it will cost too much to change them; so many other teams or services now depend on them.

Code should *never* stay still. No code is sacred. No code is ever perfect. How could it be? The world is constantly changing around it. Requirements are always in a state of flux, no matter how diligently they were captured. Product version 2.4 is so radically different from version 1.6 that it's entirely possible the internal code structure *should* be totally different. And we're always finding new bugs in our old code that need to be fixed.

When your code becomes a straightjacket then you are fighting with the software, *not* developing it. You will be permanently dancing around necrotic logic and plotting ever more arcane courses around dodgy design.

> KEY ▶ You are the master of your software; it's under your control. Do not let the code, or the processes around it, dictate how the code grows.

Fearless Change

Of course, it is perfectly sensible to fear breaking software. Large software projects contain myriad subtleties and complexities that must be mastered. We don't want to introduce bugs through reckless modification. Only fools would glibly make changes without actually knowing what they're doing. That's cowboy coding.

So how do we reconcile courageous modification with fear of error?

- Learn how to make good changes—there are practices that increase the safety of your work and reduce the chance of error. Courage comes from a confidence that your modification is safe.

- Learn what makes software easy to change, and strive to craft software with these attributes.

- Make daily improvements to your code that make it more malleable. Refuse to compromise code quality.

- Embrace healthy attitudes that lead to flourishing code.

But ultimately: *just make the change!* Fearlessly. You may fail; it may go wrong. But you can always revert the code back to a working state and try again. There is no shame in trying, and you will always learn from your mistakes. Just make sure that any change you make is backed up by sufficient testing and inspection before it hits production.

Nothing is set in stone. Not the design. Not the team. Not the process. Not the code. Understand this, and the part you can play in improving your software.

> KEY ➤ To modify code you need courage and skill. Not recklessness.

Change Your Attitude

To "enable" healthy change in your code, the programming team has to adopt the right attitudes. They must be committed to code quality and actually *want* to write good code.

Fearful, cowardly coding approaches don't make the grade. We shun: *I didn't write this. It looks rubbish. I want nothing to do with it. I will venture into this code as little as possible.* This attitude makes the coder's life a little easier now, but leads to design rot. Old code becomes stagnant whilst new driftwood washes up around its edges.

> KEY ➤ "Good code" is not somebody else's problem. It is your responsibility. You have the power to make a change and to bring about an improvement.

Here are important attitudes, both for the team and for the individual, that contribute to healthy code growth:

- Fixing wrong, dangerous, bad, duplicated, or distasteful code is not a distraction, a sidetrack, or a waste of precious time. It is positively encouraged. In fact, it is expected. You don't want to leave weak spots festering for too long. If you find code that is too scary to change, then it *must* be changed!

- Refactoring is encouraged. If you have a job that requires a fundamental code change to be done properly, then do it properly: refactor. The team understands that this is required, and that some jobs may take a little longer when we find such problems.

- No one "owns" any area of the code. Anyone is allowed to make changes in any section. Avoid code parochialism; it stifles the rate of change.

- It is not a crime to make a mistake or to write the wrong code (accidentally, at least!). If someone fixes or improves your code, then it is not a sign that you are weak or that the other programmer is better than you. You'll probably tinker with their work tomorrow. That's just the way it works. Learn and grow.

- No one's opinion should be considered more important than anyone else's. Everyone has a valid contribution to make in any part of the codebase. Sure, some people have more experience in certain areas. But they are not code "owners" or gatekeepers of the sacred code. Treating some people's work as "more accurate" or "better" than others' puts them on a false pedestal and demeans the contribution of the rest of the team.

- Good programmers *expect* change, because that is what software development is all about. You need nerves of steel and to not mind the ground changing underneath you. The code changes quickly; get used to it.

- We lean on the safety net of accountability. Again, we see reviews, pair programming, and testing (both automated unit and integration tests, and great QA/developer interactions) being key parts of ensuring our code remains supple. If you do the wrong thing, or introduce rigidity, it will be spotted before it becomes a problem.

Make the Change

An apocryphal story states that a tourist, lost in a country village, stopped a local and asked for directions to a town in a distant borough. The villager spent a moment in careful thought, and then answered slowly: *if I were going there, I wouldn't start from here!*

It sounds silly, but often the best place to start your journey from is not where you are, in a code quagmire. If you try to move forward you may sink. It may instead be best to work your way back to a sound point, leading the code on a route to a local highway, and once there press onto your destination at greater speed.

Obviously, it's important to learn how to navigate a route into code; how to map it, trace it, and understand where it hides surprising side effects.

Design for Change

We strive for code that encourages change. This is code that reveals its shape and intent, and encourages modification through simplicity, clarity, and consistency. We avoid code with side effects because it is brittle in the face of change. If you encounter a function that does two things, separate it into two parts. Make the implicit explicit. We avoid rigid coupling and unnecessary complexity.

When an ugly, rigid codebase resists change, then we need a battle strategy: we slowly improve the code day by day, making safe, piecemeal improvements; we make changes to lines of code and to the overall structure. Over a period of time, we watch it gradually slide into a malleable shape.

> KEY ➤ Often it is best to make a series of frequent, small, verifiable adjustments, rather than one large sweeping code change.

Don't try to fight with the entire codebase at once. That may be a daunting, and perhaps intractable, task. Instead, identify a bounded section of the code that you need to interact with and focus on changing that.

Tools for Change

Pay attention now! This is really important: good tooling can help you make safe changes supremely fast.

A good automated test suite allows you to work fast and work well. It enables you to make modifications and get rapid, reliable feedback on whether your modifications have broken anything. Consider introducing some kind of verifiable test for the sections of code you pick up in order to avoid errors. Just as code benefits from accountability and a careful review processes, so do these tests.

> KEY ➤ Automated tests are an invaluable safety harness that build confidence in your code changes.

The backbone of your development should be *continuous integration*: a server that continually checks out and builds the latest version of the code. If—heaven forbid—anything bad slips through to break the build, you will find out about it quickly. The automated tests should be run on the build server, too.

Pick Your Battles

Nothing is set in stone, but not everything should be fluid.

Naturally, we pick our battles. We can't possibly change all of the code all of the time, whilst simultaneously adding more new work. We will always find unpleasant code that we can't fix right now, no matter how much we'd like to. The job may be too large. Or it may be past the scope of a mammoth refactor.

There is a certain amount of *technical debt* that we live with until we get a chance to make later improvement. This should be factored back into the project plan. Significant debt becomes work items that are placed onto the development roadmap, rather than forgotten and left to fester.

Plus ça Change

It sounds like a nightmare. Who could possibly work with code that is constantly changing? It's hard enough to track many simultaneous changes, let alone join in with them!

However, we must embrace the fact that code changes: any code that stands still is a liability. No code is beyond modification. Treating a section of code as avoidably scary is counterproductive.

Questions

1. What particular attributes make software easy to change? Do you naturally write software like this?

2. How can we balance "no code ownership" with the fact that some people have more experience than others? How does this affect the allocation of tasks to programmers?

3. Every project has code that changes frequently, and code that changes little. The latter code may be staid because it's not used, because it is healthily designed for extension by external modules, or because people actively avoid the nastiness within. How much of each of these kinds of rigid code do you have?

4. Does your project tooling support your code changes? How can you improve it?

See also

- *Playing by the Rules* "Nothing is set in stone" is one of three complementary rules my team has converged on.

- *The Ghost of a Codebase Past* Expect to change code regularly, and learn from each change you make.

- *It's Done When It's Done* No software is ever "complete." It is *soft* stuff, and may change in many ways in the future. However, it's important to know when the current work on it is done.

- *Wallowing in Filth* Describes some techniques for making fearless changes.

- *The Curious Case of the Frozen Code* The very opposite of dynamic, mutable code: frozen code.

Try this....

Identify the code in your project that no one wants to touch. Is it appropriate to rework this code now? Work out how to improve it.

CHAPTER 19

A Case for Code Reuse

If it can't be reduced, reused, repaired, rebuilt, refurbished, refinished, resold, recycled or composted, then it should be restricted, redesigned or removed from production.

— Pete Seeger

We hear about a mythical thing called "code reuse." For a while it became incredibly fashionable; another software silver bullet, something new for the snake-oil vendors to peddle. I'm not sold on it.

We often talk in terms of "use cases" when developing software. We also see these *reuse cases*:

Reuse Case 1: The Copy-Pasta

Code copied out of one app is surgically placed into another. Well, in my book that's less *code reuse* and more like *code duplication*. Or, less politely: *copy-and-paste programming*. It's often evil; tantamount to *code piracy*. Imagine a bunch of swashbuckling programmers pillaging and hoarding software gems from rich codebases around the seven software seas. Daring. But dangerous. It's coding with the bad hygiene of a salty seaman.

Remember the DRY mantra: *do not repeat yourself.*

This kind of "reuse" is a *real* killer when you've duplicated the same code fragment 516 times in one project and then discover that there's a bug in it. How will you make sure that you find and fix every manifestation of the problem? Good luck with that.

Having said that, you can argue that copy-and-paste between projects actually gets stuff done. There's a lot of it about and the world hasn't come to a crashing end. Yet. And copy-and-paste code avoids the unnecessary coupling which overly DRY code can suffer.

However, copy-and-paste is a nasty business and no self-respecting programmer will admit to this kind of code "reuse."

> **KEY ➤** Avoid copy-and-paste coding. Factor your logic into shared functions and common libraries, rather than suffer duplicated code (and duplicated bugs).

Whilst it is tempting to copy-and-paste code between files in a codebase, it is even more tempting to copy in large sections of code from the Web. We've all done it. You research something online (yes, Google is a great programming tool, and good programmers know how to wield it well). You find a snippet of quite plausible-looking code in a forum or blog post. And you slap it straight into your project to see whether it works. *Ah! That seems to do it.* Commit.

Whilst it's awesome that kind souls provide online tutorials and code examples to enlighten us, it's dangerous to take these at face value, and not apply critical judgment before incorporating them into our work.

Consider first:

- Is the code genuinely *completely* correct? Does it handle all errors properly, or was it only illustrative? (Often we leave error handling and special cases as an *exercise for the reader* when publishing examples.) Is it bug free?

- Is it the best way to achieve what you need? Is it an out-of-date example? Does it come from a really old blog post, containing anachronistic code?

- Do you have rights to include it in your code? Are there any license terms applied to it?

- How thoroughly have you tested it?

> **KEY ➤** Don't copy code you find on the Web into your project without carefully inspecting it first.

Reuse Case 2: Design for Reuse

You design a library from the outset for inclusion in multiple projects. That's *clearly* more theologically correct than yucky copy-and-paste programming. However, I'm sorry: this is not code "reuse." It's code *use*. The library was designed to be used like this from the very start!

This approach could also be a huge unnecessary sidetrack.

Even if you suspect that a section of code will be used by more than one project, it's usually not worth engineering it for multiple uses from the start. Doing so can lead to overly complex, bloated software, with high-ceremony APIs that try to cover all general use cases. Instead, employ the *YAGNI* principle: if *you aren't going to need it* (yet), then then don't write it (yet).

Focus on constructing the simplest code that satisfies the requirements right now. Write only what's needed, and create the smallest, most appropriate API possible.

Then, when another program wants to incorporate this component, you can add or extend the existing, working code. By only producing the smallest amount of software possible, you will reduce the risk of introducing bugs, or of constructing unnecessary APIs that you'll have to support for years to come.

Often your planned second "use" never materialises, or the second user has surprisingly different requirements than anyone expected.

Reuse Case 3: Promote and Refactor

Write small, modular sections of code. Keep it clean and neat.

As soon as you realise that it needs to be used in more than one place, refactor: create a shared library or a shared code file. Move the code in there. Extend the API *as little as possible* to accommodate the second user.

It's tempting at this stage to think that the interface must be dusted off, reworked, and filled out. But that might not be a good idea at all. Aim to keep your changes minimal and simple, because:

- Your existing code works. (It does work well, doesn't it? And you have the tests to prove it?!) Every gratuitous change you make moves it further from this working state.

- It's possible that a third client will appear shortly with slightly different requirements. It would be a shame (as well as a waste of effort) to have to rip up the adjusted API again and adapt it.

> KEY ➤ Code should be "shared" because it is useful to multiple clients, not because the developers want to create a nifty shared library.

Reuse Case 4: Buy In, or Reinvent the Wheel

When you need to add a new feature, there may already be third-party libraries available that provide the functionality.

Carefully consider whether it is economically more sensible to roll your own code, to pull in an open source version (if license terms permit), or to buy in a third-party solution with vendor support.

You need to weigh the ownership costs against build costs, the likely code quality, and the ease of integration and maintenance of each solution. Developers tend to want to write things themselves, not just for the intellectual exercise, but also due to a distrust of the unknown. Make an informed decision.

> KEY ➤ Don't dismiss other people's code. It may be better to use existing libraries rather than write your own version.

Questions

1. How much duplication is there in your codebase? How often do you see code copied and pasted between functions?

2. How can you determine how different sections of code have to be before it is acceptable to consider it *not* duplication, and to not try to refactor the versions together?

3. Do you often copy code examples from books or websites into your work? How much effort do you invest in "sanitising" the code for inclusion? Do you mercilessly update the layout, variable names, etc.? Do you add tests?

4. When you add code from the web, should you place comments around it stating the source of the implementation? Why?

See also

- *Keep It Simple* Appropriate reuse maintains simplicity in your code and avoids the kind of problems we see in Chapter 7.

- *Navigating a Route* Unnecessary duplication makes it hard to navigate around a codebase.

Try this....

If you are working on any unnecessarily general code, work out how to remove that generality and only keep the essential husk of useful logic.

CHAPTER 20

Effective Version Control

Everything changes, nothing perishes.

— Ovid

Version control, to the developer, is like eating and breathing; like a source editor and compiler. It's an essential part of daily development life.

Version control is the process of managing multiple revisions of a set of files. These are commonly the source files for a software system (so it is often called *source control*), but it could just as easily be revisions of a document tree, or of anything else you'd store in a filesystem.

This is a simple enough facility. But a good version control system, used well, brings us many benefits:

- It provides a central collaboration hub, orchestrating how developers work together.
- It defines and publishes the state of the art; no code has been integrated unless it is stored in the system. Other tools link into this update feed—for example, continuous integration, release engineering, and code audit systems.
- It maintains a history of the work on a project, archiving the exact contents that went into each specific release. It is a code time machine.

  This facilitates *software archaeology*, tracing the changes in files to work out the changes that comprised a particular feature. It catalogues who changed each file, and why.
- It provides a central backup of your work.
- It provides the developer with a safety net. It leaves room to experiment, to try changes, and roll them back if they do not work.
- It fosters a rhythm and cadence of work: you do a chunk of work, test it, and then check it in. Then you move on to the next chunk of work.

- It enables multiple concurrent streams of development to occur on the same codebase without interference.

- It enables reversibility: any change in the history of the project can be identified and reversed if it is found to be wrong.

Use It or Lose It

That's an impressive list. Version control is the backbone of your development process; without it you lack structural support.

So the first, golden rule of version control is: *do it*. Right from the very beginning of any project, employ version control. No ifs, no buts.

Most modern VCSs (*version control systems*) require practically no effort to set up, so there is no real excuse to defer version control.[1] Even the simplest prototypes (those pernicious things that all too often grow into production systems) can start off with their own repository and tracked history.

> KEY ➤ Use version control. It is not optional or a nice-to-have tool. It is the backbone of development. Your work is at risk without it.

Software is not inherently safe; source code on a disk is like digital smoke: all too easily blown away by a move of the hand. I've lost count of the times over the years that I've deleted the wrong thing, or made a mistaken change, but didn't have a checkpoint to roll back to. Version control alleviates this. A decent, lightweight VCS encourages small, frequent check-ins, providing a serious level of insulation against your own stupidity.

War Story: Distributed Data Loss

Standing outside a restaurant, I asked the members of a team I was collaborating with where I could get their source code. Implicitly, I meant, "which server hosts the repository that I should check out?" These guys worked out of their homes, distributed around a city.

They thought for a while, looking at each other quizzically. Then Dave said: *Bill, it's on your computer, isn't it?* Surprised by the response, I probed further.

It turns out, they weren't fans of source control—it was "too much work." They thought a VCS was heavy-handed and process-driven. They preferred to take turns "looking after" the code. All changes were emailed at the end of every week for the owner to wind up into a big ball, and send it back around again.

---

1. For example, a single `git init` command in a directory establishes a Git repository in a heartbeat.

Yes, there were often many code conflicts to resolve; these were dealt with by guesswork, not always successfully. Yes, things got lost or forgotten every now and again. Yes, there were no backups. And yes, the source code had been lost catastrophically a couple of times over the years.

But even so, they were convinced that version control was too high ceremony, too much work. Yes, they were happy working like this.

That wasn't very many years ago. I've avoided the team since.

Pick One, Any One

There have been many different VCS systems produced over the years, from the pioneer days of Unix's rcs command (dating from the early 1980s), through the centralised CVS (popular in the 1990s), its modernising cousin Subversion (which held sway in the 2000s), and into the world of modern distributed systems like Git and Mercurial (which now rule the 2010s). Some tools are commercial, many are open source. They differ by license, cost, ease of use, platform support, maturity, scalability, and feature set.

A key differentiator is the mode of operation. The historical *centralised* systems funnel all communication through a central server that hosts the *repository* of all version-controlled files. This is a simple model, but requires access to that server for any non-trivial operation. The most recent VCS development is the *distributed* model, a peer-to-peer approach where each computer can host its own copy of the repository. This enables more impressive workflows, and allows you to interact with the repository even when away from a network connection.

Which tool should you use, if you have a choice?

Favour a modern, supported, and conventional system. Until recently, Subversion was probably the default choice due to its cost (free), range of supported platforms (practically everything, including your toaster), and ease of use. However, recently Git has taken over this crown. Distributed version control systems have become more popular, and for good reason. They provide more capable workflows that are genuinely useful. However, this power comes at a cost: Git definitely has a steeper learning curve.[2]

Storing the Right Things

We create so many files that we have them coming out of our ears. We have source files, configuration files, binary assets, build scripts, intermediate build files, object files,

---

2. I am now so entrenched in the distributed Git workflow that I will now only ever consider using a Subversion repository if I can use Git as the "frontend" connection client. Everyone I speak to shares this experience.

bytecode, compiled executables, and more. Which of these should be stored under version control?

For our source-code projects there are two different answers. They are not entirely contradictory.

Answer One: Store Everything

You must store *every* file that's required to re-create your software. It doesn't matter if it's a "binary" or a "source" file. Version control it. A good VCS can handle large binaries in a reasonable way, and so you should not have to worry about managing binary files. (And if you didn't store your binaries under a VCS, you'd still have to archive them and manage revisions elsewhere, anyway.)

Starting with an appropriately configured build machine, and with the correct OS and compilation environment (the build tools, standard libraries, etc., plus sufficient disk space), one simple checkout operation should get you a good buildable source tree.

That means your repository must include:

- All source code files
- All documentation
- All build files (makefiles, IDE setup, scripts)
- All configuration files
- All assets (graphics, sounds, install media, resource files)
- Any third-party–supplied files (e.g., code libraries you depend on, or DLLs from an outside company)

Answer Two: Store as Little as Possible

You clearly have to store a lot of stuff. But don't include unnecessary cruft that will confuse, bloat, and get in the way. Keep the repository file structure as simple as you can. Specifically:

- Don't store IDE configuration files or cache files. Avoid checking in precompiled header files or dynamically created code information, ctags files, user preference settings files, etc.
- Don't store generated artefacts—you needn't check in object files, library files, or application binaries if they are a result of the build process. You needn't even check in automatically generated source files.

Sometimes auto-generated files do get checked in: if they are particularly hard to generate or take a long time to create. This decision must be made very carefully—don't pollute your repository with unnecessary rubbish.

- Don't store things that are not a part of your project, like the installers for development tools, or an operating system image for the build server.
- Don't check in test or bug reports. They should be managed in a bug reporting system elsewhere.
- "Interesting" project emails do not belong in the repository. If they contain useful information, then it should be placed into more structured documentation files.
- Don't store personal settings, like the colour scheme for your editor, view configuration for your IDE, or (particularly) any setup that describes the location of build files on your computer.[3] This is especially nasty when your settings will fight with another user's computer.
- Don't keep things in the repository that you *think* you might need one day. Remember: you *can* delete stuff under version control if it isn't related to the current state of the art (it's perfectly safe—it's still there in the archives). Don't hold on to digital baggage that can be thrown away.

> KEY ➤ Store *every* file that comprises your software project under version control. But store as *little as possible*; do not include any unnecessary files.

Storing Software Releases

Should you version control the software releases that you build? Some shops put all their releases into a repository. This is usually a separate "release" repository; the binaries do not really belong beside the source files.

Consider archiving these in a simple static directory structure elsewhere. Version control does not buy you much when recording less dynamic file structures for posterity. It can be easier to navigate a file server for this kind of archiving.

Repository Layout

Think carefully about the layout of your repository. Ensure that the directory structure is clear and reveals the shape of the code. Include a helpful "read me" document at the top level.

---

3. No build system should rely on fixed locations on a computer. This is bad build system design. Fix it!

Mercilessly avoid duplication. Just as duplication in your code leads to bugs, so does duplication of files within a repository.

Manage third-party code carefully. Keep it separate from your own source files. Place it in clearly marked subdirectories. This helps you to be able to track changes from a third party without getting confused by your files.

Ensure that your repository is configured to ignore inappropriate files. You can instruct most systems to ignore certain files based on pattern-matching rules. This helps to prevent you from accidentally checking in personal settings files, derived files, and the like.

Use Version Control Well

> *To change and change for the better are two different things.*
>
> — Proverb

If the golden rule is: "use version control," then the silver rule is: "use version control *well*." It's important to truly understand how your version control system works and the best practices for working with it.

A number of these practices are universal.

Make Atomic Commits

The changes you commit to a repository tell a story of your work on the code. Consider how you tell this story so that the recorded history is clear.

Make small, atomic commits. They are easier to understand, and easier to inspect for correctness. This is the *little and often* check-in strategy.

> KEY ➤ Check in changes *little and often.*

Don't accumulate a week's worth of work before you check in. Or even a day. It leads to problems:

- It's harder to track the changes made in the code, as the changes are larger and coarser-grained.
- The rest of the code repository could have changed massively between your updates. Your new work might not be valid anymore.
- If the world changes around you, you are more likely to have conflicts: where you've changed the same section of code as someone else and now have to resolve a common set of changes.

Atomic commits are cohesive and coherent, presenting related changes as an individual step. Do not create a check-in that covers more than one change. If you find yourself writing the commit message: *Refactor internal structure and turn button green*, then it's clear that you've done two things. Do them in two separate commits. As a specific, and common, example, do not change code layout and functionality at the same time.

An atomic commit is complete. Don't check in half-done work. Each commit must stand as an entire step.

Sending the Right Messages

With each commit, provide a good *check-in message*. This should start with a *brief* summary of what has changed, ideally one clear sentence. Then follow up with the reasons why you made the change, if these are of interest. If appropriate, include a bug reference number or other supporting information.

Make the message clear, succinct, and unambiguous, just like good code. Remember the DRY principle: don't repeat yourself. There is no need to list the files that you've changed; the VCS already records this for you.

Aim for messages that sum up the change in the first sentence. These scan well in a list of commits as you browse the repository history.

Here are some examples of real check-in messages from a single codebase. Which ones do you think are good or bad?

- fix #4507: Utility windows load behind ACVS
- add some credits.. fix a bug that caused sample edit mode tab not to work..
- " " " (...*yes, an empty string; this is a surprisingly common commit message*)
- adjusted a deviance
- Documented some super-scary code in program loading whilst looking at a crasher. You know, sometimes I really despair at what I see in this codebase.
- seriously, does anybody read this stuff?

Craft Good Commits

A diligent programmer is considerate, and makes appropriate check-ins. Just as the commit message should be well-crafted, so should the contents of the commit.

- Don't break the build. Before you check in any code, first test it against the latest version of the repository. This will ensure that your new code won't break the build and annoy other developers. Other components it depends on might have changed since you wrote the code, causing your new work to be erroneous.

  The simple process is: make a change, test that it builds against the head of the repository, test that it works, check it in. In that order. Always. When you're dashing out the door to catch a bus it can be very tempting to rush a check-in of code that "should work." Take it from me: it rarely does.

- Don't trash or move a file unless you know that everyone is done with it. This is particularly important on cross-platform multibuild system projects.
- Don't let editors fight over line endings; this is another easy trap to fall into on cross-platform projects.

Branches: Seeing the Wood for the Trees

Branches are a fundamental and important VCS facility. They enable you to "fork" your development effort and work on different features simultaneously, without those development lines interfering with one another. Once complete, each code branch can be merged back onto the mainline to synchronise the forks with their parent. This is an immensely powerful development tool.

Branches can be used for personal work (as a playground for an individual's development or for risky experiments), to aid in team collaboration (defining integration or test areas), and for release management.

Many common tasks are made much easier with branches. Consider using them for:

- Encapsulating revisions of the source tree. For example, each feature can be developed on its own branch.
- Exploratory development work—the stuff you're not sure will work. Don't risk breaking the main development line: tinker on a branch and then merge down if the experiment is a success. You can create multiple branches to test out different ways of implementing the same functionality; merge down the most successful attempt (a form of code natural selection).
- Major changes that cut across a lot of the source tree and will take a while to complete, requiring many QA tests, and many individual check-ins to get right. Doing this work on a branch prevents other developers from stalling for days on end with a broken code tree.
- Individual bug fixes. Open a branch to work on a bug fix, test the work, and then merge the branch down once the fault has been closed.
- Separating volatile development from stable release lines. For example, we use *release branches* to "freeze" the code that comprises a software release. Release branches are described in *Please Release Me*.

Branches are an excellent organisation facility just waiting to be used. Don't be afraid of them. Don't pollute your main development line with unnecessary distraction that can be hived off into a branch.

However, be aware that branches are not always the most appropriate concurrent development technique. Sometimes it is better to eschew multiple, practically invisible, concurrent development efforts (with the consequent periodic integration overhead) in favour of a simple *feature-toggle* based approach on the main line of code development.[4]

The Home for Your Code

A version controlled repository is the home for your code. Be careful that it doesn't become a nursing home. Or a morgue.

After seeing enough large projects, you'll observe that any reasonably complex project's source code tends to become accustomed to the VCS it's stored in.

This happens as the project and its infrastructure grows up. As code passes infancy into adolescence, build scripts and release tools become deeply integrated with the repository. For example, automated version update scripts drive the version control machinery. Certain file structure conventions are followed because the VCS mandates them (e.g., the existence of empty directories, or whether you can create symbolic links).

These things tend to shape the way you work with the code, for better or for worse.

> KEY ➤ Source code inhabits the VCS it is stored in. The more mature a project, the more deeply it relies on this habitat.

We don't tend to migrate projects between VCSs frequently, as we value the revision history that the repository records. Migration is possible, but often it's a lossy and messy process. This is a key reason to choose an appropriate VCS at the beginning of a project.

Conclusion

To improve is to change; to be perfect is to change often.

— Sir Winston Churchill

Version control is one of our fundamental software development tools. Every programmer should know how to wield a VCS well, just as you should have a good working knowledge of a powerful source code editor.

Version control forms the backbone of team collaboration. It is essential for software development but can be used for many other purposes: for example, for managing document trees. This book was written as a set of AsciiDoc files held under Git. This

---

4. A *feature toggle* is a configuration file that selectively enables or disables functionality in your software. It might be a run-time-parsed XML config file, or a set of compile-time preprocessor flags.

has allowed me to back up my work easily, to move files between computers with no hassle, to track the changes I have made, and to share the manuscript with my publisher.

Version control is even useful for non-collaborative scenarios; most important information will benefit from being stored in a repository. By default, I create a repository for every prototype project I start, even if it's a pet personal project. I manage many other things with Git, like the personal settings saved in my computer's home directory. This makes it super easy to set up a new computer to my personal taste by just cloning that repository.

Questions

1. Version control systems come with GUI and command-line tools. What are the pros and cons for each? Is it important to know how to use both? Why?

2. What are the possible problems that distributed VCSs introduce over the simpler centralised model? How can you avoid these problems?

3. Are you using the right version control system? What facilities does your current system lack that you have seen in an alternative VCS?

4. Does using a version control system mean that you do not need to back up a personal development machine?

5. Which is a safer mechanism for concurrent working: *feature-toggles* or concurrent *branches*? Which involves the least management and integration overhead?

6. You are about to commit your changes to a repository and realise that you've worked on two separate things. Should you stop and rework the changeset, or just commit the code because you've done it already? Why? How do different VCS tools help this situation?

See also

- *Improve Code by Removing It* Version control allows you to delete code with confidence. You can always get it back from the archives.

- *Please Release Me* Version control is an essential part of a good release and deployment pipeline. This chapter describes *release branches* in more detail.

- *The Curious Case of the Frozen Code* Release branches are the VCS mechanism used to enforce a *code freeze* whilst work can continue on the development mainline.

- *Navigating a Route* Your repository history can contain valuable information that will help you to navigate your way around and gauge the quality of a codebase.

Pay attention to the quality of your commits. Are they frequent, atomic, small, and coherent? Work on creating better changes.

CHAPTER 21

Getting One Past the Goalpost

Fights would not last if only one side was wrong.

— François de la Rochefoucauld

The mid-twentieth-century philosophers and purveyors of jaunty, tuneful hair, The Beatles, told us *all you need is love*. They emphasised the point: *love is all you need*. Love; that's it. Literally. Nothing else.

It's incredible how long a career they had given that they didn't need to eat or drink.

In our working relationships with other inhabitants of the software factory, we would definitely benefit from more of that sentiment. A little more love might lead to a lot better code! Programming in the real world is an interpersonal endeavour, and so is inevitably bound up in relationship issues, politics, and friction from our development processes.

We work closely with many people. Sometimes in stressful scenarios.

It is not healthy for our working relationships, nor for the consequent quality of our software, if our teams are not working smoothly together. But many teams suffer these kinds of problem.

As a tribe of developers, one of our rockier relationships is with the QA enclave; largely because we interact with them very closely, often at the most stressful points in the development process. In the rush to ship software before a deadline, we try to kick the software soccer ball past the testing goalkeepers.

So let's look at that relationship now. We'll see why it's fraught, and why it must not be.

What Is QA Good for?

To some it's obvious what they do. To others it's a mystery. The "QA" department (that is, *Quality Assurance*) exists to ensure that your project ships a software product of sufficient quality. They are a necessary and vital part of the construction process.

What does this entail? The most obvious and practical answer is that they have to test the living daylights out of whatever the developers create in order to ensure:

- That it matches the specification and requirements—that every feature that should be implemented has been implemented.

- That the software works correctly on all platforms—that is, it works on all OSes, on all versions of those OSes, on all hardware platforms, and on all supported configurations (e.g., meeting minimum memory requirements, minimum processor speeds, network bandwidth, etc.).

- That no faults have been introduced in the latest build—the new features don't break any other behaviour, and no regressions (the reintroduction of previous bad behaviour) have been introduced.

Their name is "QA," not just "the testing department," and for a reason. Their role is not just pushing buttons like robots; it's baking quality into the product.

To do this, QA must be deeply involved throughout, not just a final adjunct to the development process.

- They have a hand in the specification of the software, to understand—and shape—what will be built.

- They contribute to design and construction, to ensure that what's built will be testable.

- They are involved heavily in the testing phase, naturally.

- And also in the final physical release: they ensure that what was tested is what is actually released and deployed.

Software Development: Shovelling Manure

In unenlightened workplaces, the development process is modelled as a huge pipe: conveying raw materials pumped in the top, through various processes, until perfectly formed software gushes (well, perhaps dribbles) out the end. The process goes something like this:

1. Someone (perhaps a *business analyst* or *product manager*) pours some requirements into the mouth of the pipe.

2. They flow through architects and designers, where they turn into specifications and pretty diagrams (or good intentions, and smoke and mirrors).

3. This flows through the programmers (where the *real* work gets done, naturally), and turns into executable code.

4. Then it flows into QA. Where it hits a blockage as the "perfectly formed" software magically turns into a nonfunctioning disaster. These people *break* the code!

5. *Eventually* the developers push hard enough down the pipe to break this blockage, and the software finally flows out of the far end of the pipe.

In the fouler development environments, this pipe more closely resembles a sewer. QA feels like the developers are pumping raw sewage down to them, rather than handing them a thoughtfully gift-wrapped present. They feel they are being dumped on, rather than worked with.

Is software development really this linear? Do our processes really work like this simple pipeline (regardless of how pure the contents)?

No. They don't.

The pipe is an interesting first approximation (after all, you can't test code that hasn't been written yet), but far too simplistic a model for real development. The linear pipeline view is a logical corollary of our industry's long fascination with the flawed *waterfall* development methodology.[1]

> KEY ➤ It is wrong to view software development as a linear process.

However, this view of the development process does explain why the development team's interaction with the QA team isn't as smooth as it should be. Our processes and models of interaction are too often shaped by the flawed sewage-based development metaphor. We should be in constant communication, rather that just throwing them software towards the end of the development effort.

A False Dichotomy

Our inter-team interactions are hindered because they are just that: interactions between *separate* teams. The QA people are considered a different tribe, distinct from the "important" developers. This bogus, partitioned vision of the development organisation inevitably leads to problems.

---

1. This model is often attributed to Winston Royce. Although he wrote about it in the 1970s, it was as an illustration of a *flawed* development process, not a laudable one. See Winston Royce, "Managing the Development of Large Software Systems," *Proceedings of IEEE WESCON* 26 (1970): 1–9.

When QA and development are seen as separate steps, as separate activities, and therefore as very separate teams, an artificial rivalry and disconnect can too easily grow. This is reinforced physically by our building artificial silos between testers and developers. For example:

- The two teams have different managers and different reporting lines of responsibility.
- The teams are not colocated, and have very different desk locations (I've seen QA in separate desk clusters, on different floors, in different buildings, and even—in an extremely silly case—on another continent).
- There are different team structures, recruiting policies, and expected turnover of staff. Developers are valued resources, whereas testers are seen as replaceable cheap mercenaries.
- And most pernicious: the teams have very different incentives to complete tasks. For example, the developers are working with the promise of bonus pay if they complete a job quickly, but the testers are not. In this case, the developers rush to write the code (probably *badly*, because they're hurrying). They then get very cross when the QA guys won't sanction it for a timely release.

We reinforce this chasm with stereotypes: developers *create*, testers *break*.

There *is* an element of truth there. There are different activities and different skills required in both camps. But they are not logically separate, silo-ed activities. Testers don't find software faults to just break things and cause merry hell for developers. They do it to improve the final product.

They are there to bake in quality. That's the Q in QA. And they can only do this effectively in tandem with developers.

> KEY ▶ Beware of fostering an artificial separation between development and testing efforts.

By separating these activities, we breed rivalry and discord. Often, development processes pit QA as the *bad guy* against the developer *hero*. Testers are pictured standing in the doorway, blocking a plucky software release getting out. It's as if they are *unreasonably* finding faults in our software. They are nit-picking over minutiae.

It's almost as if they're running into the forests, catching wild bugs, and then injecting them into our otherwise perfect code.

Does that sound silly?

Of course it does when you read it here, but it's easy to start thinking that way: *The code is fine; those guys just don't know how to use it.* Or: *They've been working far too long to find such a basic bug; they really don't know what they're doing.*

Software development is not a battle. (Well, it shouldn't be.) We're all on the same side.

Fix the Team to Fix the Code

Conway's famous law describes how an organisation's structure—and specifically the lines of communication between its teams—dictates software structure.[2] It is popularly paraphrased as "if you have four teams writing a compiler, it'll be a four-pass compiler." Experience shows this to be pretty accurate. In the same way that team *structure* affects the code, so does the *health* of the interactions within the software.

> KEY ➤ Unhealthy team interactions result in unhealthy code.

We can improve the quality of our software, and the likelihood of producing a great release, by addressing these health issues: by improving the relationship between developers and QA. Working *together* rather than waging war. *Love*, remember, *is all you need.*

This is a general principle and applies far more broadly than just between developers and QA. Cross-functional teams in all respects are very helpful.

This comes down to the way we interact and work with QA. We should not treat them as puppets whose strings we pull, or to whom we throw ropey software to test. Instead, we treat them as coworkers. Developers *must* have good rapport with QA: a friendship and camaraderie.

Let's look at the practical ways we can work better with these inhabitants of the QA kingdom. We'll do this by looking at the major places that developers interact with QA.

But We Have Unit Tests!

We are conscientious coders. We want to make rock-solid software. We want to craft great lines of code with a coherent design, that contribute to an awesome product.

That's what we do.

So we employ development practices that ensure our code is as good as possible. We review, we pair, we inspect. And we *test*. We write automated unit tests.

We have tests! And they pass! The software must be good. Mustn't it?

Even with unit tests coming out of our ears, we still can't guarantee that our software is perfect. The code might operate as the developers intended, with green test lights all the way. But that may not reflect what the software is *supposed* to do.

---

2. Melvin E. Conway, "How Do Committees Invent?" *Datamation* 14:5 (1968): 28–31.

The tests may show that all input the developers envisioned was handled correctly. But that may not be what the user will actually do. Not all of the use cases (and *abuse cases*) of the software have been considered up front. It is hard to consider all such cases—software is a mightily complex thing. Thinking about this is exactly what the QA people are great at.

Because of this, a rigorous testing and QA process is still a vital part of a software development process, even if we have comprehensive unit tests in place. Unit tests act as our responsible actions to prove that the code is good enough before we hand it over to the testers to work on.

Releasing a Build to QA

We know that the development process isn't a straight line; it's not a simple pipeline. We develop iteratively and release incremental improvements: either a new feature that needs validation or a fixed bug that should be validated. It's a cycle that we go around many times. Over the course of the construction process, we will create numerous builds that will be sent to QA.

So we need a smooth build and handoff process.

This is vital: the handoff of our code must be flawless—the code must be responsibly created and thoughtfully distributed. Anything less is an insult to our QA colleagues.

We must build with the right attitude: giving something to QA is not the act of throwing some dog-eared code, built on any old machine, over the fence for them. It's not a slapdash or slipshod act.

Also, remember that this is not a battle: we don't aim to *slip* a release past QA, deftly avoiding their defence. Our work must be high quality, and our fixes correct. Don't cover over the *symptoms* of the more obvious bugs and hope they'll not have time to notice the underlying evils in the software.

Rather, we must do everything we can to ensure that we provide QA with something worthy of their time and effort. We must avoid any silly errors or frustrating sidetracks. Not to do so shows a lack of respect to them.

> KEY ➤ Not creating a QA build thoughtfully and carefully shows a lack of respect to the testers.

This means that you should follow the guidelines covered in the following sections.

Test Your Work First

Prior to creating a release build, the developers should have done as good a job as possible to prove that it is correct. They should have tested the work they've done beforehand. Naturally, this is best achieved with a comprehensive suite of regularly run unit tests. This helps catch any behavioural *regressions* (reoccurrences of previous errors). Automated tests can weed out silly mistakes and embarrassing errors that would waste the tester's time and prevent them from finding more important issues.

With or without unit tests, the developers *must* have actually tried the new functionality, and satisfied themselves that it works as well as is required. This sounds obvious, but all too often changes or fixes that should "just work" get released, and cause embarrassing problems. Or a developer sees the code working in a simple case, considers it adequate for release, and doesn't even think about the myriad ways it could fail or be mis-used.

Of course, running a suite of unit tests is only as effective as the quality of those tests. Developers take full responsibility for this. The test set should be thorough and representative. Whenever a fault is reported from QA, demonstrative unit tests should be added to ensure that those faults don't reappear after repair.

Release with Intent

When a new version is being released to QA, the developer must make it clear exactly *how* it is expected to work. Don't produce a build and just say, *"see how this one works."*

Describe clearly exactly what new functionality is and isn't implemented: exactly what is known to work and what is not. Without this information you cannot direct what testing is required. You will waste the testers' time. You communicate this in *release notes*.

It's important to draw up a set of good, clear *release notes*. Bundle them with the build in an unambiguous way (e.g., in the deployment file, or with a filename that matches the installer). The build must be given a (unique) version number (perhaps with an incrementing *build number* for each release). The release notes should be versioned with this same number.

For each release, the release notes should clearly state what has changed and what areas require greater testing effort.

More Haste, Less Speed

Never rush out a build, no matter how compelling it seems. The pressure to do this is greatest as a deadline looms, but it's also tempting to sneak a build out before leaving the office for the evening. Rushing work like this encourages you to cut corners, not check everything thoroughly, or pay careful attention to what you're doing. It's just too easy. And it's not the right way to give a release to QA. Don't do it.

If you feel like a school kid desperately trying to rush your homework and get "something" in on time, in the full knowledge that the teacher will be annoyed and make you do it again, then something is wrong! Stop. And think.

> KEY ➤ Never rush the creation of a build. You will make mistakes.

Some products have more complex testing requirements than others. Only kick off an expensive test run across platforms or OSes if you think it's worthwhile, when an agreed number of features and fixes have been implemented.

Automate

Automation of manual steps always removes the potential for human error. So automate your build or release process as much as possible. If you can create a single script that automatically checks out the code, builds it, runs all unit tests, creates installers or deploys on a testing server, and uploads the build with its release notes, then you remove the potential for human error for a number of steps. Avoiding human error with automation helps to create releases that install properly each time and do not contain any regressions. The QA guys will love you for that.

Respect

The delivery of code into QA is the act of producing something stable and worthy of potential release, not the act of chucking the latest untested build at QA. Don't throw a code grenade over the fence, or pump raw software sewage at them.

On Getting a Fault Report

We give the test guys a build. It's our best effort yet, and we're proud of it. They play with it. Then they find faults. Don't act surprised. You knew it was going to happen.

> KEY ➤ Testing will only reveal problems that software developers added to the system (by omission or commission). If they find a fault, it was *your fault!*

On finding a bug, they lodge a *fault report*: a trackable report of the problem. This report can be prioritised, managed, and once fixed, checked for later regression.

It is *their* responsibility to provide accurate, reliable fault reports, and to send them through in a structured and orderly way—using a good bug tracking system, for example. But faults can be maintained in a spreadsheet, or even by placing stories in a work backlog. (I've seen all these work.) As long as there's a clear system in place that records and announces changes to the state of a fault report.

So how do we respond to a fault report?

First, remember that QA *isn't* there to prove that you're an idiot and make you look bad. The fault report isn't a personal slight. So don't take it personally.

Our "professional" response is "thanks, I'll look into it." Just be glad it was QA who they found it, and not a customer. You *are* allowed to feel disappointed that a bug slipped through your net.

You should be worried if you are swamped by so many fault reports that you don't know where to start—this is a sign that something very fundamental is wrong and needs addressing. If you're in this kind of situation, it's easy to resent each new report that comes in.

Of course, we don't leap onto every single fault as soon as it is reported. Unless it is a trivial problem with a super-simple fix, there are almost certainly more important problems to address first. We must work in collaboration with all the project stakeholders (managers, product specialists, customers, etc.) to agree which are the most pressing issues to spend our time on.

Perhaps the fault report is ambiguous, unclear, or needs more information. If this is the case, work *with* the reporter to clarify the issues so you can both understand the problem fully, can reproduce it reliably, and know when it has been closed.

QA can only uncover bugs from development, even if it's not a fault that *you* were the direct author of. Perhaps it stems from a design decision that you had no control over. Or perhaps it lurks in a section of code that you didn't write. But it is a healthy and professional attitude to take responsibility for the *whole product*, not just your little part of the codebase.

Our Differences Make Us Stronger

Whenever you're in conflict with someone, there is one factor that can make the difference between damaging your relationship and deepening it. That factor is attitude.

— William James (philosopher and psychologist)

Effective working relationships stem from the right developer attitudes. When we're working with QA engineers, we must understand and exploit our differences:

- Testers are very different from developers. Developers often lack the correct mindset to test effectively. It requires a particular way of looking at software, particular skills and peccadilloes to do well. We must respect the QA team for these skills— skills that are essential if we want to produce high-quality software.

- Testers are inclined to think more like a user than a computer; they can give valuable feedback on perceived product quality, not just on correctness. Listen to their opinions and value them.

- When a developer works on a feature, the natural instinct is to focus on the *happy path*—on how the code works when everything goes well (when all input is valid, when the system is working fully with maximum CPU, no memory or disk space issues, and every system call works perfectly).

  It's easy to overlook the many ways that software can be used incorrectly, or to overlook whole classes of invalid input. We are wired to consider our code through these natural cognitive biases. Testers tend not to be straightjacketed by such biases.

- Never succumb to the fallacy that QA testers are just "failed devs." There is a common misconception that they are somehow less intelligent, or less able. This is a damaging point of view and must be avoided.

> KEY ➤ Cultivate a healthy respect for the QA team. Enjoy working with them to craft excellent software.

Pieces of the Puzzle

We need to see testing *not* as the "last activity" in a classic waterfall model; development just doesn't work like that. Once you get 90% of the way through a waterfall development process into testing, you will likely discover that *another* 90% of effort is required to complete the project. You cannot predict how long testing will take, especially when you start it far too late in the process.

Just as code benefits from a test-first approach, so does the entire development process. Work with the QA department and get their input early on to help make your specifications verifiable, ensure their expertise feeds into product design, and that they will agree that the software is maximally testable before you even write a line of code.

> KEY ➤ The QA team is not the sole owner of, nor the gatekeeper of "quality." It is everyone's responsibility.

To build quality into our software and to ensure that we work well together, all developers should understand the QA process and appreciate its intricate details.

Remember that QA is part of the *same* team; they are not a rival faction. We need to foster a holistic approach, and maintain healthy relationships to grow healthy software. *All we need is love.*

Questions

1. How close do you think your working relationship with your QA colleagues is? Should it be better? If so, what steps can *you* take to improve it?

2. What is the biggest impediment to software quality in your development organisation? What is required to fix this?

3. How healthy are your release procedures? How can you improve them? Ask the QA team what would help them most.

4. Who is responsible for the "quality" of your software? Who gets the "blame" when things go wrong? How healthy is this?

5. How good do you think your testing skills are? How methodically do you test a piece of code you're working on before you check in or hand off?

6. How many silly faults have you let slip through your coding net recently?

7. What could you add to your development regimen *in addition to unit tests* to ensure the quality of the software you hand to QA?

See also

- *Testing Times* Development testing: writing automated unit, integration, and system tests.

- *People Power* Working well with excellent QA folk is an example of the important working relationships we must foster.

- *Please Release Me* The testing/QA process and the QA team are vital to making effective software releases.

Try this....

Commit to working more closely with your QA department. Adjust your working relationships with them, so you construct better software together.

CHAPTER 22

The Curious Case of the Frozen Code

> *There she blows!—there she blows!*
>
> *A hump like a snow-hill! It is Moby Dick!*
>
> — Herman Melville
> *Moby Dick*

Managers pronounce it in planning meetings. Developers utter it in reverent awe. Process ceremonies build up around it. And I have to stifle the gag reflex.

It's a shout I imagine coming from a sailor in *Moby Dick*. Not *"There she blows!"* but *"Code freeze!"* It's about as likely, and just as fictitious.

Our hunt for another mythical state of code.

Hunting the Code Freeze

Code freeze is a term bandied around with, presumably, good intentions. But often people don't intend to say what the words actually imply.

A code freeze denotes the period between some "done" point—when no further work is expected to be performed—and the release date.

Exactly when are these points? And what happens in the middle?

The *release date* is pretty easy to define: sometimes called *release to manufacture* or RTM. It's when the *Gold Master* of an installer disk is burnt and sent for duplication. In the enlightened twenty-first century we may not always ship physical media, but we tend to follow the mechanical conventions dictated by such a release schedule nonetheless. Is this useful and appropriate? Sometimes yes; sometimes no. It does lend a useful cadence to the delivery schedule.

But what is the preceding *"done" point* that initiates code freeze? Clearly, it should be the point when we consider the code to be complete, with all features implemented and no egregious outstanding bugs. However, some "freeze" their code at:

- The *feature complete* point, when all functionality has been written, but not fully tested, and no bugs necessarily addressed.
- The point of the first *alpha or beta release* being made (of course, the definition of these states is also beautifully ambiguous).
- When a *release candidate* build is first made.

During this period, we "freeze" the code so that no further work ought to be performed on it. However, this notion is *pure bunk*; the code never stands still. Whatever happens to the code, this is the phase when a final, exhaustive regression test sweep is run on the software to ensure that it is adequate for release.

> KEY ▶ "Code freeze" is the period leading up to a release when no changes are anticipated.

At best: *frozen* is figurative term. The code is considered frozen for development work, but is still open for final testing. We *anticipate* some changes being made in light of these tests—if it was not possible to change the code at all, we could just release it *now* regardless.

Because we're testing to find problems, we will probably uncover a few nasty things that need remedial work. What happens then? You must fix the faults, which implies that the code isn't as frozen as all that! It's not a very deep freeze.

At worst: the code freeze metaphor isn't particularly useful. It's a misnomer. Even glaciers move; just very slowly.

> KEY ▶ "Code freeze" is a misleading term. Code never stands still, even if you'd like it to.

A New World Order

So, at code freeze, we do anticipate some final work will be required. But we carefully monitor the software's development, selectively including or excluding changes in the release code.

Rather than a complete lockdown on changes, "code freeze" really signifies a new rule of order is in place for the development effort. Changes cannot be applied blindly. Even worthwhile changes must be added with careful agreement.

We work very hard to maintain the integrity of the release, so each change is reviewed very carefully before inclusion. We only include changes that are strictly necessary for the release. Not all issues or bugs found in the "frozen" code will be considered for fixing post code freeze. Only "showstoppers" that will prevent a release from being made will be addressed. Some lower priority issues may be queued for a later release, depending on their priority. We balance the risk: it may be more important to release the product than invest time and energy finding and fixing these faults.

Specifically, there is absolutely no more work on new features. No bugs are "fixed" without prior agreement; we prioritise the issues that have to be addressed. This is a discipline; we do this because even the simplest feature addition or bug fix may introduce unexpected and unwanted side effects.

So this stage of development is not so much a "freeze" of the code; it is more a very intentional deceleration. It is a mindful reduction of the rate of change of the code line.

> KEY ➤ We slow down development work to carefully shepherd a code
> line to release, managing the final fixes and changes carefully.

Careless speed costs lines (of code).

During the freeze period, some larger (and more departmental) organisations will invoke the services of the "installer team" to create the install/distribution systems, or get to work on any remaining collateral (artwork, text files, etc.) for the final release. Personally, I believe this is wrong—by the time you enter a "freeze," *all* work should have been completed, ready for final test.

Forms of Freeze

It helps to consider the three different forms of "freeze," and to be specific in the terms we use. *Code freeze* itself is a bit too woolly and misleading:

Feature freeze
A feature freeze declares that only bug fixes may now be committed—no new features will be developed. This helps to avoid "feature creep"—as we get near a scheduled release, it's always tempting to sneak that one extra little facility in without fully considering the risk or potential bugs that the change may introduce.

Code freeze
We no longer work on any features, nor on any bugs that have not been highly prioritised. We only accept fixes for "showstopping" issues. We dearly need a better, less ambiguous, name for this state.

"Hard" code freeze
No changes are allowed *at all*. Any change required after this point is tantamount to bringing out the defibrillators and trying to revivify the development team. We never really consider this state, because by the time you get here the software has shipped, and the party has moved on to another code line.

Branches Make It Work

Typically, when a code freeze is declared, we *branch* the code in the revision control system. Specifically, we create a *release branch*. This allows the release's development code line to be frozen, without delaying other work that can continue on the main code branch.

It is best practice, when working with a release branch, that *absolutely no* code work takes place on the branch itself. The release branch remains, always, stable with no speculative changes applied.

Instead, all work takes place on a spongier branch, perhaps the development mainline. Each fix is tested and verified there and, only when ready, is *merged* to the release branch. By doing this, only acceptably good code ever arrives on the release branch.

Code should always flow between branches *towards* points of stability. We "promote" change sets based on their proven quality.

Every change that is incorporated into the frozen branch goes through more rigour than previous development changes:

- They are each carefully reviewed.
- They are given focused testing effort.
- They are risk-analysed, so any potential differences they introduce are well understood and, if necessary, mitigated.
- They are prioritised—they will be carefully reviewed for appropriateness in the release.

Branches are pivotal to a team being able to manage code freezes. Without a release branch, all the developers would physically have to put down their tools, and stall work for the duration of the freeze. This isn't a good use of time or expensive resources. Developers like to develop; soon they'll get itchy feet, and write code anyway.

> **KEY** ▶ Branch or bust.

That said, it's a good idea to avoid concurrent work as much as possible—it can be confusing and lead to conflicting goals and aims for the team.

But It's Not Really Frozen!

Be careful that the "code freeze" misnomer doesn't lead you into a false sense of confidence. Often the term code freeze is pronounced to managers to imply a more stable project state, to garner their confidence. It *sounds* great, doesn't it?

But don't believe your code is in a better state than it is. At all times it's important to have a realistic appraisal of the state of your project.

Be wary that the word "freeze" doesn't tempt you to keep things rigid when they should not be. When changes must be made, they *must* be made.

Length of the Freeze

You must declare a digital winter for the right length of time. Like the Narnian winter, you don't want an unnecessarily lengthy freeze where Christmas never comes! But have it too short, and the freeze is a pointless exercise.

The correct period depends on the complexity of your project, the test demands it imposes (both on people and resources: do we need to install or configure a whole separate test platform with administrators and boffins to keep it spinning?), the scope of the changes that have gone into this release (which may influence the level of regression testing performed), and the resources available to devote to test and verification.

A typical freeze period length is two weeks.

Beware the Pareto principle: we often see in IT projects where the "last" 20% of effort expands to take up 80% of the total time (or thereabouts). To avoid this, make sure you enter the freeze at the right point. Don't declare a freeze when you think you just need to "finish off" a few things. You freeze once everything *is* finished off.

Feel the Freeze

A code freeze is the hard road to release—not a picnic in the park. Set your expectations accordingly.

During a code freeze period, expect to find bugs that you *will not be able to fix* because they are not important enough to risk inclusion. This is no longer a coding free-for-all where any code change is permissible; otherwise you wouldn't have declared freeze. Therefore expect to be disappointed, and to ship a product that you'd hoped would be better!

> KEY ➤ It's not unusual (or wrong) to ship software that you know could be better.

Look on the bright side: because you've found them, you can fix those bugs in the next release.

Also expect to rack up *technical debt* during a freeze.[1] This is one of the few valid times to do so: when there's no scope to make wide-ranging repairs, you have to fix problems with stopgap "paper over the cracks" techniques to get a "good enough" shipping product. But do remember to consider this kind of work as *debt*, not normal practice, and plan to pay this off in the development cycles after the release.

> KEY ➤ During code freeze you will accrue technical debt. Monitor this, and be prepared to pay the debt off soon after the release ships.

If you make a change during freeze that has serious implications, consider if the code should be thawed and refrozen, with a thorough test cycle kicked off from scratch. Postpone the release and restart your code freeze period if you have to.

Scientists tell us that freezing-thawing-freezing is bad for your health. So be careful not to do this too many times, or you'll end up with food poisoning!

A long freeze period is a warning sign that you don't have a stable enough codebase.

The End Draws Near

At the end of a code freeze period, when we reach the RTM point, the code line is really, *honestly* frozen. No changes will now occur as the release has (finally) been made. Close the release branch. Archive the code line. Go and celebrate.

Any further changes will be made to a different code line.

> KEY ➤ The only true "code freeze" is when an acceptable release is made. This is the point that the code is finally *set in stone*.

This point is the real honest-to-goodness code freeze. But no one ever talks about this!

Antifreeze

If you work well, it is possible to avoid code freeze periods altogether. You *can* skip this sordid dance.

Many development teams are no longer constrained by a physical manufacturing process—they ship software over the Internet, or create web services that can be deployed into production servers in a heartbeat. The "disaster" of a bug making it through to an external release is minimised here—an online software update can be deployed to remedy the issue in the field before many users even spot the problem.

---

1. For more on the *technical debt* metaphor, see *http://martinfowler.com/bliki/TechnicalDebt.html*.

However, this is no excuse to chuck code out without testing. Rapid code-freeze-less releases require a new mind-set, and discipline. We strive to release fast by writing reliable, provably bug-free code from the start.

We can minimise, and even remove, code freeze periods by:

- Employing continuous delivery; setting up a pipeline that ushers each build into a full deployable state. This ensures that you are always ready to deploy.

- Establishing a good *automated* test harness with good coverage. These tests must cover the code, the integration, and final user-facing aspects of the system to give reliable feedback on the state of the product.

- Good acceptance criteria testing—tools like Cucumber (*http://cukes.info*) can be used to ensure that the full set of high-level user requirements have been met by the software.

- Reduce the test period—reduce the scope or size of project so that you don't need a lengthy lockdown for each release.

- Develop a simple and reliable "release pipeline" that will take your code and deploy it into production with little effort and no human intervention.

With this kind of discipline it's perfectly possible to "release" code into production regularly, with far less ceremony than the traditional release engineering process. Many teams can make a software release every week. Some are capable of deploying code onto their production systems daily.

These super-short development cycles require a coding mind-set that is more disciplined throughout, so you don't need to switch gears and apply more care at the frozen end of a development phase.

> KEY ➤ Aim for code that never "freezes," but is permanently ready to release to production.

Conclusion

Code freeze is a problematic term; it is a misleading metaphor. Code doesn't really freeze or thaw. Code is a malleable substance, constantly changing and adapting to the world around it. What really happens is that the rate of change of development slows, and we change the focus of our work.

However, it is true that as we get near a software release we need more discipline in the development regimen to ensure that the software is of a releasable quality.

Questions

1. Do you have a formal code freeze period in your development practice? How diligently is it observed?

2. How do you ensure that changes applied in the freeze period are safe and appropriate?

3. Is a single person responsible for the quality of the build, or is it a team concern? Which is the right approach, and why?

4. Does it take your project a long time to get to the code freeze point? Why? How can you shorten this?

See also

- *Please Release Me* A "code freeze" exists to help you stablise your software in the run up to a release.

- *Effective Version Control* A *release branch* is used to encapsulate frozen code.

Try this....

Consider how to improve your release process. How can you minimise (or eliminate) the code freeze period?

Please Release Me

Creating a *software release* is an incredibly important step in your software development process, and not one that should left to the last minute. It requires discipline and planning.

Many times I have run into silly, perfectly avoidable problems that were caused by a lackadaisical approach to the construction of software releases.

Most of these were caused by the sloppy habit of creating a "release" from a local working directory, rather than from a clean checkout. (Hint: this is not a real software release, it's a "build" of your code, you need a *lot* more process and diligence to create a proper release.)

Some examples:

- A software release was made from a developer's local working directory. The developer hadn't cleaned the code first, and the directory contained uncommitted source file changes. He noticed, but made the "release" anyway. When problems were reported, we had no record of exactly *what* went into that build. The result: debugging the software was a nightmare, mostly guesswork.

- A software release was made from a local directory that wasn't up-to-date; the developer hadn't updated to the HEAD of the Subversion code repository. So the release was missing features and bug fixes. Helpfully, the developer tagged the

HEAD of the repository as the "release point," claiming he'd build that version. The result: much confusion, embarrassment, and a dent in the project's reputation.

- A project was released whose code was not under source control; it lived locally on the hard disk of one machine which—as I'm sure you can guess—was not being backed up. The code was based upon an original software release by another organisation. We had no record of where the original code came from, which version it was based on, or how it had been subsequently modified. For bonus points, the machine's exact build environment was unknown—the result of years of tweaks and adjustments. Murphy's law struck. The machine died. The result: all copies of the source were lost, along with the understanding of how to build it for the target platform. Game over.

Each was an incredibly frustrating experience.

Creating a serious high-quality software release is a lot more work than just hitting "build" in your IDE and shipping whatever comes out. If you are not prepared to put in this extra work, then you should *not* be creating releases.

> KEY ➤ Creating software releases requires discipline and planning. It is more than hitting "build" in a developer's IDE.

In the previous chapter we looked at "code freeze," where we attempted to stabilise our code in the run up to a release. We also questioned whether a code freeze period should exist at all. Once you have your code ready to release, be it a snapshot of your mainline, or a frozen branch of development, you need rigour and discipline to construct a sound release from it.

Part of the Process

Most people write software for the benefit of others as well as themselves. So it has to get into the hands of your "users" somehow. Whether you end up rolling a software installer shipped on a CD, a downloadable installer bundle, a zipfile of source code, or deploy the software on a live web server, this is the important process of creating a *software release*.

The software release process is a critical part of your software development regimen, just as important as design, coding, debugging, and testing. To be effective, your release process must be:

- Simple
- Repeatable
- Reliable

Get it wrong, and you will be storing up some potentially nasty problems for your future self. When you construct a release you must:

- Ensure that you can get the exact same code that built it back again from your source control system. (You do use source control, don't you?) This is the only concrete way to prove which bugs were and were not fixed in that release. Then when you have to fix a critical bug in version 1.02 of a product that's five years old, you can do so.

- Record exactly how it was built (including the compiler optimisation settings, target CPU configuration, etc.). These features may subtly affect how well your code runs and whether certain bugs manifest.

- Capture the build log for future reference.

A Cog in the Machine

The bare outline of a good release process, specifically for a "shrink-wrap" distributable application, is shown next.[1]

Step 1: Initiate the Release

Agree that it's time to spin a new release. A formal release is treated differently than a developer's test build, and should *never* come from an existing working directory.

Agree what the name and type of the release is (e.g., "5.06 Beta1" or "1.2 Release Candidate").

Step 2: Prepare the Release

Determine exactly what code will constitute this release. In most cases, you will already be working on a *release branch* in your source control system, so it's the state of that branch right now. You should rarely release code directly from your source control system's mainline of code development (i.e., *trunk* or *master*).

A release branch is a stable snapshot of the code that allows you to continue development of "unstable" features on the trunk. You can merge in the good, stable, known work from the mainline into the release branch once it is proven. This maintains the integrity of the release codebase whilst allowing other new work to continue on the mainline.

If you run unit tests and a continuous integration system on your code's mainline, then you must also arrange to run these on the release branch, for as long as the branch is alive. The release process should be short, and so release branches should be short-lived.

---

1. Other kinds of releases—for example, to a live web server—largely follow this pattern with few adjustments.

Tag the code in source control to record what is going into the release. The tag name must reflect the release name.

Release Branches

You can make a branch in your version control system for just about any reason: to work on a new feature independent of the rest of the codebase, or to work on a bugfix or exploratory refactor without disrupting others. The branch encapsulates a set of changes. When you've completed the work, you typically merge the branch back onto the mainline. Or throw it away. Standard stuff.

"Release branches" are made for the exact opposite reason—to mark a point in the codebase where you want to ensure *stability*. Once you have made a branch for your software release, then other new features can be developed on the code mainline without fear of compromising the impending software release. This provides a mechanism for your "code freeze."

The QA department can perform regression testing of the branch code without worrying that any new work will move the goalposts under their feet. Very occasionally an important bugfix from the mainline may get merged into the release branch, but each merge is made carefully, with the consent of all people who have an interest in the quality of the software on that branch.

A release branch is not merged back down onto the trunk, as you perform no fresh development within it. All development occurs on the trunk, is sanity tested there, and then merged onto the release branch.

A good release process does not necessarily require a release branch. If you keep your code mainline in a permanently shippable state (by developing with more rigour and employing sound automated tests), then it is possible to bypass the release branch ritual altogether.

Step 3: Build the Release

Check out a virgin copy of the entire codebase at that tag. *Never* use an existing checkout. You may have uncommitted local changes that affect the build, or other untracked files that make a difference. Always tag and *then* checkout that tag. This will avoid many potential problems.

> KEY ➤ Always build your software in a fresh checkout, from scratch.
> Never reuse old parts of a software build.

Now build the software. This step *must not* involve hand-editing any files at all, otherwise you do not have a versioned record of exactly the code you built.

Ideally, the build should be *automated*: a single button press, or a single script invocation. Checking the mechanics of the build into source control alongside the code unambiguously records how the code was constructed. Automation reduces the potential for human error in the release process.

> KEY ➤ Make your build as simple as a single step that automates all parts of the process. Use a scripting language to do this.

The build script acts as unambiguous documentation on how to build the project. It also ensures that it is simple to deploy the build on a CI (*continuous integration*) server, where it can be automatically run to ensure validity of the build. Indeed, the best release builds are triggered from a CI server directly, and need never touch human hands.

> KEY ➤ Deploy your builds on a CI server to ensure their health. Make formal releases from the same system.

Step 4: Package the Release

Ideally, this is an integral part of the previous step.

Construct a set of "release notes" describing how the release differs from the previous release: the new features and the bugs that have been fixed. (This can be automated, pulled from source control logs. However, check-in messages might not be the best customer-facing notes.)

Package the code (create an installer image, CD ISO images, etc.). This step should also be part of the automated build script for the same reason.

Step 5: Deploy the Release

Store the generated artefacts and the build log for future reference. Put them on a shared file server.

Test the release! Yes, you tested the code already to prove that it was time to release, but now you should test this "release" version to ensure that everything is correct, and that the artefacts are of suitable release quality.

> KEY ➤ Never release software without testing the final artefacts.

There should be an initial smoke test to ensure that the installers work OK (on all supported deployment platforms) and that the software appears to run and function correctly.

Then perform whatever testing is appropriate for this type of release. Internal test releases may be run through test scripts by in-house testers. Beta releases may be released to select external testers. Release candidates should see suitable final regression checks. A software release should not be distributed until it has been thoroughly checked.

Finally, deploy the release. If you ship directly to an end user, then this perhaps involves putting the installer on your website, and sending out emails or press releases. Perhaps it means sending the software to a manufacturer to burn onto physical media.

If your code is deployed on a live, running production server, then we enter the world of *devops* (*development/operations*, where software development meshes with IT operations). This is the art of deploying new code onto a remote server, upgrading any required software components, upgrading datastores (e.g., performing database schema migration), and restarting the server with the new code; all with as little downtime as possible. This process needs to offer sensible fallback in case of any installation issues. As with many other software processes, automation is very much the key to an effecient and successful server deployment.

Release Early and Often

One of the worst release process sins is to think about this stuff only as you reach the end of a project, when you finally need to perform a public software release.

In the software world, it's an increasingly popular belief that you should defer any task or decision until the *last responsible moment*;[2] that is, until the point you know most about the exact requirements and have minimised the opportunity cost of what you could be doing instead. This is a sound viewpoint; however, the last responsible minute to construct a release process is a lot sooner than most developers expect.

> KEY ▶ Do not defer the planning and construction of a software release process until the last minute. Build it early, iterate through builds rapidly and frequently. Debug the build like you'd debug any other software.

We've seen that the ideal release process is entirely automated. The automated build and release plumbing should be established very *early on* in the development process. It should then be used often (daily, if not more frequently) to prove that it works, and that it is robust. This will also help to highlight and eliminate any nefarious presumptions in the code about the installation environment (hardcoded paths, assumptions about the computer's installed libraries, capabilities, etc.).

Starting the software release process early in the development effort gives you plenty of time to iron out wrinkles and flaws so that when you are in the run-up to a real public

---

2. This is originally from Mary and Tom Poppendieck's *Lean Software Development: An Agile Toolkit* (Boston: Addison-Wesley, 2003), where they describe it as: *the moment at which failing to make a decision eliminates an important alternative.*

release, you can focus on the important task of making your software work, rather than the tedious mechanics of how to ship it. Indeed, some people set up their release process as the very first thing on a new software project.

And There's More...

This is a large topic, tied intimately with configuration management, source control, testing procedures, software product management, and the like. If you have any part in releasing a software product, you really must understand and respect the sanctity of the software release process.

Questions

1. When do you decide to kick off a new software release?

2. How repeatable and reliable is your build and release process? How simple is it? How often do builds fail?

3. What is the worst release-creation failure you have seen? How could it have been avoided?

4. Does your build intermittently fail? Does this happen on developer machines, or the CI server? Which is the worse place for this to happen?

5. Should the creation and curation of the build and release process be a specific job for a specific person, or should everyone on the team be responsible for this? Why?

See also

- *The Curious Case of the Frozen Code* How we try to marshall the code development work towards a release.
- *Effective Version Control* A software release is built from virgin code taken straight out of the source repository. The VCS hosts our *release branch* of code.

Try this....

Review your project's build and release process. Work out how to improve it. If it is not automated via a single script invocation, write this script now.

PART III

Getting Personal

Becoming a better programmer requires more than a mere grasp of good coding and of good design, even though these are deep enough topics. There's a whole raft of other skills you need to pick up, and attitudes and approaches that will build you into a master.

The following chapters will help you grow in this area, presenting a selection of topics on personal development. We'll learn how to learn, consider behaving ethically, be challenged to avoid stagnation, as well as look at our physical well-being. These are all important parts of the coder's life.

CHAPTER 24

Live to Love to Learn

Learning is like rowing upstream: not to advance is to drop back.

— Chinese proverb

Programming is an exciting and dynamic field to work in; there is *always* something new to learn. Programmers are rarely forced to repeat the same task for years, only discovering new ways to develop RSI and failing eyesight. We continually face the unknown: new problems, new situations, new teams, new technologies, or a new combination of them all.

We are continually challenged to learn, to increase our skills and our capabilities. If you feel like you're stagnating in your career, one of the most practical steps you can take to get out of the rut is to make a conscious effort to *learn something new*.

> KEY ➤ Be in a state of continual learning. Always look to learn something new.

Some people are naturally better at learning; they excel at absorbing new information and can "get up to speed" rapidly. That's natural. But it is something we can all improve at, if we try. You need to take charge of your learning.

If you want to improve as a programmer, you *need* to be a skilled and seasoned learner. And you need to learn to enjoy it.

> KEY ➤ Learn to *enjoy* learning.

What to Learn?

There's a whole world of things you could attempt to pick up. So what should you look at? American political poet Donald Rumsfeld summed up this conundrum in a particularly apt way when he made an infamous White House press conference:

> *As we know, there are known knowns; there are things we know we know. We also know*
> *there are known unknowns; that is to say, we know there are some things we do not know.*
> *But there are also unknown unknowns—the ones we don't know we don't know.*

That is surprisingly profound.

You're aiming for a *known unknown*—something you'd like to learn. Or shoot for the *unknown unknowns*: spend some time investigating interesting things to learn first.

Ultimately, pick something that interests you. Pick something that will benefit you (the act of learning in itself *is* a benefit, but choosing something because it will give you fresh usable skills, broadens your insight, or brings you pleasure is a good thing). You will be investing a significant amount of time, so invest wisely!

Learn a new technology

For programmers this is the obvious choice. We're fascinated by the different ways we can make electrons dance, and there are so many ways to do it.

There is no shortage of new and interesting programming languages; you don't have to become an expert, but do get beyond *"Hello, World!"* Learn a new library, an application framework, or a software tool. Learn how to use a new text editor or IDE. Learn a new documentation tool, or a test framework. Learn a new build system, an issue tracking system, a source control system (indulge yourself in the new *distributed version control* craze that all the cool kids are going on about), a new operating system, and so on.

Learn new technical skills

Learn how to effectively read alien code, or how to write technical documentation. Learn how to architect software.

Learn how to work with people

Yes, this is tediously "touchy-feely" for most code monkeys. But it is an incredibly interesting, useful field. Study sociology, or management texts. Read about becoming a software team leader. This will help you to become a more capable team worker. It will help you to understand how to communicate well with your team and how to understand your customer better.

Learn a new problem domain

Perhaps you've always wanted to write mathematical modelling software, or work on audio DSP. Without any experience or knowledge you'd be unlikely to find a job in a new sphere, so give yourself a head start and begin to learn about it. Then work out how to get practical, demonstrable experience.

Learn how to learn

Seriously! Find new techniques that will help you absorb knowledge more effectively. Do you find there's a constant barrage of information you need to tap into, and it just seems to flow past you? Investigate ways to seek out, consume, and absorb knowledge. Practice new skills like mind mapping and speed reading.

Learn something completely different

Or, more interestingly, focus on something completely left field with no relevance to your day job, and no obvious software applicability. Learn a new foreign language, a musical instrument, a new branch of science, art, or philosophy. Even spirituality. This will widen your world view, and will inevitably inform the way you program.

Learning to Learn

Learning is a basic human skill. We all do it, all the time. When it arrives freshly formatted, the human brain rapidly absorbs information and develops skills across a wide range of experiences.

Then we hop aboard the academic train, where our learning is progressively funnelled through an increasingly restricted system. We move from a general education into a more specialised secondary education, until at university we focus on a single major topic. Post-graduate study focuses on an even more specific area of that specific topic. This increasing focus enables us to become highly proficient in an area, but in the process we train ourselves to become very narrow minded.

> KEY ➤ Our learning is often too narrowly focused. Consider a wider sphere of reference. Draw inspiration from many fields.

There are a few techniques to employ that will help you learn more successfully.

Understand how you best learn and exploit that to your advantage; your personality type affects your learning style. People who are traditionally categorised as "right-brain" learn best when presented with patterns and a holistic view of a subject; they struggle when bombarded by a serial stream of information. Their "left-brain" counterparts thrive on a linear, rational presentation of the topic. They prefer to assimilate facts than to have a grand story told to them.[1] Introverts prefer to learn on their own, whereas extroverts thrive in collaborative workshops. Understanding your particular personality type will reveal specific ways to make your learning routine maximally effective.

You may find it useful to try absorbing information from many different information sources. In the modern connected world we're presented with many media forms:

- The written (e.g., books, magazines, blogs)
- The spoken (e.g., audio books, presentations, user groups, podcasts, courses)

---

1. It's interesting to note that, although the left/right brain characterisation is prevalent in pop-psychology writing, no scientific studies have proved that such a distinction actually exists.

- The visual (e.g., video podcasts, TV shows, performances)

Some people respond better to particular media. What works best for you? For the best results, mix several of these sources. Use podcasts on a topic to reinforce what you're reading in a book. Attend a training course and read a book on the topic, too.

> KEY ▶ Use as many sources as possible to improve the quality of your learning.

Cross-sensory feedback attempts to stimulate parts of the brain that you don't normally exercise whilst learning, to increase the brain's effectiveness. Consider trying some of these actions whilst learning—some may work well for you:

- Listen to music whilst you work
- Doodle whilst you think (yes I am paying attention in your meeting, look at how many doodles I've made…)
- Fiddle with something (a pen or a paper clip, perhaps)
- Talk whilst you work (vocalising what you're doing or learning, it really does help you retain more knowledge)
- Make thought processes concrete rather than purely intellectual—like modelling things with building blocks or CRC cards
- Employ meditative practices (may help you attain greater focus and cut out distractions)

A surprisingly simple way to improve your information recall is to grab a notepad and capture information as you uncover it, rather than let it wash past you.

This serves two purposes. Firstly, it keeps you focussed and helps you to maintain concentration on the topic. It's a basic idea, but remarkably helpful. Secondly, even if you throw those notes away immediately afterwards, the cross-sensory stimulation will aid your recall of facts.

> KEY ▶ Takes notes as you learn. Even if you throw them away.

Your mental state affects the quality of your learning. Studies have shown that cultivating a positive attitude towards learning significantly enhances your recall. So find things to learn that engage you. Stress and lack of sleep will contribute to an inability to concentrate, degrading your ability to learn.

The Four Stages of Competence

You can learn falsehood and believe that it's right. This can be at best embarrassing, and at worst dangerous. This is illustrated by the *Four Stages of Competence* (a classification posited in the by 1940s by psychologist Abraham Maslow). You may have:

Conscious incompetence
> You don't know something. But you know that you're ignorant. This is a relatively safe position to be in. You probably don't care—it's not something you need to know. Or you know that you're ignorant and it is a source of frustration.

Conscious competence
> This is also a good state to be in. You know something. And you know that you know it. To use this skill you have to make a conscious effort, and concentrate.

Unconscious competence
> This is when your knowledge of a topic is so great that it has become second nature. You are no longer aware that you are using your expertise. Most adults, for example, can consider walking and balance as an unconscious competence—we just do it without a second thought.

Unconscious incompetence
> This is a dangerous place to be. You don't know that you don't know something. You are ignorant of your ignorance. Indeed, it is very possible that you think you understand the subject but don't appreciate how very wrong you are. It is a *blind spot* in your knowledge.

Learning Models

There are a number of very illuminating models of learning that have been constructed by educational psychologists. The *Dreyfus model of skill acquisition* is a particularly interesting example, postulated by brothers Stuart and Hubert Dreyfus in 1980 whilst they were working on artificial computer intelligence.[2] After examining highly skilled practitioners such as airline pilots and chess grand-masters, they identified five specific levels of understanding:

Novice
> A complete newbie. Novices want to get results fast, but have no experience to guide them in doing so. They look for rules they can follow by rote, and have no judgment

---

2. Stuart E. Dreyfus and Hubert L. Dreyfus, *A Five-Stage Model of the Mental Activities Involved in Directed Skill Acquisition* (Washington, DC: Storming Media).

to tell whether those rules are good or bad. Given good rules (or luck finding suitable resources on Google), novices can get quite far. Novices have *no* knowledge of a topic (yet).

Advanced beginner

At this level, some experience has led to learning; you can break free from rules a little and try tasks on your own. But perception is still limited, and you'll get stuck when things go wrong. At this level there is a better understanding of where to get answers (you know the best API references, for example) but you are still not at a level where you can comprehend the bigger picture. The beginner can't focus out irrelevant details; as far as they're concerned everything and anything could be important to the problem at hand. Beginners rapidly gain *explicit knowledge*—the kind of factual knowledge that can be easily written down and articulated.

Competent

This stage sees you with a mental model of the problem domain; you've mapped the knowledge base, have begun to associate its parts, and understand the relative importance of different aspects. This big picture view allows you to approach unknown problems and plan methodical routes into those problems, rather than diving in and hoping rules will get you to a solution. At this point, you actively seek out new rules to formulate a plan of attack, and begin to see the limitation of those rules.

This is a good place to be.

Proficient

Proficient people move beyond competency. They have a much better understanding of the big picture, and are frustrated with the simplifications that the novice needed. They can correct previous errors and reflect on their experiences to work better in the future. At this point you can also learn from other's experiences and assimilate them into your body of understanding. Proficient people can interpret *maxims* (as opposed to simplistic rules) and apply them to a problem (e.g., they know how and when to apply design patterns). Now it is easy to identify and focus only on the issues that really matter, confidently ignoring irrelevant details. Here we see the person has gained significant *tacit knowledge*—knowledge that's hard to transfer by exposition, that is only gained by experience and deep understanding.

Expert

This is the pinnacle of the learning tree. There are very few experts. They are authorities on a subject; they know it completely, and can use this skill interlinked with other skills. They can teach others (although they probably teach competents better than novices as there is less of a disconnect). Experts have *intuition*, so rather than needing rules, they naturally see an answer, even if they can't articulate why it's the best solution.

Why is the Dreyfus model interesting? It's a revealing framework to understand where you currently stand in the mastery of a topic, and helps determine where you need to get to. Do you need to be an *expert*? Most people are *competent* and this is satisfactory (indeed, a team of experts would be far too top-heavy, and probably dysfunctional).

It also illustrates how you should expect to be solving problems at each stage of your learning. Are you looking for simple rules to apply, hungrily gathering maxims to draw experience from, or intuitively sensing answers? How much of a "big picture" view do you have of the topic?

The Dreyfus model is also a very useful aid for teamwork. If you know where a colleague sits on the novice-expert spectrum, you can better tailor your interaction with them. It will help you learn how to work with other people—whether you should give them some simple rules, explain some maxims, or leave them to weave new information into their broader understanding.

Note that the Dreyfus model applies *per skill*. You may be an expert in a particular topic, and a complete notice in another. This is natural. And should also be a source of humility —even if you know all there is to know about behaviour-driven design, you may know nothing about the Joe Bloggs test framework. It should excite you that there is something more to learn that may enhance your expertise in BDD, whilst keeping you humble that you aren't an infallible expert in every subject! No one likes a know-it-all.

The Knowledge Portfolio

The Pragmatic Programmers describe a vivid and potent metaphor for learning—they talk about your *knowledge portfolio*.[3] Consider your current working set of knowledge like a portfolio of investments. This metaphor beautifully highlights how we should *manage* the information we have gathered, prudently investing to keep our portfolio current, and bringing in new investments to strengthen it. Consider which items you should retire from your portfolio to make room for other things.

Be aware of the risk/reward balance of the items in your portfolio. Some things are common knowledge, but a safe investment to hold—they are low risk, easy to learn about, and guaranteed to be useful in the future. Other investments are riskier—they may not be mainstream technologies and practices, so studying them may *not* pay off in the future. But if they do become mainstream, then you will be one of a smaller set of people experienced in that niche, and so able to exploit that knowledge more. These higher risk knowledge investments may pay much greater dividends in the future. You need a good spread of risk and a healthy range of knowledge investments.

> KEY ➤ Purposefully manage your knowledge portfolio.

3. Hunt and Thomas, *The Pragmatic Programmer*.

Teach to Learn

To teach is to learn twice.

— Joseph Joubert

One of the most effective ways to learn anything is to *teach* it; explaining a topic to someone else solidifies the knowledge in your head. When you have to explain something, you are encouraged to go deeper so you truly understand the topic. Teaching forces you to review the material, reinforcing it in your memory.

Write a blog post on what you learn, give a talk, teach a friend, or start to mentor a colleague. Each of these will benefit you just as much as they benefit the other person.

Einstein said: *If you can't explain it simply, you don't understand it well enough.* When reading a book, or listening to a teacher, it's easy to fool yourself that you "know" a topic. You've heard about it, but nothing has yet tested where the limits of your knowledge lie. Teaching pushes on this boundary: you'll have to answer tricky questions that stretch your knowledge. If you're asked a question that you can't answer, the right response is: *I don't know, but I'll find out for you.* You've both learnt.

> KEY ▶ Teach a topic to learn that topic well.

Act to Learn

I hear and I forget. I see and I remember. I do and I understand.

— Confucius

An essential learning technique is to learn by *doing*. Reading books and articles, watching online tutorials, and attending programming conferences are all very well. But until you actually try to use that skill, it's just an abstract collection of concepts in your head.

Make the abstract concrete—dive in. Try it.

Ideally, do this *whilst* you're studying. Kick off a test project and try to use the knowledge as you amass it. When learning a new language, start writing code in it immediately. Take the code examples you read and try them out. Play around with the code; make mistakes, see what works and what doesn't.

> KEY ▶ Using what you just learned cements it in your memory. Try examples, answer questions, create pet projects.

Using information is a sure way to gain understanding about it. It will generate more questions that will guide you in your learning.

What Have We Learnt?

Tell me, and I will forget. Show me, and I may remember. Involve me, and I will understand.

— Confucius

You have to take responsibility for your own learning. It's not up to your employer, your state education system, an assigned mentor, or any other person.

You are in charge of your own learning. It's important to continually improve your skills to improve as a developer. And to do that you have to *learn* to learn. To make it rewarding you have to learn to *love* doing it.

Learn to live to love to learn.

Questions

1. When were you last in a situation that required learning? How did you approach it?

2. How successful were you?

3. How quickly did you learn?

4. How could you have performed better?

5. Did you learn, then work, or learn as you worked? Which do you think is most effective?

6. When was the last time you taught someone? How did it affect your understanding of that topic?

7. How can you find the time to learn new things when you are under pressure to produce work?

See also

- *A Love for Languages* One of the things a programmer frequently learns: a new language.

- *Many-festos* Learn about the latest thoughts, trends, fashions, fads, and movements in the software development world.

- *Test-Driven Developers* Considers how to *prove* that you know a programming skill well. Is examination and certification valuable?

- *Navigating a Route* Sharp learning skills help you learn new codebases more effectively.

CHAPTER 25

Test-Driven Developers

Logic will get you from A to B. Imagination will take you everywhere.

— Albert Einstein

After years trapped in the software factory and many long hours of bitter experience, software development becomes second nature. Once you are familiar with the syntax of your programming language, understand the concepts of program design, and have learnt to appreciate the difference between good and bad code, you find yourself naturally making reasonable coding decisions without discernible effort. Daily coding activities and "design in the small" become instinctive. Correct syntax flows from your fingers' muscle memory.

A mindless "shoot from the hip" approach is symptomatic of the cowboy coder, but experienced programmers can work incredibly effectively without much deep thought. This is the benefit that experience brings you.

Have you reached this stage?

According to the Four Stages of Competence model, described in *Live to Love to Learn*, this idealic state is *unconscious competence*. It is an act we are able to do without needing to consciously think, a task we can perform effectively without even realising exactly what we're doing and how difficult it is.

There are many activities in which we achieve a state of unconscious competence. Some are professional. Some are far more mundane: most humans can walk and eat without careful concentration. A common task in which people see their skills progress through the four stages of competency is driving a car.

Driving is an interesting analogue of programming. Learning to drive has many parallels with learning our craft, and there are lessons we can learn from a comparison of the two.

Driving the Point Home

It takes a significant amount of learning to become a competent driver. It requires effort to learn the mechanics of the car, as well as the etiquette and rules of the road. Driving well requires a concert of actions and skills; it's an intricate process. You must invest a lot of effort and practice to achieve competence.

When new drivers first pass their driving test they are at the *conscious competence* stage of learning. They know that they can drive, and they have to pay attention to carefully coordinate all the contending forces. The selection of a new gear is a conscious process (for those enlightened drivers with manual transmission). Mastery of the clutch requires thoughtful balance.

But with experience, a lot of these actions become automatic reactions. We gain confidence. The controls and handling of the vehicle become second nature. We become accustomed to how the vehicle responds to our control. We naturally adopt the correct road positioning. We become masters of the operation of the vehicle.

Once a driver reaches this stage, their attention is freed to concentrate on the remaining unknown: the road itself, and the decisions that it constantly presents.

Similarly, once software developers gain a mastery of their tools and languages, they are freed to see the bigger shape of the problem to be solved. They are able to plan a route without having to concentrate on the minutiae of how they will manage it.

Some drivers are better than others. Some are more conscientious. Some have more natural ability.

Similarly, some developers are "naturals." Others have to invest serious effort to work effectively. Some developers are more thoughtful and careful than others. Others lack diligence and an appreciation of what's going on around them.

The majority of problems on the road—the accidents, delays, and so on—are due to *driver error*. Crashes happen to cars but they are caused by the people who learnt to use them.

The majority of coding disasters are due to *programmer error*. Crashes happen to programs, but they are caused by the people who learnt to write them.

Success Breeds Complacency

> *Success breeds complacency. Complacency breeds failure. Only the paranoid survive.*
>
> — Andy Grove

The state of conscious competence can, if you're not careful, lead to complacency. Complacent drivers do not concentrate on the road, but end up "coasting": driving without due care and attention. Rather than look for hazards on the road ahead, you're thinking about what to eat for dinner, or singing along with the radio.

To become a better driver, it is important to overcome this complacency. Otherwise you are a liability: a very real danger. You could easily collide with something or run someone over.

Programming presents parallel pitfalls. Unless you take care, you'll craft a code catastrophe. Remember: careless code costs lives!

> KEY ➤ Beware of becoming complacent when you reach a state of "competence." Always code with your brain fully engaged to avoid silly, potentially dangerous, errors.

Testing Times

Before you are let loose in a vehicle, you have to prove that you are capable. You have to pass a *driving test*. It's illegal to drive on public roads without having first passed this test. The driving test proves that you have the necessary skills, and the responsibility, to drive. It demonstrates that you can not only handle a car, but can make good decisions under the pressured conditions of the road.

The existence of a test ensures that all drivers on the road have reached a certain standard, and have completed a certain amount of training. This training means that:

- Learner drivers must amass hours of *real-world* driving experience before they are ready to attempt the test. They don't just study the theory of driving, and understand the mechanics of a car, but gain practical hands-on experience on the road. Whilst learning, they are effectively "driving apprentices" studying under a master.
- There is a reduced risk of accidents on the road; drivers are taught the dangers and pitfalls inherent in driving and how to avoid them.
- Trained, experienced drivers have more confidence in their abilities and can make mature decisions.
- Drivers understand how the road is shared between all types of users, and are considerate to other road users.
- Drivers are aware of the limitations of their equipment. They know how to react in emergency situations when things go wrong.

The driving test ensures that a complex human activity does not end in disaster. It doesn't just *encourage* people to be good drivers based on good intentions, but *mandates* it.

Some countries go further, with an additional "advanced" driving test—a higher standard of driving capability. This test is a requirement for certain jobs.

Test-Driven Developers

Now, there isn't a direct equivalent of a driving test in the programming world; certification is not a legal prerequisite to write code (nor should it be, in the author's opinion). But to enter gainful employment you *do* usually have to demonstrate a reasonable level of skill: having passed a reputable training course, or showing tangible prior experience.

So here is the obvious thought experiment: what would the equivalent of a driving test for software developers look like? How can you realistically demonstrate competence? Does it even make sense to try to?

I'm sure there are coders whom you respect and *recognise* as advanced. But is it possible, or practical, or useful, to certify them as such?

We debate the true value of certification in our industry. Certainly, much of the certification pedalled by training organisations is pure bunk, snake oil that helps you tick boxes on a job application form but that means very little. Are you a *certified scrum master*? How marvellous. I hope it didn't cost too much to buy that certificate.

Would a physical coding test be of any use? What would it look like? How tailored would it have to be to specific technology areas? Would the many specialisations make it impractical to create? How would you measure engineers who don't predominantly work in code?

As we've seen, the majority of programmer skills are gained by experience garnered on the job. So recognising progression through the *apprentice-journeyman-craftsman* model may suit us better. Not every long-serving coder continues to learn and hone his skills; not everyone becomes a master craftsman. Time on the job is not enough.

Indeed, advancing coding skills can be orthogonal to the typical developer promotion path. If you serve faithfully in a job for *n* years, then your company might give you a pay raise and allow you to climb another step up the corporate ladder. But that doesn't necessarily mean that you're any better a programmer than when you started.

It is not at all clear that the benefits of the driving test can be brought to our profession in a meaningful way.

Conclusion

> *Think for yourself and let others enjoy the privilege of doing so too.*
>
> — Voltaire

This is a little thought experiment, a rhetorical question. Nothing more. But it's interesting to think about this kind of thing, to provide a framework that will help us become better programmers.

It's certainly valuable to consider the stages of coding ability we progress through. Determine when you have moved from conscious competence to unconscious competence. And beware of mindlessness and complacency.

Questions

1. What do you think? What is the programmer's equivalent of a driving test? Could there be such a thing?

2. Are your programming skills at the standard test level or at the advanced level? Do you think you frequently achieve *unconscious competence*?

3. Do you want to maintain your current skill level? Do you want to improve it? How will do you this?

4. How could you test a programmer's ability to perform an "emergency stop"?!

5. Is there any extra value to be gained from investing in your skills? If good drivers enjoy lower insurance premiums, how does being a "safer coder" materially benefit you?

6. If coding is like driving, do we treat code testers like crash test dummies?

See also

- *Live to Love to Learn* Describes models of learning and the *Four Stages of Competence* model in detail.

- *Relish the Challenge* Whether or not our knowledge is formally tested, we should strive to continually improve our skills.

Try this....

Consider how to change your habits to become a more mindful and less complacent programmer. Ensure you do not slip from *unconscious competence* into *cowboy coding*.

CHAPTER 26

Relish the Challenge

Success is not final, failure is not fatal: it is the courage to continue that counts.

— Winston Churchill

We are "knowledge workers." We employ our skill and knowledge of technology to make good things happen. Or to fix it when they don't. This is our joy. It's what we live for. We revel in the chance to build things, to solve problems, to work on new technologies, and to assemble pieces that complete interesting puzzles.

We're wired that way. We relish the challenge.

The engaged, active programmer is constantly looking for a new, exciting challenge.

Take a look at yourself now. Do you actively seek out new challenges in your programming life? Do you hunt for the novel problems, or for the things that you're really interested in? Or are you just coasting from one assignment to the next without much of a thought for what would motivate you?

Can you do anything about it?

It's the Motivation

Working on something stimulating, something challenging, on something that you enjoy getting into helps keep you motivated.

If, instead, you get stuck in the coding "sausage factory"—just churning out the same tired code on demand—you will stop paying attention. You will stop learning. You will stop caring and investing in crafting the best code you can. The quality of your work will suffer. And your passion will wane.

You will stop becoming better.

Conversely, actively working on coding problems that *challenge* you will encourage you, excite you, and help you to learn and develop. It will stop you from becoming staid and stale.

Nobody likes a stale programmer. Least of all, yourself.

What's the Challenge?

So what is it that particularly interests you?

It might be that new language you've been reading about. Or it might be working on a different platform. It might just be trying out a new algorithm or library. Or to kick off that pet project you thought about a while ago. It might even be attempting an optimisation or refactor of your current system; just because it looks elegant, even if—shudder to think—it doesn't actually provide business value.

Often this kind of personal challenge can only be gained on a side project; something you work on alongside the more mundane day-to-day tasks. And that's *perfect*—it's the antidote to dull "professional" development. A programming panacea. The crap code cure.

What excites you about programming? Think about what you'd like to work on right now, and why:

- Are you happy to be paid for producing any old code, or do you want to be paid because you produce particularly exceptional work?
- Are you performing tasks for the kudos; do you seek the recognition of your peers or the plaudits of managers?
- Do you want to work on an open source project; would sharing your code give you a sense of satisfaction?
- Do you want to be the first person to provide a solution in a new niche, or to a tricky new problem?
- Do you solve problems for the joy of the intellectual exercise?
- Do you like working on a particular kind of project, or do certain technologies suit your strange peccadilloes?
- Do you want to work alongside and learn from certain types of developers?
- Do you look at projects with an entrepreneurial eye—seeking something you think will one day make you millions?

As I look back over my career, I can see that I've tried to work on things in many of those camps. But I've had the most fun, and produced the best software, when working on projects that I've been invested in; where I've *cared* about the project itself, as well as wanting to write exceptional code.

Don't Do It!

Of course, there are potential downsides to seeking out cool coding problems for "the fun of it." There are perfectly valid reasons not to:

- It's selfish to steer yourself towards exciting things all the time, leaving boring stuff for other programmers to pick up.

- It's dangerous to "tinker" a working system just for the sake of the tweak, if it's not introducing real business value. You're adding unnecessary change and risk. In a commercial environment, it's a waste of time that could be invested elsewhere more profitably.

- If you get sidetracked on pet projects or little "science experiments," then you'll never get any "real" work done.

- Remember: not every programming task *is* going to be glamorous or exciting. A lot of our day-to-day tasks are mundane plumbing. That's just the nature of programming in the real world.

- Life is too short. I don't want to waste my spare time working on code as well!

- Rewriting something that already exists is a gross waste of effort. You are not contributing to our profession's corpus of knowledge. You are likely to just re-create something that already exists, possibly not as good as the existing implementations, and full of new terrible bugs. What a waste of time!

Yada. Yada. Yada.

These positions do have some merit. But they should not become excuses that prevent us from becoming better programmers.

It is exactly *because* we have to perform dull tasks all day that we should also seek to balance them with the exciting challenges. We must be responsible in how we use our time do this, and whether we use the resulting code or throw it away.

Get Challenged

So work out what you'd like to do. And then do it:

- Perform some code katas—short practice exercises—that will provide valuable deliberate practice. Throw the code away afterwards.

- Find a coding problem you'd like to solve, just for the fun of it.

- Kick off a personal project. Don't waste all your spare time on it, but find something you can invest effort in that will teach you something new.

- Maintain a broad field of personal interest, so you have good ideas of other things to investigate and learn from.

- Don't ignore other platforms and paradigms. Try rewriting something you know and love on another platform or in another kind of programming language. Compare and contrast the outcome. Which environment lent itself better to that kind of problem?

- Consider looking for a new job if you're not being stretched and challenged where you're currently working. Don't blindly accept the status quo! Sometimes the boat needs to be rocked.

- Work with, or meet up with other motivated programmers. Try going to programming conferences, or join local user groups. Attendees come back with a head full of new ideas, and invigorated from the enthusiasm of their peers.

- Make sure you can see the progress you're making. Review source control logs to see what you've achieved. Keep a daily log, or a to-do list. Enjoy knocking off items as you make headway.

- Keep it fresh: take breaks so you don't get overwhelmed, stifled, or bored by bits of code.

- Don't be afraid of reinventing the wheel! Write something that has already been done before. There is no harm in trying to write your own linked-list, or standard GUI component. It's a really good exercise to see how yours compares to existing ones. (Just be careful how you employ them in practice.)

Conclusion

It's impractical and dangerous to just chase shiny new things all the time and not write practical, useful code. But it's also personally dangerous to get stuck in a coding rut, only ever working on meaningless, tedious software, without being challenged and having fun.

Do you have something you're engaged in and love to work on?

Questions

1. Do you have projects that challenge you and stretch your skills?

2. Are there some project ideas you've thought about for a while, but not started? Why not start a little side project?

3. Do you balance "interesting" challenges with your day-to-day work?

4. Are you challenged by other motivated programmers around you?

5. Do you have a broad field of interest that informs your work?

See also

- *Live to Love to Learn* When you are enthused to learn a new skill, you need to employ effective learning techniques.

- *Avoid Stagnation* Maintain motivation and seek new challenges to prevent your skills and your career from stagnating.

> **Try this....**
>
> Consider what you'd really *like* to be working on right now. Is it your current job? Lucky you! Otherwise, how can you work on this now? Should you start a "pet project" or change jobs?

CHAPTER 27

Avoid Stagnation

Iron rusts from disuse; water loses its purity from stagnation...
even so does inaction sap the vigor of the mind.

— Leonardo da Vinci

When was the last time you learnt something new and exciting enough to put on your résumé? When was the last time you were stretched beyond your capabilities? When was the last time your work made you feel uncomfortable? When was the last time you discovered something that delighted you? When were you last humbled by another programmer and encouraged to learn from them?

If the answers to these questions are the dim and distant past,[1] then you have entered the *comfort zone*: a place that some regard as nirvana—where your life is easy and your work days are short and predictable.

However, the comfort zone is a pernicious place. It's a trap. An easy life means you're not learning, not progressing, not *getting better*. The comfort zone is where you stagnate. Pretty soon you'll be overtaken by younger developer upstarts. The comfort zone is an express route to obsolescence.

> KEY ▶ Be wary of stagnation. Seeking to become a better programmer, by definition, is not the most comfortable lifestyle.

Few people make a conscious decision to stagnate. But it can be easy to slip into the comfort zone and coast along your development career without realising. Take a reality check: is this what you're doing right now?

---

1. The "distant past" is not so long ago when you measure in *programmer years*, which is why people find it so hard to estimate the duration of software projects!

Your Skills Are Your Investment

Beware: maintaining your skill set is hard work. It involves putting yourself in uncomfortable situations. It requires a very real investment of effort. It can be risky and hard. You might even embarass yourself. That doesn't sound entirely pleasant, does it?

It's therefore not something that many people feel naturally inclined to do. You spend so many hours of the day working, don't you deserve to have an easy life and then go home to forget all about it? It's natural to learn towards the familiar and the comfortable.

Don't do it!

You have to make a conscious decision to invest in your skills. And you have to make that decision repeatedly. Don't see it as an arduous task. Delight in the challenge. Appreciate that you are making an investment that will make you a better programmer, and a better person.

> KEY ➤ Expect to invest time and effort to grow your skill set. This is a worthwhile investment; it will repay itself.

An Exercise for the Reader

How can you shake yourself up right now? Here are some changes to make that will push you out of the comfort zone:

- Stop using the same tools; there might be better ones that will make your life easier if you'd only learn about them.

- Stop using the same programming language for every problem; you might be smashing a walnut with a sledgehammer.

- Start using a different OS. Learn how to use it properly. Even if it's one that you don't like, spend a while trying it out to really learn its strengths and weaknesses.

- Start using a different text editor.

- Learn keyboard shortcuts and see how it impacts your workflow. Make a conscious effort to stop using a mouse.

- Learn about a new topic, something that you don't currently *need* to know. Perhaps deepen your knowledge of maths or of sorting algorithms.

- Start a personal pet project. Yes, use some of your precious spare time to be geeky. Publish it as open source.

- Maneuver yourself to work on a new part of your project, one you know little about. You might not be productive immediately, but you'll gain a wider knowledge of the code and will learn new things.

Consider expanding yourself beyond the programming realm:

- Lean a new language. But *not* a programming language. Listen to audiobook teaching series on Japanese on your drive into work.
- Rearrange your desk! Try to look at the way you work in a new light.
- Start a new activity. Perhaps start a blog to journal your learning. Spend more time on a hobby.
- Take up exercise: join a gym or start running.
- Socialise more. Spend time with geeks *and* with non-geeks.
- Consider adjusting your diet. Or going to bed earlier.

Job Security

Being a better developer, one with a more rounded skillset, one who is constantly learning, will increase your job security. But ask yourself if you really need that: *are* you in the right job?

Hopefully you are in the right career: you enjoy programming. (If you don't, consider seriously if a career change might be a good option. What would you *really* like to do?)

There is a danger in staying in one job or one role too long, of doing the same thing over and over with no new challenges. All too easily, we get entrenched in what we're doing. We like being local experts; the king of our little coding castle. It's comfortable.

Perhaps it's now time to move on to a new employer? To face new challenges and move on in your coding journey. To escape the comfort zone.

Staying put is usually easier, more familiar, and more convenient. In the recent rocky economic climate, it's also the safer bet. But it might not be the best thing for you. A good programmer is courageous, both in their approach to the code and their approach to their career.

Questions

1. Are you currently stagnating? How can you tell?
2. What was the last new thing you learnt?
3. When did you last learn a new language? When did you last learn a new technique?
4. What new skill should you learn next? How will you learn it? What books, courses, or online material will you use?
5. Are you in the right job at the moment? Do you enjoy it, or has all the joy been sucked out? Are you working the 9-to-5, or are you enthused and engaged to see your project succeed? Should you look around for new challenges?

6. When did you last get a promotion? Or a pay raise? Does a job title have any real meaning? Does your job title bear any relation to your skills?

See also

- *Relish the Challenge* Avoid stagnation by seeking new challenges.

Try this....

Commit now to avoiding stagnation. Make an honest assessment of how "stuck in the mud" you currently are. Construct a practical plan to better yourself.

CHAPTER 28

The Ethical Programmer

I might fairly reply to him, "You are mistaken, my friend, if you think that
a man who is worth anything ought to spend his time weighing up the prospects
of life and death. He has only one thing to consider in performing any action—
that is, whether he is acting rightly or wrongly, like a good man or a bad one."

— Socrates
The Apology

I often describe how the quality of a coder depends more on their *attitude* than their technical prowess. A recent conversation on this subject led me to consider the topic of *the ethical programmer*.

What does this mean? What does it look like? Do ethics even have an appreciable part to play in the programmer's life?

It's impossible to divorce the act of programming from any other part of the coder's human existence. So, naturally, ethical concerns govern what we, as programmers, do and how we relate to people professionally.

It stands to reason, then, that being an "ethical programmer" is a worthwhile thing; at least as worthwhile as being an ethical *person*. You'd certainly worry about anyone who aspired to be an *unethical programmer*.

Many professions have specific ethical codes of conduct. The medical profession has the Hippocratic oath, binding doctors to work for the benefit of their patients, and to not commit harm. Lawyers and engineers have their own professional bodies conferring chartered status, which require members to abide by certain rules of conduct. These ethical codes exist to protect their clients, to safeguard the practitioners, as well as to ensure the good name of the profession.

In software "engineering" we have no such universal rules. There are few industry standards that we can be usefully accredited against. Various organisations publish their own crafted code of ethics, for example the ACM (*http://www.acm.org/about/code-of-*

ethics) and the BSI (*http://www.bcs.org/server.php?show=nav.6030*). However, these have little legal standing, nor are they universally recognised.

The ethics of our work are largely guided by our own moral compass. There are certainly many great coders out there who work for the love of their craft and the advancement of the profession. There are also some shadier types who are playing the game predominantly for their own selfish gain. I've met both.

The subject of computer ethics was first coined by Walter Maner in the mid-1970s. Like other topics of ethical study, this is considered a branch of philosophy.

Working as an "ethical" programmer has considerations in a number of areas: notably in our attitudes towards code, and towards people. There are also a bunch of legal issues that need to be understood. We'll look at these in the following sections.

Attitude to Code

Do not write code that is deliberately hard to read, or designed in such a complex way that no one else can follow it.

We joke about this being a "job security" scheme: writing code that only you can read will ensure you will never get fired! Ethical programmers know that their job security lies in their talent, integrity, and value to a company, not in their ability to engineer the company to depend on them.

> KEY ➤ Do not make yourself "indispensable" by writing unreadable or unnecessary "clever" code.

Do not "fix" bugs by putting sticking-plaster workarounds or quick bodges in place, hiding one issue but leaving the door open for other variants of the problem to manifest. The ethical programmer finds the bug, understands it, and applies a proper, solid, tested fix. It's the "professional" thing to do.

So, what happens if you're within a gnat's whisker of an unmovable deadline and you simply *have* to ship code, when you discover an awful, embarrassing, showstopping bug? Is it ethical to apply a temporary quick-fix in order to rescue the imminent release? Perhaps. In this case, it may be a perfectly pragmatic solution. But the ethical programmer does not let it rest here: he adds a new task to the work pool to track the "technical debt" incurred, and attempts to pay it off shortly after the software ships. These kinds of Band-Aid solutions should not be left to fester any longer than necessary.

The ethical programmer aims to write the best code possible. At any point in time, work to the best of your ability. Employ the most appropriate tools and techniques that will lead to the best results—for example, use automated tests that ensure quality, pair programming, and/or code review to catch mistakes and sharpen designs.

Legal Issues

An ethical, professional programmer understands pertinent legal issues and makes sure to abide by the rules. Consider, for example, the thorny field of software licensing.

Do not use copyrighted code, like GPL (*http://www.gnu.org/licenses/gpl.html*) source, in proprietary code when the license does not permit this.

> **KEY** ➤ Honour software licenses.

When changing jobs, do not take source code or technology from an old company and transplant parts of it into a new company. Or even show parts of it in an interview with another company.

This is an interesting topic, as it leads to a large gray area: copying private intellectual property or code that has a clear copyright notice is clearly stealing. However, we hire programmers based on their prior experience—the things they have done in the past. Is rewriting the same kind of code from memory, without duplicating exact source lines, ethical? Is re-implementing another version of a proprietary algorithm that conferred competitive advantage unethical if you've hired the designer of that algorithm specifically for their experience?

Often code is published online with a very liberal license, merely asking for attribution. The ethical programmer takes care to make sure attribution is given appropriately for such code.

> **KEY** ➤ Ensure appropriate credit is given for work you reuse in your codebase.

If you know that there are legal issues surrounding some technology you're using (e.g., encryption or decryption algorithms that are encumbered by trade restrictions), you have to make sure your work does not violate these laws.

Do not steal software, or use pirated development tools. If you are given a copy of an IDE make sure that there is a valid license for you to use it. Just as you would not pirate a movie, or share copyrighted music online, you should not use illegally copied technical books.

Do not hack or crack your way into computers or information stores for which you do not have access authority. If you realise it's possible to access such a system, let the administrators know so they can remedy the permissions.

Attitude to People

Treat others as you would want them to treat you.

— Matthew 7:12

We've already considered some "ethical attitudes" towards people, as we write code primarily for the audience of other programmers, not for the compiler. Programming problems are almost always people problems, even if the solutions have a technical nature.

> KEY ▶ Good attitudes towards code are *also* good attitudes to other programmers.

Imagine yourself as a heroic coder. The kind of programmer who wears your underwear atop your trousers, and not simply as a geeky fashion faux pas. Now: *do not abuse your super powers for evil*. Only write software for the good of mankind.

In practice, this means: don't write viruses or malware. Don't write software that breaks the law. Don't write software to make people's life worse, either materially, physically, emotionally, or psychologically.

Don't turn to the dark side.

> KEY ▶ Do not write software that will make another person's life worse. This is an abuse of power.

And here we open a wonderful new can of worms: is it ethical to write software that makes some people very rich at the expense of poorer people, if it doesn't break any laws? Is it ethical to write software to distribute pornographic content, if the software itself breaks no laws? You can argue that people are exploited as a byproduct of both activities. Is it ethical to work in these industries? This is a question that I can only leave for the reader to answer.

What about working on military projects? Would an ethical programmer feel comfortable working on weapons systems that could be used to take a life? Perhaps such a system will actually *save* lives by acting as a deterrent against attack. This is a great example of how the ethics of software development is a philosophical topic, not an entirely black-and-white affair. You have to reconcile yourself with the consequences that your code has on other people's lives.

Teammates

The people you encounter most frequently in your programming career are your teammates—the programmers, testers, and so on, that you work with closely day by day. The ethical programmer works conscientiously with all of them, looking to honour each team member, and to work together to achieve the best result possible.

Speak well of all people. Do not engage in gossip or backbiting. Do not encourage jokes at the expense of others.

Always believe that anyone, no matter how mature or how experienced, has something valuable to contribute. They have an opinion that is worth hearing, and should be able to put forward points of view without being shot down.

Be honest and trustworthy. Deal with everyone with integrity.

Do not pretend to agree with someone when you believe they are wrong; this is dishonest and rarely useful. Constructive disagreements and reasoned discussions can lead to genuinely better code design decisions. Understand what level of "debate" a team member can handle. Some people thrive on intense, passionate intellectual debate; others are frightened by confrontation. The ethical programmer seeks to engage in the most productive discussion result without insulting or offending anyone. This isn't always possible, but the goal is to always treat people with respect.

Do not discriminate against anyone, on any grounds, including gender, race, physical ability, sexual orientation, mental capability, or skill.

The ethical programmer takes great care to deal with "difficult people" in the most fair, transparent way, attempts to diffuse difficult situations, and works to avoid unnecessary conflict.

> KEY ➤ Treat others as you would like them to treat you.

Manager

Many issues that may be seen as agreements between you and your manager can also be seen as ethical contracts between you and the other members of the team, as the manager acts as a bridge with the team.

Do not take credit for work that is not yours, even if you take someone else's idea and modify it to fit the context a bit. Give credit where it's due.

Do not give an unnecessarily high estimate for the complexity of a task, just so that you can slack off and do something more enjoyable on the pretence of working hard on a tricky problem.

If you see looming issues that will prevent the smooth running of the project, report them as soon as you notice. Do not hide bad news because you don't want to worry or offend someone, or be seen to be a pessimistic killjoy. The sooner issues are raised, planned around, and dealt with, the smoother the project will go for everyone.

If you spot a bug in the system, report it. Put a bug in the fault tracking system. Don't turn a blind eye and hope that no one else will notice it.

> KEY ➤ The ethical programmer takes responsibility for the quality of the product at all times.

Do not pretend to have skills or technical knowledge that you do not possess. Don't put a project schedule in danger by committing to a task you cannot complete, just because you think it's interesting and you'd like to work on it.

If you realise that a task you're working on is going to take significantly longer to complete that you expected, voice that concern as soon as possible. The ethical programmer does not keep it quiet in order to save face.

When given responsibility for something, honour the trust placed in you. Work to the best of your ability to fulfill that responsibility.

Employer

Treat your employer with respect.

Do not reveal company confidential information, including source code, algorithms, or inside information. Do not break the terms of your employment contact.

Don't sell work you have done for one company to another, unless you have express permission to do so.

However, if you realise that your employer is engaged in illegal activities, it is your ethical duty to raise it with them, or report their malfeasance as appropriate. The ethical programmer does not turn a blind eye to wrongdoing just to keep her own job secure.

Do not falsely represent, or bad-mouth your employer in public.

Yourself

As an ethical programmer, you should keep yourself up-to-date on good programming practice.

Ethical programmers do not work so hard that they burn themselves out. This is not only personally disadvantageous, but also bad news for the whole team. Hours and hours of extra work, week in, week out, will lead to a tired programmer, which will inevitably lead to sloppy mistakes, and a worse final outcome. The ethical programmer understands that although it's nice to look like a hero who works incredibly hard, it's not a good idea to set unrealistic expectations and to burn yourself out.

> KEY ➤ A tired programmer is of no use to anyone. Do not overwork. Know your limits.

You have a right to expect the same ethical conduct from others you work with.

The Hippocodic Oath

What would the ideal programmers' *code of ethics* look like? The ACM and BSI ethics documents are formal, lengthy, and hard to recall.

We need something pithier; more of a mission statement for the ethical programmer.

I humbly suggest:

> *I swear to cause no harm to the code, or to the business; to seek personal advancement, and the advancement of my craft. I will perform my allotted tasks to the best of my ability, working harmoniously with my team. I will deal with others with integrity, working to make the project, and the team, maximally effective and valuable.*

Conclusion

Ethics is in origin the art of recommending to others the sacrifices required for cooperation with oneself.

— Bertrand Russell

How much you care about this kind of thing depends on your level of diligence, your professionalism, and your personal moral code. Are you in the programming game for fun, enjoyment, and the development of great code? Or are you in it for yourself, for career development (at the expense of others, if necessary), to make as much money as you can, and to hoist yourself above others on the professional ladder?

It's a choice. You can choose your attitude. It will shape the trajectory of your career.

I find my attitudes shaped by my desire to write good code and to participate in a community that cares about working well. I seek to work amongst excellent developers whom I can learn from. As a Christian, I have a moral framework that encourages me to prefer others over myself and to honour my employers. This shapes the way I act.

I conclude from what we've seen here that there are (at least) two levels to the ethical programming career: the mandate to "do no harm" is the base level, to not tread on people, or be involved in work that exploits others. Beyond this is a more involved ethical mantra: to only work on projects that provide sound social benefits, to specifically *make the world better* with your talents, and to share knowledge in order to advance the programming craft. I suspect that many people ascribe to the first camp of ethics. Fewer feel the urge, or are able to devote themselves to the cause of the second.

How do your beliefs and attitudes shape the way you work? Do you think you are an ethical programmer?

Questions

1. Do you consider yourself an "ethical" programmer? Is there a difference between being an ethical programmer and an ethical person?

2. Do you agree or disagree with any of the observations in this chapter? Why?

3. Is it ethical to write software that makes bankers fabulously wealthy if the money they make comes at the expense of other people, who are not able to exploit the same computing power? Does it make a difference whether the trading practice is legal or not?

4. If your company is using GPL code in its proprietary products, but is not fulfilling the obligations of the license terms (by withholding its own code), what should you do? Should you lobby for the license terms to be met by open sourcing the company's code? Or should you ask for that GPL code to be replaced with a closed source alternative? If the product has already shipped, should you be a "whistle-blower" and expose the license violation? What if your job security depended on keeping quiet?

5. What should you do if you identify another programmer acting "unethically"? How does this answer differ if that programmer is a coworker, a friend, someone whom you've been asked to give a reference for, or a coder you've met but do not work directly with?

6. How do software patents fit into the world of ethical programming?

7. Should your passion for software development have any bearing on how much you care about ethical issues? Does a passionate programmer act more ethically than a career coder?

See also

- *It's the Thought That Accounts* Being accountable to another programmer will motivate you to act virtuously.

- *People Power* Treat the people you work with with respect. Learn from them; encourage them to improve.

Try this....

Review the issues mentioned in this chapter. How can you ensure that you are acting ethically in each area? Which area makes you feel the least comfortable? Make a specific step to address this.

CHAPTER 29

A Love for Languages

Those who know nothing of foreign languages know nothing of their own.

— Johann Wolfgang von Goethe
Maxims and Reflections

No two problems are the same. No two challenges are identical. And so no two programs are exactly alike. Thankfully, this makes our job interesting.

Now, some tasks *are* suspiciously similar. For us, that's the easy money; reusing the skills we've already learnt. This is experience—what makes you valuable on the job market. But it's also what makes you a staid developer, a one-trick pony. A dog that knows no new tricks.

We must continually face new challenges, continually learn, continually solve new problems, and continually use new technologies.

That's how you become a better programmer.

> KEY ➤ Don't become a *one-trick pony*. Position yourself to face new challenges, learn, and grow as a developer.

Love All Languages

Part of this growth regime is to work in more than one language. Getting stuck in a single language rut will force your problem solving to be one-dimensional. Too many developers plough a career knowing only one thing and miss out on a world of opportunity.

Learn multiple languages so you are fluent in multiple kinds of solutions. Learn scripting languages, learn compiled languages. Learn simple languages with minimal tooling, learn languages with vast and comprehensive libraries. Most importantly, learn languages that follow different idioms and paradigms.

These days, the bread-and-butter work is still in *imperative languages* (usually procedural languages),[1] most often object-oriented: C#, Java, C++, Python, and their ilk. Smalltalk is an interesting OO language that has some different ideas worth learning; it has fed directly into Objective-C's design. There are non-OO procedural languages knocking about, although most have had OO warts bolted on these days: Basic or Pascal, for example. Most shell scripting languages are still pure procedural contraptions.

Functional languages provide a particularly rich seam to learn from. Even if you don't use one daily, understanding the concepts espoused by functional languages will inform procedural programmers and help them write more solid, expressive, and robust code. Lisp, Scheme, Scala, Clojure, Haskell, and Erlang are all very worth studying.

Logic languages, like Prolog, teach an entirely different way of thinking about and expressing a solution. *Formal specification languages* like Z, whilst rarely in active use, illustrate how much more rigorous we can be. This rigour moved toward a more practical application in the language Eiffel, which wraps the notion of strong contracts into an OO language.

Consider also learning some "dead" languages that are no longer commonly used, to understand the history of your craft. BCPL was the forerunner to the C-type curly brace family of languages. Simula's concepts fed into the design of C++. COBOL, a real veteran language, was historically used in business applications. Many such systems still run today. (COBOL programmers earned a fortune fixing Y2K bugs.)

Gain an understanding of assembly language: speaking (almost) directly to CPU. Most programmers rarely need to resort to opcodes and cryptic mnemonics, but understanding what your high-level languages are built atop helps you to write better software.

---

1. These are the languages where you give a serial list of instructions detailing *how* the code should work. In the opposite, *declarative languages*, you describe *what* should be done. The language works out how.

Whilst knowing many languages is laudable, it's hard to be super-proficient in every one. You will likely focus most of your talent on a couple, else you risk becoming a *jack of all trades, master of none.*

Love Your Language

Day to day, I use C++ more than any other language. So I'll use it as an example. Many people spurn C++ as overly complex and archaic. It's not. It's powerful, expressive, and performant. But it does allow you to blow your own leg off if you want to.

Having used C++ in anger for many years (sometimes, quite literally in anger) has been a great deal of fun, and a very enlightening experience. So much so, I now have a love/hate relationship with the language.

It's not perfect. C++ is a very sharp tool and, like all sharp tools, it has sharp edges. Often you can wield the language to produce incredible, expressive code in a way that no other language can. But sometimes you accidentally cut yourself on one of its sharp edges, and end up staring at pages of inexplicable template errors, mumbling expletives under your breath.

These mumbled expletives don't prove that C++ is a bad language (although some would claim that they do). Every language has its flaws. It's just a language that you have to learn to live with. A language that you have to understand well to work with properly. You must *grok* how it works under the covers, and what makes it tick. It's more demanding than some alternatives.

I was musing about this, and then it struck me....

We are very much involved in a real *relationship* with our language. It can even be akin to marriage; it's a rewarding relationship, but it requires work.

You have to be careful how you treat C++. It's a fickle beast: it gives you many wonderful and exciting techniques to play with, and in doing so it gives you plenty of rope to hang yourself with. With templates come unfathomable type-related error messages. With multiple inheritance comes greater potential for bad class design and the *deadly diamond*. With new and delete come memory leaks and dangling pointers.

Does this mean that C++ is *bad*? Should we ditch C++ now and all use Java or C# instead? Of course not! Some programmers argue for this, but it's a misguided and myopic viewpoint. You don't get anything in life for free; you must expect to invest something costly to achieve a fulfilling relationship. It's hard to live with someone (or something) day by day, to share your most intimate (programming) thoughts, and to not get upset with them occasionally. You can expect a certain amount of friction as you get close and become accustomed to one another. Any relationship leads you along a path of constant learning about each other, of working out how to accommodate each other's foibles, and how to bring out the best in each other.

Admittedly, C++ isn't going to put much effort into learning about you, but many clever people (the guys who designed and standardised the beast) already did.

Becoming proficient in any language requires commitment. Many programmers are averse to putting in the required effort, or get frustrated too easily when things go wrong. So they prostitute themselves with other languages which they think will be more fulfilling, or take up with a younger, more glamorous alternative. (It's always a big ego boost to be seen with a young trophy language on your arm. Is this the programmers' equivalent of a mid-life crisis?[2])

Cultivating Your Language Relationship

There are a few generally accepted hallmarks of a healthy marriage. They can shed some light on a healthy relationship with your language.

A good marriage requires love and respect, commitment, communication, patience, and shared values. Let's take a closer look.

Love and Respect

For a marriage to succeed, the partners must like each other, value each other, and want to spend time with each other. There must be a level of attraction. They must love each other.

Most code monkeys program because it's their passion. They love to write code. And they usually pick a language because they genuinely enjoy using it.

> KEY ➤ Love your language! Work in a language you enjoy.

Now, many people are forced to use a certain language at work because the existing codebase is written in it—in this sense, they enter an arranged marriage. At home they'd rather tinker with a cool bit of Ruby or Python. Remember, some arranged marriages work perfectly well. Some do not. They aren't common or popular in Western culture.

---

2. How many people ditch their first relationship in the hope of trading it for something that requires less maintenance, only to discover that the replacement model is *just* as fickle, equally as hard to live with, and not as fulfilling?

But sometimes you are forced into bed with a language you don't think you'll enjoy only to discover, with time and experience, that it is profoundly enjoyable.

How much does your appreciation of a language shape the quality of the code you write, or the way you'll improve your skills working with it? How much of this is born from acceptance, respect, and a growing familiarity? Understand that love and respect can grow over time.

Commitment

A good marriage requires *commitment*: a determination to stick with it through good and bad, rather than jump out when things get uncomfortable.

To become an expert programmer in any given language, or with any technology, you must have a commitment to learn about it, to spend time with it, and to work with it. You can't be selfish and expect *it* to pander to your every need, especially when it is specifically designed to suit many diverse situations and requirements.

Commitment may also mean that you have to sacrifice. You must give up some of your preferred ways of working in order to accommodate the other party. The language has particular idioms and ways of working that suit it best. You might not like them, or would prefer to work in other ways. But if they are the definition of "good" code, then they are the idioms you should adopt.

Does your commitment to writing good code in the current language supersede your desire to do things your own way? *Good code* or *an easy life*? It's all about commitment.

> KEY ▶ To write the best code in a language, you should commit to its styles and idioms rather than force your own upon it.

Communication

In a good marriage you constantly communicate. You share facts, feelings, hurts, and joys. You don't just talk superficially as you would with acquaintances you meet in the street, but at a real heart-to-heart level. It's deep. You share things with your partner that you would share with no one else. This kind of communication requires an immense level of trust, acceptance, and understanding.

This isn't necessarily easy; people communicate in very different ways. Communication can be very easily misconstrued or misinterpreted. It takes a huge effort to communicate successfully in a marriage. It's something that you have to pay attention to and make a constant effort with. Communication is very much a skill that you learn, not just something you *can* or *can't* do.

The act of programming is entirely about communication. The code we write is as much a communication of the intent of our program (both to ourselves and to other programmers who might pick it up) as it is a list of instructions for a computer to execute.

In this sense, we communicate both *to* the language—to tell it what to do, in a clear, concise, unambiguous, correct way—and also to *others* using the programming language as the medium.

Good communication is a vital (and often lacking) skill in high-quality software developers. It takes a huge amount of effort, and constant attention, to do this well. Remember: communication is as much about listening as it is about talking.

> KEY ➤ Good programmers are good communicators. They talk, write, code, listen, and read well.

Patience

Good marriages aren't created overnight. They are cultivated. They grow. Gradually.

In our fast food culture we have learnt to expect everything *now*: instant food, instant cash, instant downloads, instant gratification. But relationships never work like this.

It's the same with our programming relationship. You can learn of the existence of a language in an instant. You might even have an instant attraction: programming lust. But it can take a long time to master a language fully, to be able to honestly claim that you really know how to write "good" code in it. It can take a long time, and an awful lot of patience, until you fully appreciate the beauty of a language.

> KEY ➤ Don't expect to become a language master overnight, and don't get frustrated whilst you work at it.

Of course, the most enjoyable languages have a shallow initial learning curve, so you feel that you're making good progress as you start your relationship.

Shared Values

A strong glue that holds many relationships together is a common sense of morals, values, and beliefs. For example, research shows that couples with shared strong religious beliefs are far more likely to stay together than those without them; it acts as a solid foundation to build the relationship upon.

If you don't agree with a languages' basic values—the many facilities and idioms it provides—then you'll always have a skewed relationship with the language.

A Perfect Metaphor?

This is illuminating. But no metaphor is perfect. Is faithfulness to your language as important to healthy coding as it is to a healthy marriage? No. It is actually very useful to "play the field" and mess around with other languages on the side. Make C# your muse, and Python your bit on the side. It'll teach you about different programming skills and techniques, and help you to avoid getting stuck in a programming rut.

Or *is* that actually very like marriage? I'll leave that for you to decide.

Conclusion

This colourful marriage metaphor shows us that knowledge of a programming language isn't all there is to programming. Consider how you work with your tools, the kind of relationship you have with them.

Good programmers think about more than mere lines of code, or an isolated code design. They care about how they use and interact with their tools, and how to get the best out of them, as much as they care about simple fact-based knowledge of them.

Good programmers don't expect quick-fix answers to problems, but learn to live with and appreciate the strong and weak points of their tools. They commit to a life with them, and invest time and effort getting to know them. They appreciate and value them.

Questions

1. What are the rough edges with your current language? List its strong and weak points.

2. What other languages and tools do you work with? How much commitment have you shown to learning them intimately?

3. They say married couples grow more alike over time. Have you adjusted to be shaped by your language? Is that for better, or for worse?

4. Which languages most rapidly show signs of neglect if programmers fail to commit to them? (You come home via one too many indirected pointers, and find your object inside the dog. And try as you might, you can't see *what* you've done to offend the language.)

See also

- *Care About the Code* You care about languages because you love to learn and you care about code.

- *Live to Love to Learn* These techniques will help you to learn new languages.

- *Software Development Is…* More metaphors for software development. (In case you were running out of them.)

Try this....

Determine how to deepen your relationship with your language(s) of choice.

CHAPTER 30

Posturing Programmers

A good stance and posture reflect a proper state of mind.

— Morihei Ueshiba

As modern software development project pressures increase, the demand placed on programmers grows, moving us from the once traditional 15-hour working day closer to the continental 26-hour working day. In such a climate, it's becoming increasingly important to ensure that you have a comfortable and ergonomically sound working environment.

This is perhaps as vital an issue to the twenty-first-century programmer as good code design or any other software development practice. After all, you can't be an Agile developer with a bad back; no one wants to employ a *rigid* programmer. And you can't navigate a complex UML class diagram with failing eyesight.

In order to improve the quality of the life you spend in front of a computer, and to safeguard your physical well-being, we'll look in this chapter at how to optimise your working environment.

Pay close attention; if you don't get this stuff right, you could end up with large medical bills. You'll thank me one day.

Basic Computer Posture

First, let's look at the most basic case of day-to-day computer use: sitting in front of a monitor (or as old-school Human Resources departments like to call it: a "VDU"[1]). You probably do this for many, many hours a day, so it's vital to make sure that you sit correctly. Surprisingly, sitting down is a quite complicated task. It requires hard work

---

1. VDU: Vision Destruction Unit

and determination to master. Practice makes perfect. As you work through this section, remember to take regular breaks—go for a run or something equally relaxing.

The way you sit at a computer has implications for not just your productivity (bad posture can have a significant effect on your concentration and, therefore, your productivity) but also your health. Poor posture can lead to neck pain, back pain, headaches, digestive problems, breathing difficulties, eye strain…the list goes on. An example of good sitting posture is illustrated in Figure 30-1.

Figure 30-1. Good posture

These are the ergonomic experts' recommendations:

- Adjust your chair and monitor position so that your eyes are level with the top of your screen and your knees are slightly lower than your hips. Adjust the monitor so that it is a comfortable distance from you (say about 18 to 24 inches).
- Your elbows should rest at an angle of about 90 degrees. You should not need to significantly move your shoulders when typing or using the mouse. To achieve this, your keyboard should be at about elbow height.
- The angle of your hips should ideally be 90 degrees, or slightly more. (You're thinking about this as you read, aren't you?)
- Your feet should rest flat on the floor; do not tuck them under your chair. Don't sit on them, either—you'll get terrible leg-ache and a footprint on your rump.
- Your wrists should rest on the desk in front of you. (It's certainly very poor posture to let them rest on a desk behind you. Unless you are severely double-jointed.) Your wrists should remain straight when typing.
- Adjust your chair to support the lower back.

To avoid problems:

- Shift your position throughout the day to keep your muscles loose and to ease tension in your body.

- Take plenty of breaks, and walk around the office. You may find it beneficial to talk to other people. After a little practice, oral communication can become second nature, even to the seasoned programmer.
- Don't collapse your neck as you read the screen. Hold your head high, and be proud to be a programmer.
- Defocus your eyes occasionally. Try those auto-stereogram thingies that were popular in the 1990s. Or look up from the screen and focus on a distant object (perhaps you could look longingly at the door, or glace at the deadlines that are receding into the distance).
- In truly extreme cases of muscle fatigue, you may find it necessary to take drastic action: step outside of the building (yes, it is perfectly safe to do this) and take an extended stroll. If the stroll gets too relaxing, you'll find plenty of seats in the local park where you can practice sitting down momentarily.

> KEY ➤ Take care of yourself. Maintain good posture as you work.

Having determined a good posture for the basic case of computer use, let's now look at some of the less-considered postures required by the modern programmer. After all, it's important to ensure that we remain ergonomically sound during the *entire* day.

The Debugging Posture

Code got you down? Are the gremlins refusing to budge? Have you been concentrating for six hours flat, yet you still can't work out why there's an ugly brown rectangle on the screen when you should have an elegant turquoise octagon?

In this case, your body needs a slightly different posture to accommodate the weight of the world on your shoulders and the shift of your cerebral cortex from the top of your body to somewhere inside your shoe. To adequately support your body and prevent further strain (unfortunately, the brain-strain is unavoidable), follow these steps:

- Lean forward slightly (a hip angle of 45 to 60 degrees is best).
- Place your elbows on the desk on front of you (ideally, they should rest at your wrists' positions when typing).
- Extend your forearms vertically upwards.
- Lean your head against your arms.
- Sigh.

Figure 30-2 illustrates this. In these situations, you may also find it more comfortable to move the monitor a little closer to the front of the desk than you would ordinarily have it. You'll find that this makes it much easier to repeatedly bang your head against it when you're feeling particularly frustrated.

Figure 30-2. The pondering posture

When It's Really Going Badly

Sometimes, despite adopting a careful debugging poise, you won't be able to solve that thorny problem. The bugs just won't budge. You can look as nonchalant as you want, they just don't seem to respect your determined (yet comfortable) posture. Programming is not always plain sailing, and sometimes all that straight-back, slack-shoulder nonsense can take a running jump.

If you find that it *is* going really badly, then adopt the position shown in Figure 30-3, and brace yourself for when it all crashes and burns around you.

Figure 30-3. The predicament posture

The All-Nighter

When deadlines loom you may find yourself working heroic hours to get everything finished in time. Of course, you know that no one is going to thank you for it, but a sense of moral obligation and a pride in your work will compel you to stay up three nights in a row and to live off a diet of caffeine and stale doughnuts.

In these situations, you will find the posture in Figure 30-4 particularly useful, especially after the fourth all-night stint. Like any other ergonomic consideration, the really important thing here is to adjust your working environment to help you. If possible, shut the blinds and close the door to block out extraneous noise or anything that might distract you from your current task. If you work in a loud communal area with many people walking past all day, then arrange your desk and chair so as to offer maximum potential to not be seen.

Try not to snore too loudly. You may find it useful to insert the mouse firmly into your mouth to plug the airway. (Remember not to do this if you have a blocked nose, or you might asphyxiate yourself.)

Figure 30-4. The power nap posture

Intervention from Above

Occasionally a boss feels compelled to prowl around to ensure that his minions are working as hard as pack mules. In order to ensure *his* maximum comfort and to prevent him from straining his delicate aggravation muscle, you should adopt the posture shown in Figure 30-5. It's for his own good:

- Employ a taught, pained posture. Tighten all your muscles, and look like you are poised to chase after a burglar.

- Adopt a screwed-up facial expression (if this is not already your natural appearance after years of programming). Something along the lines of severe constipation conveys an adequate appearance of extreme concentration.

- For the best effect, purchase some dry ice (this can be readily obtained from a stage supplies store) and leave it under your desk. The boss will be impressed at the perspiration generated by your fervent work. Don't be tempted to overdo this though, or your colleagues may become concerned at your flatulence problems, or security may call the fire department.

Ideally, orient your workspace so that your back is against a wall so that no one can walk up behind you unawares. Adopting the posture shown in Figure 30-5 at very short notice can lead to sprained muscles (especially if you have to rapidly remove your feet from the desk) and fused nerves.

Figure 30-5. The "perfect" posture

The All-Clear

Be careful when adopting the above posture to not screw your eyes up too much. It's important to be able to see your boss walk away so you know when it is safe to relax, and adopt the posture in Figure 30-6.

You will find that using a joystick to play network games requires rather less wrist strain than a keyboard, and so it is preferable to use one, where available. Creative filing of expense claim forms should enable you to justify the purchase of a very good quality gaming device. Do not consider Nintendo Wii controllers in the office—they are not especially subtle.

Figure 30-6. The playful posture

Design Time

Our final programmer posture should be employed when designing new code, or working on extremely hard problems. At these times it is important to ensure maximum comfort so that you will not be distracted by your surroundings.

You should find that Figure 30-7 is fairly self-descriptive.

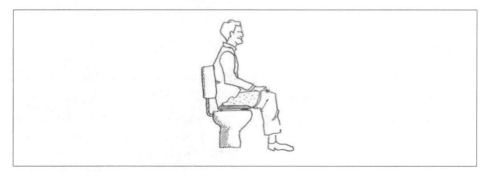

Figure 30-7. The powder room posture

Eye Strain

Finally, it is valuable to spend a little time considering the health of your eyes. Make sure that as you peer at your monitor you don't strain your eyesight. Take frequent breaks. Ensure that your screen doesn't suffer excessive reflections from windows or lights; move the screen if this is a problem. Make sure that direct light sources (a window or a lamp) are not directly pointing at you, too.

Every now and again, stare wistfully out of the window at the joy of the real world outside.

Regular eye tests are essential. Here's one simple test you can try in the comfort of your swivel chair, which doubles as a good regular eye exercise. Print a copy of Figure 30-8 and hang it on the wall above your desk (you may need to experiment to work out the best distance you should be from the chart). From time to time during the day, move your focus away from the computer screen and look at the chart. Start by reading the top letter, and work steadily downwards. Read as far as you can to the bottom.

Figure 30-8. iTest

Conclusion

Yes, I'm being flippant. But this *is* an important topic that you have to think about. Many programmers don't take enough care of themselves physically.

It's vital to ensure that your workstation is ergonomically sound and that you don't ruin your eyes, develop RSI, or strain your back spending long days sitting on your backside, staring at a computer screen. You only get one body: look after it.

No, I'm not your dad nagging you not to slouch. (But take your feet off the desk, you're making the place look untidy.)

Consider using a standing desk (these are quite popular at the moment). Ensure that your chair is not a cheap-and-nasty wreck, but something appropriately adjustable, with suitable lumbar support. Perhaps you would benefit from an ergonomic keyboard and mouse?

Take regular breaks. Stay hydrated throughout the working day. Avoid eye strain with appropriate eye exercises. Work a reasonable number of hours and get sufficient rest at night.

Look after yourself!

Questions

1. How well is your workspace set out? Is it comfortable? Do you feel any strain as you work?

2. How can you improve your workspace? For example, is your monitor at a comfortable height? Is your chair adjustable so you can keep straight wrists as you type?

3. How many hours do you work a day? Do you work long hours to get things done? What effect does this have on your body?

4. Do you maintain a good level of hydration as you work? (Not drinking enough will lead to a reduction in your ability to concentrate.)

Try this....

Survey how your workstation is set up. Take appropriate measures to avoid bad posture and to reduce eye strain. You only get one body: look after it.

PART IV

Getting Things Done

Life in the software factory can be hectic and fast-paced, with many unreasonable demands. "Make it super-elegant." "Make it feature-rich." "Make it bug-free." "And make it *now!*" With the pressures of unrealistic deadlines and tricky coding tasks looming over your head, it can be easy to lose focus, and deliver the wrong thing, or fail to deliver at all.

In these chapters, we'll explore ways of cutting excellent code in the best ways possible —the art of getting things done.

CHAPTER 31

Smarter, Not Harder

Battles are won by slaughter and maneuver. The greater the general,
the more he contributes in maneuver, the less he demands in slaughter.

— Winston Churchill

Let me tell you a story. It's all true. A colleague, working on some UI code, needed to overlay pretty rounded arrows over his display. After he struggled to do it programmatically using the drawing primitives provided, I suggested he just overlay a graphic on the screen. That would be much easier to implement.

So off he went. He fired up Photoshop. And fiddled. And tweaked. And fiddled some more. In this, the Rolls-Royce of image composition applications, there is no quick-and-easy way to draw a rounded arrow that looks halfway decent. Presumably an experienced graphic artist could knock one up in two minutes. But after almost an hour of drawing, cutting, compositing, and rearranging, he still didn't have a convincing rounded arrow.

He mentioned it to me in frustration as he went to make a cup of tea.

On his return, tea in hand, he found a shiny new rounded arrow image sitting on his desktop ready for use.

"How did you do that so quickly?" he asked.

"I just used the right tool," I replied, dodging a flying mug of tea.

Photoshop *should* have been the right tool. It's what most image design work is done in. But I knew that Open Office provides a handy configurable rounded arrow tool. I had drawn one in 10 seconds and sent him a screenshot. It wasn't elegant. But it worked.

The moral?

There is a constant danger of focusing too closely on one tool, or on a singular approach to solve a problem. It's tantalisingly easy to lose hours of effort exploring its blind alleys when there's a simpler, more direct route to your goal.

So how can we do better?

Pick Your Battles

To be a productive programmer, you need to learn to work *smarter* rather than *harder*. One of the hallmarks of experienced programmers is not just their technical acumen, but how they solve problems and pick their battles.

Good programmers get things done quickly. Now, they *don't* bodge things like a shoot-from-the-hip cowboy coder. They just work smart. This is not necessarily because they are more clever; they just know how to solve problems *well*. They have an armoury of experience to draw from that will guide them to use the correct approach. They can see lateral solutions—the application of an unusual technique that will get the job done with less hassle. They know how to chart a route around looming obstacles. They can make informed decisions about where best to invest effort.

Battle Tactics

Here are some simple ideas to help you work smarter.

Reuse Wisely

Don't write a lump of code yourself when you can use an existing library, or can repurpose code from elsewhere.

Even if you have to pay for a third-party library, it is often far more cost effective to take an off-the-shelf implementation than to write your own. And test your own. And then debug your own.

> KEY ▶ Use existing code, rather than writing your own from scratch. Employ your time on more important things.

Overcome *"not invented here"* syndrome. Many people think that they can do a much better job themselves, or fashion a more appropriate version for their specific application. Is that *really* the case? Even if the other code isn't designed exactly how you prefer, just use it. You don't necessarily need to rewrite it if it's working already. Make a facade around it if you must to integrate into your system.

Make It Someone Else's Problem

Don't work out how to do a task yourself if someone already knows how to do it. You might like to bask in the glory of the accomplishment. You might like to learn something new. But if someone else can give you a leg up, or complete the job much faster than you, then it may be better to put the task in their work queue instead.

Only Do What You Have To

Consider sacrilege: Do you *need* to refactor? Do you *need* to unit test?

I'm a firm advocate of both practices, but sometimes they might not be appropriate or a worthwhile investment of your time. Yes, yes: refactoring and unit testing both bring great benefits and should never be tossed aside thoughtlessly. However, if you're working on a small prototype, or exploring a possible functional design with some throwaway code, then you might be better off saving the theologically correct practices for later.

If you do (laudably) invest time in unit tests, consider exactly *which* tests to write. A stubborn "test every method" approach is not sensible. (Often you'll think you have better coverage than you expect). For example, you need not test every single getter and setter in your API.[1] Focus your testing on usage, not methods, and pay particular attention to the places you would likely expect brittleness.

Pick your testing battles.

Put It on a Spike

If you're presented with multiple design options and you're not sure which solution to pick, don't waste hours cogitating about which is best. A quick *spike* solution (a throwaway prototype) might generate more useful answers in minutes.

To make this work well, set a specific Pomodoro-like (*http://www.pomodorotechni que.com*) time window within which you will perform the spike. Stop when the time elapses. (And in true Pomodoro style, get yourself a nice hard-to-ignore windup timer to force you to stop.)

Use tools that will help you backtrack quickly (e.g., an effective version control system).

Prioritise

Prioritise your work list. Do the most important things first.

> KEY ➤ Concentrate effort on the most important things first. What is most urgent, or will produce the most value?

---

1. It's another issue whether you *should* have getters and setters in your APIs in the first place.

Be rigorous about this. Don't get caught up on unimportant minutiae; it's incredibly easy to do. Especially when one simple job turns out to depend on another simple job. Which depends on another simple job, which depends on.... After two hours you'll surface from a rabbit hole and wonder why on earth you're reconfiguring the mail server on your computer when what you wanted to do was modify a method on a container class. In computer folklore, this is referred to as *yak shaving (http://bit.ly/Y1J0fB)*.

Beware of the many small tasks you do that aren't that important; email, paperwork, phone calls—the administrivia. Instead of doing those little things throughout the day, interrupting and distracting you from your flow on important tasks, batch them together and do them at one (or a few) set times each day.

You may find it helps to write these tasks down on a small "to do" list, and at a set time start processing them as quickly as possible. Ticking them off your list—the sense of accomplishment can be a motivating reward.

What's Really Required?

When you are given a new task, check what's *really* needed now. What does the customer actually need you to deliver?

Don't implement the Rolls-Royce full bells-and-whistles version if it's not necessary. Even if the work request asks for it, push back and verify what is genuinely required. To do this, you need to know the context your code lives in.

This isn't just laziness. There is a danger in writing too much code too early. *The Pareto principle*[2] implies that 80% of required benefit could come from just 20% of the intended implementation. Do you really need to write the remainder of that code, or could your time be better employed elsewhere?

One Thing at a Time

Do one thing at a time. It's hard to focus on more than one job at once (especially for men with our uni-tasking brains). If you try to work concurrently, you'll do both jobs badly. Finish one job then move on to another. You'll get both jobs completed in a shorter space of time.

Keep It Small (and Simple)

Keep your code and design as small and as simple as possible. Otherwise, you'll just add a lot more code that will cost you time and effort to maintain in the future.

---

2. For many events, roughly 80% of the effects come from 20% of the causes. For more on this, see *http://en.wikipedia.org/wiki/Pareto_principle*.

You *will* need to change it; you can never foretell exactly what the future requirements are. Predicting the future is an incredibly inexact science. It is easier and smarter to make your code malleable to change now than it is to build in support for every possible future feature on day one.

A small, focused body of code is far easier to change than a large one.

Don't Defer and Store Up Problems

Some things that are hard (like code integration) should *not* be avoided because they are hard. Many people do so; they defer these tasks to try to minimise the pain. It sounds like picking your battles, doesn't it?

In reality, the smarter thing is to start sooner and face the pain when it is smaller. It's easier to integrate small pieces of code early on, and then to frequently integrate the subsequent changes, than it is to work on three major features for a year and then try to stitch them together at the end.

The same goes for unit testing: write tests now, alongside your code (or before). It'll be far harder, and less productive, to wait until the code is "working" before you write the tests.

As the saying goes: *If it hurts, do it more often.*

Automate

Remember the classic advice: *if you have to do it more than once, write a script to do it for you.*

Automating a common, tedious task could save you many hours of effort. Consider also a single task that has a high degree of repetition. It might be faster to write a tool and run that once, than to do the repetitive job by hand yourself.

This automation has an added advantage: it helps others to work smarter, too. If you can run your build with *one* command, rather than a series of 15 complex commands and button presses, then your entire team can build more easily, and newcomers can get up to speed faster.

To aid this automation, experienced programmers will naturally pick automatable tools, even if they don't intend to automate anything right now. Favour workflows that produce plain text, or simple structured (e.g., JSON or XML) intermediate files. Select tools that have a command-line interface as well as (or instead of) an inflexible GUI panel.

It can be hard to know whether it's worth writing a script for a task. Obviously, if you are likely to perform a task multiple times then it's worth considering. Unless the script is particularly hard to write, you are unlikely to waste time writing it.

Error Prevention

Find errors sooner, so you don't spend too long doing the wrong thing.

To achieve this:

- Show your product to customers early and often, so you'll find out quickly if you're building them the wrong thing.
- Discuss your code design with others, so you'll find out if there's a better way to structure your solution earlier. Don't invest effort in bad code if you can avoid it.
- Code review small, understandable bits of work often, not large dense bits of code.
- Unit-test code from the outset. Ensure the unit tests are run frequently to catch errors before they bite you.

Communicate

Learn to communicate better. Learn how to ask the right questions to understand unambiguously. A misunderstanding now might mean you'll end up reworking your code later on. Or suffer delays waiting for more answers to outstanding questions. This is particularly important, and we'll spend a whole chapter on Communication.

Learn how to run productive meetings so your life is not sucked out by the demons who sit in the corners of meeting rooms.

Avoid Burnout

Don't burn yourself out working silly hours, leading people to expect unrealistic levels of work from you all the time. Make it clear if you are moving beyond the call of duty, so people learn not to expect it too often.

Healthy projects do not require reams of overtime.

Power Tools

Always look out for new tools that will boost your workflow.

But don't become a slave to finding new software. Often new software has sharp edges that could cut you. Favour tried-and-tested tools that many people have used. You can't put a price on the collected knowledge of these tools available via Google.

Conclusion

Pick your battles. (Yeah, yeah.) *Work smarter, not harder.* (We've heard it all before.)

They are trite maxims. But they are true.

Of course, this doesn't mean *don't work hard*. Unless you want to get fired. But that's not smart.

Questions

1. How do you determine the right amount of testing to apply to your work? Do you rely on experience or guidelines? Look back over your last month's work; was it really tested adequately?

2. How good are you at prioritising your workload? How can you improve?

3. How do you ensure you find issues as soon as possible? How many errors or re-workings have you had to perform that could have been avoided?

4. Do you suffer from *not invented here* syndrome? Is everyone else's code rubbish? Could you do better? Can you stomach incorporating other's work in your own?

5. If you work in a culture that values the number of hours worked over the quality of that work, how can work reconcile "working smart" with not looking lazy?

See also

*   *This Time I've Got It* A cautionary tale: it's easy to not work as *smart* as you are able.

*   *A Case for Code Reuse* Employ the "smart" approach to code reuse. Don't make a duplicated mess, but don't write more code than you have to.

*   *It's Done When It's Done* Don't do more work than necessary—learn how to define when it's "done."

Try this....

Identify three techniques that will help you become a *more productive* programmer. Aim for two new practices to adopt, and one thing to stop doing. Start employing these techniques tomorrow. Become accountable to someone over them.

10,000 MONKEYS
(OR THEREABOUTS)

HAIRLINE-DRIVEN DEVELOPMENT

YOUR RATE OF HAIR LOSS IS INVERSELY PROPORTIONAL TO THE DISTANCE FROM YOUR PROJECT DEADLINE.

THEREFORE, CHOOSE SMALLER PROJECTS THE BALDER YOU GET.

It's Done When It's Done

In the name of God, stop a moment, cease your work, look around you.

— Leo Tolstoy

A program is made of a number of subsystems. Each of those subsystems is composed of smaller parts—components, modules, classes, functions, data types, and the like. Sometimes even boxes and lines. Or clever ideas.

The jobbing programmer moves from one assignment to the next; from one task to another. The working day is composed of a series of construction and maintenance tasks on a series of these software components: composing new parts, stitching parts together, and extending, enhancing, or mending existing pieces of code.

So our job is simply a string of lots of smaller jobs. It's recursive. Programmers love that kind of thing.

Are We There Yet?

So there you are, getting the job done. (You think.)

Just like a small child travelling in the back of a car constantly brays *are we there yet?*, pretty soon you'll encounter the braying manager: *are you done yet?*

This is an important question. It's essential for a software developer to be able to answer that one simple request: to know what "done" looks like, and to have a realistic idea of how close you are to being "done." And then to communicate it.

Many programmers fall short here; it's tempting to just keep hacking away until the task seems complete. They don't have a good grasp on whether they're nearly finished or not. They think: *There could be any number of bugs to iron out, or unforeseen problems to trip me up. I can't possibly tell if I'm almost done.*

But that's simply not good enough. Usually, avoiding the question is an excuse for lazy practice, a justification for "coding from the hip," without forethought and planning. It's not methodical.

It's also likely to create problems for you. I often see people working far too hard:

- They are doing more work than necessary, because they didn't know when to stop.

- Without knowing when they'll be done, they don't actually *complete* the tasks they think are finished. This leads to having to pick things back up later on, to work out what's missing and how to stitch it in. Code construction is far slower and harder this way.

- The wrong bits of code get polished, as the correct goal was never in sight. This is wasted work.

- Developers working too hard are forced to put in extra hours. You'll not get enough sleep!

Let's see how to avoid this and to answer "are we there yet?" effectively.

Developing Backwards: Decomposition

Different programming shops manage their day-to-day development efforts differently. Often this depends on the size and structure of the software team.

Some place a single developer in charge of a large swath of functionality, give them a delivery date, and ask them for occasional progress reports. Others follow more agile processes, and manage a backlog of granular tasks (perhaps phrasing them as *stories*), divvying those out to programmers as they are able to move into a new task.

The first step towards defining "done" is to know *exactly* what you're working on. If it's a fiendishly large and complex problem, then it's going to be fiendishly complex to say when you'll be done.

It's a far simpler exercise to answer how far you are through a small, well-understood problem. Obvious, really.

So if you have been allotted a monster task, before you begin chipping away at it, break it down into smaller, understandable parts. Too many people rush headlong into code or design without taking a step back to consider how they will work through it.

> KEY ➤ Split large tasks up into a series of smaller, well-understood tasks. You will be able to judge progress through these more accurately.

Often this isn't a complex task, at least for a top-level decomposition. (You may have to drill down a few times. Do so. But take note: this is an indication that you've been handed a task at far too high a granularity.)

Sometimes such a decomposition is hard to do, and is a significant task itself. Don't let that put you off. If you don't do it up front for estimation purposes, you'll only end up doing it later on in less focused ways as you battle to the finish line.

Make sure that at any point in time, you know the smallest unit you're working on; rather than just the big target for your project.

Define "Done"

You've got an idea of the big picture; you know what you're ultimately trying to build. And you know the particular sub-task you're working on at the moment.

Now, make sure that for whatever task you are working on, you know *when to stop*.

To do this, you have to define what "done" is. You have to know what "success" means. What the "complete" software will look like.

> KEY ➤ Make sure you define "done."

This is important. If you haven't determined when to stop, you'll keep working far past when you needed to. You'll be working harder and longer than you needed to. Or, you won't work hard enough—you'll not get everything done. (Not getting *everything* done sounds easier, doesn't it? But it's not…the half-done work will come back to bite you, and will make more work for you later down the line, whether that's bugs, rework, or an unstable product.)

Don't start a piece of coding work until you know what success is. If you don't yet know, make your first task determining what "done" is. Most often it's not the programmer who defines this, but a product owner, system designer, customer, or the end user.

Only then, get going. With the certainty of knowing where you're headed, you'll be able to work in a focused, directed manner. You'll be able to make informed choices, and to discount unnecessary things that might sidetrack or delay you.

> KEY ➤ If you can't tell when it's done, then you shouldn't start it.

So how does this look in practice? How do you define "done"? Your "done" criteria needs to be:

Clear
> It must be unambiguous and specific. A list of all the features to be implemented, the APIs added or extended, or the specific faults to be fixed.

If, as you get into the task, you discover things that might affect the completion criteria (e.g., you discover more bugs that need fixing, or uncover unforeseen problems) then you must make sure that you reflect this in your "done" criteria.

This criteria is usually directly traceable to some software requirements or a user story—if you have them. If this is the case, make sure that this connection is documented.

Visible

Make sure that the success criteria is seen by all important parties. This probably includes your manager, your customers, the downstream teams using your code, or the testers who will validate your work.

Make sure everyone knows and agrees on this criteria. And make sure they'll have a way of telling—and agreeing—when you are "done."

Achievable

Define the "done" criteria carefully. An unachievable "done" definition is useless: if it's beyond the reach of the current team then it will become an albatross around their neck, rather than a goal to strive for. For example, a goal of 100% code coverage in a low-test environment is not realistic.

The nature of each task will clearly define what "done" means. However, you should consider:

- How much code must be completed. (Do you measure this in units of functionality, APIs implemented, or user stories completed?)
- How much design is done, and how it's captured.
- Whether any documents or reports must be generated.

When it's a coding task, you can mostly clearly demonstrate "being done" by creating an unambiguous test set. Write tests that will show when you've fashioned the full suite of code required.

> **KEY ➤** Use tests written in code to define when your code is complete and working.

There are some other questions that you may have to consider when you describe what "done" is:

- Where is the code delivered to? (To version control, for example.)
- Where is the code deployed to? (Is it "done" when it's live on a server? Or do you deliver testable product ready for a deployment team to roll out?)
- What are the economics of "done"? The exact numbers required that may lead to certain trade-offs or measurements. For example, how well should your solution

scale? It's not good enough if your software only manages 10 simultaneous users if 10,000 are required. The more precise your done criteria, the better you understand these economics.

- How will you signal that you're done? When you think you're done, how will you let the customer/manager/QA department know? This probably looks different for each person. How will you garner agreement that you are indeed done—who signs off on your work? Do you just check in, do you change a project reporting ticket, or do you raise an invoice?

Just Do It

When you've defined "done," you can work with focus. Work up to the "done" point. Don't do more than necessary.

Stop when your code is good enough—not *necessarily* perfect (there may be a real difference between the two states). If the code gets used or worked on an awful lot, it may eventually be refactored to be perfect—but don't polish it yet. This may just be wasted effort. (Beware: this is not an excuse to write *bad code*, just a warning against unnecessary over-polishing.)

> KEY ➤ Don't do more work than necessary. Work until you're "done."
> Then stop.

Having a single, specific goal in mind helps you to focus on a single task. Without this focus, it's easy to hack at code randomly trying to achieve a number of things and not managing any of them successfully.

Questions

1. Do you know when your current task will be "done"? What does "done" look like?
2. Have you decomposed your current task into a single goal, or a series of simple goals?
3. Do you decompose your work into achievable, measurable units?
4. How does your current development process determine how you break up and estimate work? Is it sufficient?
5. How much variation in accuracy is there between the estimates made by people on your team? Why do you think this is? What makes the most accurate estimators better?

See also

- *Smarter, Not Harder* Define "done" and don't do more. That's working *smart*, not *hard*.

- *Nothing Is Set in Stone* No software is ever completely "done." By definition, software is *soft*, the requirements may change tomorrow and require us to change it.

Try this....

Review your current code task. Is it the right size? Is it correctly decomposed? Define a clear "done" point. Work out how to track your progress through it more accurately.

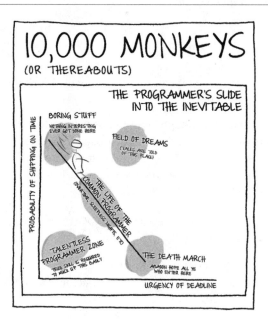

CHAPTER 33

This Time I've Got It...

It is easier to prevent bad habits than to break them.

— Benjamin Franklin

"Just one more minute," Jim said. "I think I really do know what the problem is now. This time I'll fix it."

Julie had been watching him trying to solve the problem for almost a whole day now, with increasing amusement.

Jim had been hunched over the keyboard for hours straight. He'd hardly glanced up. He'd certainly not eaten. And he'd only had the one cup of coffee that Julie had brought mid-morning, mostly out of pity.

It wasn't like him at all. He was a man on a mission.

A sense of urgency, if not mild panic, had been brought about by a "level 1" bug discovered in the live system. How it had got through the QA process was anyone's guess.

It was thought to be a problem in some of Jim's code, and so Jim sprang into action. It was partly pride that stopped him from asking for help, but there was also a hint of naiveté—he thought he'd have it tracked down in 10 minutes, and he would then look like a hero for fixing the running system.

So far that plan had failed.

With every minute that passed, the pressure increased. Reports from customers were trickling in about the problem. One or two reports early in the morning had become a steady stream. Before long, that stream would become a flood, and then the whole team would be dumped in it. Indeed, if the problem wasn't fixed soon, the company could suffer as a result.

No one wants that on their conscience.

Or their resumé.

Jim had to get this fixed. And fast. The pressure was building.

By now they surely should have rolled the code back to a previously known good release and taken more time over the diagnosis and the fix, but at every turn Jim assured Julie that he was "almost there." And he truly believed it. But each time he got close to the cause of the problem, each time he thought he had it cornered, it seemed to back off into a darker recess of the system.

The problem was clearly now not solely in Jim's code. All his unit tests showed that the module functioned as well as had been expected. No, this was a gnarly integration issue; something strange happening at the boundary of a number of software modules. And it was intermittent, too. The problem was related to some subtle timing or ordering of events flowing around the system.

Jim's prey, like a shy deer, was evading his sights. He just couldn't quite find it.

"I think I know where it is now. It's not in the event dispatcher itself. I think there's some nastiness in the communication between it, the database, and the processing backend," said Jim. "I've got it down to those three components. I haven't fixed it yet, but the next fix really *has* to work." He tried to sound more certain than he really was.

"Really? Are you sure?" chimed Julie. There was a hint of mocking in her tone. It wasn't missed. Normally Jim would play along, but he wasn't in the mood today. He gave her the glare that he normally reserved for traffic wardens and turned his gaze back to the scores of source code windows open on his screen.

"If I could just…"

"Wait a minute," interrupted Julie. "Seriously, just *wait*. Stop and think about what you're doing." Her calm voice cut across Jim and he looked up again. He looked tired. And stressed. "Come on, walk with me to the coffee machine. Tell me what you think the problem is."

Jim *had* been thinking. All day. But he did need a coffee, so he acquiesced. He'd been too proud to ask for help; increasingly so as the day wore on. But now he realised that he needed a listening ear and a fresh perspective. He was out of good ideas, and was now operating on educated guesses and adrenaline.

Jim had been too close to the problem. He'd tried every first thing that entered his head without seeing (or yet understanding) the bigger picture. He had started with a pre-conception of the issue, and hadn't focused on detecting the fault before applying sticking-plasters. Each one was a "little fix" that should have been the solution, but just masked, or moved the problem around—like smoothing an air bubble trapped under wallpaper.

And he'd spent a whole day doing it. He felt no closer to the solution, and he felt the rest of the teams eyes boring into the back of his head as he worked frantically on a fix.

"Don't worry," said Julie. She had seen it many times over. She'd done it herself enough times in the past. And she knew well enough that she was still perfectly capable of doing it again. "Tell me what you've found so far." Jim started to describe the situation.

One coffee, and one chat later Jim felt refreshed and had a new focus. As he had explained the full problem to Julie, without her saying a single word, it dawned on him that he'd missed a large piece of the puzzle. As he described what he was going to do next, he realised how he'd not seen the real problem. He described what he'd do instead.

"That makes perfect sense," said Julie encouragingly. "Do you want me to pair with you?"

"I think I've got this covered now," said Jim. "But do come back in 10 minutes and check that I'm not going off on one again." Then he added, thoughtfully, "And, when I'm done, would you mind reviewing the fix?"

"Of course not," said Julie. She smiled.

Jim was like her in many respects. She knew that he'd only learn by making mistakes. At the end of the day, she'd ask him to reflect on what had happened, a little personal retrospective. Hopefully he wouldn't be doing that again in a hurry.

Jim fixed the issue, they reviewed the fix, and deployed it by the end of the day (which was spent celebrating over a drink, when it could have been spent hunched over a keyboard working late into the night).

Desert Island Development

No developer is an island. Beware the peril of getting so narrowly focused, and so close to a part of the problem that you're not really able to see the whole issue, or be able to effectively work on it.

Watch yourself. Check whether you're going down a coding blind alley, and make sure that you will notice and can get back out. How can you do this? Work out some practical mechanisms. Set yourself short time limits and deadlines, and review your progress as you go. Make yourself accountable to someone else as you work, either by pairing, reviewing, or informally reporting progress to them.

> KEY ➤ Be accountable to another programmer. Review progress with them regularly.

Never be too proud to ask for help. As we just saw, it's often in describing a problem that you'll explain to yourself how to fix it. If you've never tried doing this, you'll be amazed at how frequently it happens. You don't even need to talk to another programmer. It could even be a rubber duck.[1]

Stood at the Bottom of the Mountain

Many software design issues, coding decisions, or bug fixes feel like a huge mountain you have to climb. Running directly to the foot of the mountain and starting to clamber up is often the wrong approach.

Often it is better (i.e., easier, more time- or money-effective) to approach the mountain in a team. The team can help each other up. One person can point out when another is going to climb into a difficult situation. The team can work together in ways that an individual can't.

It always pays to take a step back first and plan a route before starting your ascent. Round the far side of the mountain there may be a far easier route to get up, if you'd only look for it. Indeed, there may already be a path laid. With signposts. And lights. And an escalator. Your first route into a problem is rarely the best.

> KEY ▶ When facing a problem, make sure you've considered more than one approach to solve it. Only then should you start working on it.

This is one example, of many, of how software development is often more of a human problem than a technical problem. We have to learn how to enable ourselves to solve problems most effectively, and overcome our natural instincts to solve problems quickly —but ineffectively.

Questions

1. How effectively do you work with others in your team?

2. Can you ask for help, or to discuss problems?

3. How often do you "code yourself into a dead end"? When did you last do this? How long did it take you to notice?

4. Are you *accountable* to others? If not, to whom could you become accountable?

5. Do you think sharing your progress and discussing problems would make you look like a weaker programmer to others in the team?

See also

- *Smarter, Not Harder* This tale highlights how important it is to work *smarter, not harder.*

---

1. Hunt and Thomas, *The Pragmatic Programmer.*

- *Use Your Brain* Don't suffer tunnel vision, racing towards a goal down the wrong path. Stop, and *use your brain*.
- *It's the Thought That Accounts* Accountability, and daily (or more frequent) conversations about what you are working on can help avoid mindless mistakes.

Try this....

Before starting your next coding task, write down a "plan of attack" for how you will solve/diagnose/design/approach the code. Use this to prevent you from running in head-first without due consideration.

PART V

The People Pursuit

Software development is rarely a lone activity; it is a social sport, a people pursuit. A good programmer is able to work well with the other inhabitants of the software factory. To become a better programmer, you must learn how to work effectively with others, and how to learn from them.

CHAPTER 34

People Power

Two things are infinite: the universe and human stupidity;
and I'm not sure about the universe.

— Albert Einstein

Programming is a people pursuit.

Almost since the first programs were constructed we have realised that programming is not a solely technical challenge. It is also a social challenge. Software development is a pastime that involves writing code *with* other people, *for* other people to understand. It means working with other people's code, joining and leaving software teams, working under your boss' supervision, managing developers (which is rather like herding cats), and so on.

Many of the most enduring programming tomes are devoted to the people problem, for example, *The Mythical Man Month*[1] and *Peopleware*.[2]

Just as the people working with a codebase will inevitably shape the code they produce, the people who work with you will inevitably shape *you*.

> KEY ➤ Purposefully place yourself beside excellent programmers.

That is, if you want to be an exceptional programmer, then you must consciously place yourself daily amongst people who are exceptional programmers. It's a really simple but profound way to make sure that you improve your skills and attitudes.

We are products of our environment, after all. Just as plants need good soil, fertiliser, and the correct atmosphere to grow healthily, so do we.

---

1. Frederick P. Brooks Jr., *The Mythical Man Month* (Boston: Addison Wesley, 1995).

2. Tom Demarco and Timothy Lister, *Peopleware* (New York: Dorset House Publishing, 1999).

Spending too long with depressing people will make you feel depressed. Spending too long with run-down people will make you feel tired and lethargic. Spending too long with sloppy workers will encourage you to work sloppily yourself—why bother trying if no one else is? Conversely, working with individuals who are passionate about good code and strive to make better software will encourage you to do the same.

By immersing yourself in the environment of excellent programmers, you will treat yourself to:

- Enthusiasm that is infectious
- Motivation that is inspirational
- Responsibility that is contagious

Find people like that and marinate yourself in their company. Consciously seek out the people who care about good code, and about writing it well. In that kind of environment, you won't fail to be nurtured and encouraged.

By working with high calibre developers you will gain far more than technical knowledge; although that knowledge itself is very valuable. You'll enjoy positive reinforcement of good programming habits and attitudes. You'll be encouraged to grow, and be challenged to improve in your weaker areas. This isn't always comfortable or easy, but it *is* worthwhile.

So make a point of seeking out the best programmers and work with them. Design code with them. Pair program with them. Socialise with them.

What to Do

You could make this kind of relationship formal with *mentorship*; indeed many good workplaces try to put mentorship schemes into practice formally. Carve out specific chunks of time to work together.

Or you may pursue it informally: get yourself assigned on the same projects as great programmers. Change jobs to work with them. Go to conferences, talks, or user groups to meet with them. Or just make a point of hanging out with other great programmers.

As you do this, learn from them. Watch out for:

- How they think and solve puzzles
- How they plan a route into problems
- The attitude they adopt when things get hard
- How they know to keep pushing on a problem, when to take a break, or when try a different approach

- Their specific coding skills and techniques that you don't yet understand

Know Your Experts

Consider carefully what you think an excellent programmer looks like.

You specifically *don't* want to get alongside people who work too hard, filling all the hours God sends with code. Those people are almost certainly not the exceptional programmers! Managers often think that employees who spend every waking hour on a project are the programming heroes, but often this really hints at their lack of ability. They can't get things right the first time, so they have to spend many more hours getting the code to "work" than was actually necessary.

Experts make it look easy and get things done on time.

20/20 Hindsight

As I look back over my career, I realise that the most enjoyable and personally productive times I've encountered have been when I've been working alongside excellent, motivated, interesting developers. And because of this, I will now always attempt to place myself alongside people like that.

I've learnt that they make me better at what I do, and I have more fun whilst I'm doing it.

An interesting and beneficial side effect of working with good coders is that you are far more likely to end up working with good code.

Questions

1. Are you around people you think are excellent programmers right now? Why? Or why not?

2. How can you move yourself nearer better coders? Can you move to a new project or team? Is it time to look for a new job with a different company?

3. How can you tell who is an excellent developer, and who isn't?

See also

- *Relish the Challenge* Seek out good colleagues who can encourange and challenge you.
- *It's the Thought That Accounts* Become accountable to them.
- *Speak Up!* Learn to communicate well; listening is essential if you are to learn.
- *An Ode to Code* Not every colleague is a saint.

Identify some "coding heroes" you'd like to learn from, and plan a way to work alongside them. Consider asking to be mentored by them.

10,000 MONKEYS
(OR THEREABOUTS)

CHAPTER 35

It's the Thought That Accounts

Thinking well is wise; planning well, wiser; doing well, wisest and best of all.

— Persian Proverb

I run. Every week. It's my waistline, you see. Perhaps it's guilt, but I feel I need to do something to keep it under control.

Now, let's be clear: I'm no masochist. Exercise is *not* my favourite thing in the world. Far from it. It ranks marginally above hot pokers being stuck in my eyes. There are plenty of things I'd rather do with my evenings. Many of them involve sitting down, preferably with a glass of wine.

But I know that I *should* run. It's good for me.

Is that fact alone enough to ensure I go regularly, every week, for the full distance? With no slacking or slowing of the pace?

It is not.

I dislike exercise and would gladly employ the weakest of excuses to get out of a run. "Oh no, my running shorts have a loose thread." "Oh no, I have a runny nose." "Oh no, I'm a bit tired." "Oh no, my leg has fallen off."

(Ok, some excuses *are* better than others.)

What unseen force coaxes me to continue running regularly when guilt alone can't drag me out the door? What magical power leads me on where willpower fails?

Accountability.

I run with a friend. That person knows when I'm slacking, and encourages me out of the house even when I don't fancy it. That person turns up at the door, as arranged, before my lethargy sets in. I perform the same service back. I've lost count of the times that I wouldn't have run, or would have given up halfway around had I not had someone there, watching me and running alongside me.

And, as a by-product we enjoy the run more for the company and shared experience.

Sometimes we *both* don't feel like going on the run. Even if we admit it to each other, we won't let each other off the hook. We encourage ourselves to push through the pain. And, once we've run, we're always glad we did it, even if it didn't feel like a great idea at the time.

Stretching the Metaphor

Some metaphors are tenuous literary devices, written to entertain, or for use as contrived segues. Some are so oblique as to be distracting, or form such a bad parallel as to be downright misleading.

However, I believe this picture of accountability is directly relevant to the quality of our code.

We hear our industry experts, speakers, writers, and code prophets talk about producing good, well-crafted code. They extol the virtues of "clean" code and explain why we need well-factored code. But it matters not one jot if, in the heat of the workplace, we can't put that into practice. If the pressures of the codeface cause us to shed our development morals and resort to hacking like uninformed idiots, what use is their advice?

The spirit is willing, but when the deadline looms, all too often the flesh is weak. We can complain about the poor state of our codebases, but who do we look at to blame?

We need to bake into our development regimen ways to avoid the temptation for short-cuts, bodges, and quick fixes. We need something to lure us out of the trap of thoughtless design, sloppy, easy solutions, and half-baked practices. The kind of thing that costs us effort to do, but that in retrospect we're always glad we *have* done.

How do you think we'll achieve this?

Accountability Counts

I know that in my career to date, the single most import thing that has encouraged me to work to the best of my abilities has been *accountability,* to a team of great programmers.

It's the other coders that make me look good. It's those other coders that have *made* me a better programmer.

> KEY ▶ Being accountable to other programmers for the quality of your work will dramatically improve the quality of your coding.

That is a single simple, but powerful idea.

Code++

To ensure you're crafting excellent code, you need people who are checking it at every step of the way. People who will make sure you're working to the best of your ability, and are keeping up to the quality standard of the project you're working on.[1]

This needn't be some bureaucratic big-brother process, or a regimented personal development plan that feeds back directly into your salary. In fact, it had better not be. A lightweight, low-ceremony system of accountability, involving no forms, no lengthy reviewing sessions or formal reviews is far superior, and will yield much better results.

Most important is to simply recognise the need for accountability; that being answerable to other people for the quality of your code encourages you to work your best. Realise that actively putting yourself into the vulnerable position of accountability is not a sign of weakness, but a valuable way to gain feedback and improve your skills.

How accountable do you currently feel you are for the quality of the code you produce? Is anyone challenging you to produce high-quality work, to prevent you from slipping into bad, lazy practices?

Accountability is worth pursuing not only in the quality of our code output, but also in the way we learn, and how we plan our personal development. It's even beneficial in matters of character and personal life (but that's a whole other book).

Making It Work

There are some simple ways to build accountability for the quality of code into your development process. In one development team we found it particularly useful when all the coders agreed on a simple rule: *all code passed two sets of eyes before entering source control*. With this as a peer-agreed rule, it was *our choice* to be accountable to one another, rather then some managerial diktat passed down from faceless suits on high. Grassroots buy-in was key to this success of the scheme.

To satisfy the rule, we employed pair programming and/or a low-ceremony one-on-one code review, keeping each checked-in change small to make the scheme manageable. Knowing another person was going to scrutinise your work was enough to foster a resistance to sloppy practice and to improve the general quality of our code.

---

1. This is one of the reasons open source code is often of higher quality than proprietary code: you know that many other programmers will be looking at your work.

> **KEY ▶** If you know that someone else *will* read and comment on your code, you're more likely to write good code.

This practice genuinely improved the quality of the team, too. We all learnt from one another, and shared our knowledge of the system. It encouraged a greater responsibility for and understanding of the system.

We also ended up with closer collaboration, enjoyed working with each other, and had more fun writing the code as a consequence of this scheme. The accountability led to a pleasant, more productive workflow.

Setting the Standard

When building developer accountability into your daily routine, it is worth spending a while considering the benchmark that you're aiming for. Ask yourself the following questions:

How is the quality of your work judged? How do people *currently* rate your performance? What is the yardstick they use to gauge its quality? How do you think they *should* rate it?

- The software works, that's good enough.
- It was written fast, and released on schedule (internal quality is not paramount).
- It was well-written, and can be maintained easily in the future.
- Some combination of the above.

Which is seen as most important?

Who currently judges your work? Who is the audience for your work? Is it only seen by yourself? Your peers? Your superiors? Your manager? Your customer? How are they qualified to judge the quality of your handiwork?

Who *should* be the arbiter of your work quality? Who really knows how well you've performed? How can you get them involved? Is it as simple as asking them? Does their opinion have any bearing on the company's current view of your work's quality?

Which aspects of your work should be placed under accountability?

- The lines of code you produce?
- The design?
- The conduct and process you used to develop it?
- The way you worked with others?
- The clothes you wore when you did it?

Which aspect matters the most to you at the moment? Where do you need the most accountability and encouragement to keep improving?

The Next Steps

If you think that this is important, and something you should start adding to your work:

- Agree that accountability is a good thing. Commit to it.
- Find someone to become accountable to. Consider making it a reciprocal arrangement; perhaps involve the entire development team.
- Consider implementing a simple scheme like the one described above in your team, where every line of code changed, added, or removed must go past two sets of eyes.
- Agree on how you will work out the accountability—small meetings, end-of-week reviews, design meetings, pair programming, code reviews, etc.
- Commit to a certain quality of work, be prepared to be challenged on it. Don't be defensive.
- If this happens team-wide, or project-wide, then ensure you have everyone's buy-in. Draft a set of team standards or group code of conduct for quality of development.

Also, consider approaching this from the other side: can you help someone else out with feedback, encouragement, and accountability? Could you become another programmer's moral software compass?

Often this kind of accountability works better in pairs of peers, rather than in a subordinate relationship.

Conclusion

Accountability between programmers requires a degree of bravery; you have to be willing to accept criticism. And tactful enough to give it well. But the benefits can be marked and profound in the quality of code you create.

Questions
1. How are you accountable to others for the quality of your work?
2. What should you be held accountable for?
3. How do you ensure the work you do today is as good as previous work?
4. How is your current work teaching you and helping you to improve?
5. When have you been glad you kept quality up, even when you didn't feel like it?

6. Does accountability only work when you *choose* to enter into an accountability relationship, or can it effectively be something you are *required* to do?

See also

- *The Ethical Programmer* You should be accountable for the quality of your conduct as well as the quality of your code.

- *People Power* When working alongside excellent coders, you cannot help but be challenged to improve your skills.

- *This Time I've Got It* Accountability can help avoid embarrassing and silly mistakes.

- *Playing by the Rules* Employ accountability between team members to encourage everyone to stick with your team "rules."

Try this....

Find a colleague to become accountable to. Commit to a certain quality of work. Ask them to keep an eye on your code. Consider making this a two-way relationship.

CHAPTER 36

Speak Up!

The single biggest problem in communication is the illusion that it has taken place.

— George Bernard Shaw

It's the classic stereotype of a programmer: an antisocial geek who slaves alone, in a stuffy room with dimmed lights, hunched over a console tapping keys furiously. Never seeing the light of day. Never speaking to another person "in real life."

But nothing could be further from the truth.

This job is *all* about communication. It's no exaggeration to say we succeed or fail based on the quality of our communication.

This communication is more than the conversations that kick off at the water cooler. Although those are essential. It's more than conversations in a coffee shop, over lunch, or in the pub. Although those are all also essential.

Our communication runs far deeper; it is multifaceted.

Code Is Communication

Software itself, the very act of writing code, is a form of communication.

This works several ways....

Talking to the Machines

When we write code we are *talking to* the computer, via an interpreter. This may literally be an "interpreter" for scripting languages that are interpreted at runtime. Or we communicate via a translator: a compiler or JIT. Few programmers these days converse in the CPU's natural language: machine code.

Our code exists to give a literal list of instructions to the CPU.

Every so often, my wife leaves me a list of jobs to do. *Make dinner, clean the living room, wash the car.* If her instructions are illegible, or unclear, I won't do what she actually wants me to. I'll iron the cutlery and hoover the bathtub. (I've learnt to not argue, and do what I'm told, even if it makes no sense to me.) If she wants the right results, she has to leave me the right kind of instructions.

It is the same with our code.

Sloppy programmers are not explicit. The results of their code can be the equivalent of ironed cutlery.

> **KEY** ➤ Code is communication with the computer. It must be clear and unambiguous if your instructions are to be carried out as you intend.

We are not talking in the CPU's mother tongue, so it's always important to know what nuances of its language get lost in translation to our programming language. The convenience of using our preferred language comes at a cost.

Talking to the Animals

Although your code forms an ongoing conversation with your mechanical friend, the computer, it does not *just* speak to a CPU.

It speaks to other humans, too—to the other people who share the code with you, and who have to *read* what you have written. It is read by the people you are collaborating with. It is read by the people who review your work. It is read by the maintenance programmer who picks up your code later on. It will be read by you when you come back in a few months to fix nasty bugs in your old handiwork.

> **KEY** ➤ Your code is communication to other humans. Including you. It must be clear and unambiguous if others are to maintain it.

This is important.

A high-calibre programmer strives to write code that clearly communicates its intent. The code should be transparent: exposing the algorithms, not obscuring the logic. It should enable others to modify it easily.

If code does not reveal itself, showing what it does, then it will be difficult to change. And the one thing we know about coding in the real world is *the only constant is change*. Uncommunicative code is a bottleneck and will impede your later development.

Good code is not terse to the point of unreadability. But neither is it lengthy and laboured. And it is most definitely not filled with comments. More comments *do not* make code better, they just make it longer—and probably worse as the comments can easily get out of sync with the code.

Good code is not trickily clever, deftly using "advanced" language features to such aplomb that it will leave maintenance programmers scratching their heads. (Of course, the amount of head scratching does depend on the quality of the maintenance programmers; this kind of thing always depends on context.)

The quality of our expression in code is determined by the programming languages we choose to use, and in how we use them. Are you using a language that allows you to naturally express the concepts you are modelling?

We must talk the same language at the same time, or we'll suffer a biblical Tower of Babel cacophony. The team working on a section of code must write in the same language; it's not a winning formula to add lines of Basic to a Python script. If your entire application is written in C++, then the first person to add code in another language had better have a compelling reason.

However, even in an environment using the same programming language, it is possible to use different dialects and end up introducing communication barriers. You may adopt different formatting conventions, or employ different coding idioms (e.g., using "modern" C++ *versus* "C++ as a better C").

Of course, using multiple programming languages is not evil. Larger projects may legitimately be composed of code in more than one language. This is a standard for big distributed systems where the backend runs on a server in one language, with remote clients implemented in other, often more dynamic, browser-hosted languages. This kind of architecture allows you to employ the right kind of language for each task. We see here yet another language in play: the language that those parts communicate through (perhaps a REST API with JSON data formatting).

Consider also the *natural language* you program in. Most teams are based in the same country, so this is not a concern. However, I often work on multi-country projects with many nonnative English speakers. We made a conscious choice to write all code in English: all variable names, comments, class or function names, everything. This affords us a degree of sanity.

I've worked on multisite projects that didn't do this, and it's a real problem having to run code comments through Google Translate to work out if they're important or not. I've been left wondering whether a variable name has a Hungarian wart at the start, is misspelled, abbreviated, or if I just have a very bad grasp of the natural language used.

Remember that code is read by humans far more often than it is written. Therefore, it should be optimised for reading, not for writing. Use a concise construct only if it's easier for someone else to understand, rather than easier for you to type. Follow a layout convention that reveals intent clearly, not one that requires fewer keystrokes.

Talking to Tools

Our code communicates even further—to other tools that work with it. Here "tools" is not a euphemism for your colleagues.

Your code may be fed into documentation generators, source control systems, bug tracking software, and code analysers. Even the editors we use can have a bearing (what character set encoding is your editor using?).

It isn't unusual to add extra directives to our code to sate these processors' whinging, or to adapt our code to suit those tools (adjusting formatting, comment style, or coding idioms).

How does this affect the readability of the code?

Interpersonal Communication

Electric communication will never be a substitute for the face of someone who with their soul encourages another person to be brave and true.

— Charles Dickens

We don't just communicate by typing code. Programmers work in teams with other programmers. And with the wider organisation.

There's a lot of communication going on here. Because we're doing this all the time, high-quality programmers *have* to be high-quality communicators. We write messages to speak with, even gesticulate at, others all the time.

Ways to Converse

There are many communication channels we use for conversations, most notably:

- Talking face-to-face
- Talking on the phone, one-to-one
- Talking on the phone in a "conference call"
- Talking on VoIP channels (which isn't necessarily different from the phone, but is more likely to be hands-free and allow you to send files over the same communication channel)
- Email

- Instant messaging (e.g., typing in Skype, on IRC channels, in chatrooms, or via SMS)
- Videoconferencing
- Sending written letters via the physical postal system (do you remember that quaint practice?)
- Fax (which has largely been replaced by scanners and common sense; however, it still has a place in our comms pantheon because it is regarded as useful for sending legally binding documents)

Each of these mechanisms are different, varying in the locations spanned, the number of people involved at each end of the communication, the facilities available and richness of interaction (can the other person hear your tone of voice, or read your body language?), the typical duration, required urgency and deferrability of a discussion, and the way a conversation is started (e.g., does it need a meeting request to set up, or is it acceptable to interrupt someone with no warning?).

They each have different etiquettes and conventions, and require different skills to use effectively. It is important to select the correct communication channel for the conversation you need to have. How urgent is an answer? How many people should be involved?

Don't send someone an email when you need an urgent answer; email can sit ignored for days. Walk over to them, ring them, Skype them. Conversely, don't phone someone for a non-urgent issue. Their time is precious, and your interruption will disrupt their *flow*, stopping them from working on their current task.

When you next need to ask someone a question, consider whether you are about to use the correct communication mechanism.

> KEY ➤ Master the different forms of communication. Use the appropriate mechanism for each conversation.

Watch Your Language

As a project evolves, it gains its own dialect: a vocabulary of project and domain-specific terms, and the prevalent idioms used to design or think about the shape of the software design. We also settle on terminology for the process used to work together (e.g., we talk about *user stories*, *epics*, *sprints*).

> KEY ➤ Take care to use the right vocabulary with the right people.

Does your customer need to be forced to learn technical terms? Does your CEO need to know about software development terminology?

Body Language

You'd be upset if someone sat beside you, sparked up a conversation, but spent the whole time facing in the opposite direction. (Or you could pretend they were from a bad spy movie; *I hear the gooseberries are doing well this year...and so are the mangoes.*[1])

If they pulled rude faces every time you spoke, you'd be offended. If they played with a Rubik's cube throughout the conversation you'd feel less than valued.

It is easy to do exactly this when we communicate electronically; to not fully respect the person we're talking with. On a voice-only conversation, it's easy to zone out, read email, surf the Web, and not give someone else your full attention.

Having fully embraced our modern, always-connected, broadband age, I now default to selecting a *video-on* communication channel. Often I'll kick off a conversation that might have been via phone or instant message with a VOIP video chat. Even if my conversant will never enable their own video, I like to broadcast a picture so that my face and body language are clearly visible.

This shows I'm not hiding anything, and fosters a more open conversation.

A video chat forces you to concentrate on the conversation. It engages the other person more strongly, and maintains focus.

Parallel Communication

Your computer is having many conversations at once: talking to the operating system, other programs, device drivers, and other computers. It's really quite clever like that. We have to make sure that *our* code communication with it is clear and won't confuse matters whilst it's having conversations with other code.

That's a powerful analogy to our interpersonal communication. With so many communication channels available simultaneously, we could be engaging in office banter, instant messaging a remote worker, and exchanging SMSs with our partner, all whilst participating in several email threads.

And then the telephone rings. Your whole tottering pile of communication falls over.

How do you ensure that each of your conversations is clear enough and well-structured so it won't confuse any other communication you're concurrently engaged in?

I've lost count of the number of times I've typed the wrong response into the wrong Skype window and confused someone. Fortunately, I've never revealed company confidential information that way. Yet.

---

1. See the "Secret Service Dentists" sketch from *Monty Python's Flying Circus*.

> KEY ➤ Effective communication requires focus.

Talking of Teams

Communication is the oil that lubricates teamwork. It is simply *impossible* to work with other people and not talk to them.

This, once more, underscores Conway's law. Your code shapes itself around the structure of your teams' communications. The boundaries of your teams and the effectiveness of their interactions shapes, and is shaped by, the way they communicate.

> KEY ➤ Good communication fosters good code. The shape of your communications will shape your code.

Healthy communication builds camaraderie, and makes your workplace an enjoyable place to inhabit. Unhealthy communication rapidly breaks trust and hinders teamwork. To avoid this, you must talk to people with respect, trust, friendship, concern, no hidden motives, and a lack of aggression.

> KEY ➤ Speak to others transparently, with a healthy attitude, to foster effective teamwork.

Communication within a team must be free-flowing and frequent. It must be normal to share information, and everyone's voice must be heard.

If teams don't talk frequently, if they fail to share their plans and designs, then the inevitable consequences will be duplication of code and effort. We'll see conflicting designs in the codebase. There will be failures when things are integrated.

Many processes encourage specific, structured communication with a set cadence; the more frequent the better. Some teams have a weekly progress meeting, but this really isn't good enough. Short *daily* meetings are far better (often run as *scrums*, or *stand-up* meetings). These meetings help share progress, raise issues, and identify roadblocks without apportioning blame. They make sure that everyone has a clear picture of the current state of the project.

The trick with these meetings is to keep them short and to the point; without care, they degrade into tedious rambling discussions of off-topic issues. Keeping them running on-time is also important. Otherwise they can become distractions that interrupt your *flow*.

Talking to the Customer

There are many other people we must talk to in order to develop excellent software. One of the most important conversations that we must hold is with the customer.

We have to understand what the customer wants, otherwise we can't build it. So you have to ask them, and work in their language to determine their requirements.

After you've asked them once, it's vital to keep talking to them as you go along to ensure that it's still what they want, and that assumptions you make match their expectations.

The only way to do this is in their language (not yours), using plenty of examples that they understand—for example, demos of the system under construction.

Other Communication

And still, the programmer's communication runs deeper than all this. We don't just write code, and we don't just have conversations. The programmer communicates in other ways; for example, by writing documentation and specifications, publishing blog articles, or writing for technical journals.

How many ways are you communicating as a programmer?

Conclusion

> *First learn the meaning of what you say, and then speak.*
>
> — Epictetus

A good programmer is hallmarked by good communication skills. Effective communication is:

- Clear
- Frequent
- Respectful
- Performed at the right levels
- Using the right medium

We must be mindful of this, and *practice* communication—we must seek to constantly improve in written, verbal, and code communication.

Questions

1. How does personality type affect your communication skills? How can an introverted programmer communicate most effectively?

2. How formal or casual should our interactions be? Does this depend on the communication medium?

3. How do you keep colleagues abreast of your work without endlessly bugging them about it?

4. How does communication with a manager differ from communication with a fellow coder?

5. What kind of communication is important to ensure that a development project runs successfully?

6. How do you best communicate a code design? They say a picture speaks a thousand words. Is this true?

7. Do distributed teams need to interact and communicate *more* than colocated teams?

8. What are the most common barriers to effective communication?

See also

- *Keeping Up Appearances* Code is communication. Here's how to communicate effectively in code.

- *Smarter, Not Harder* Keeping in constant communication with your team, manager, or customer can save you from accidentally working on the wrong thing. It's good to talk!

> **Try this....**
>
> Over the next week, keep a watch on all the ways you communicate with other people. Determine two practical things you could do to improve the quality of your communications.

10,000 MONKEYS
(OR THEREABOUTS)

subject: <project foo>
to: bob, sue, frank, bill, hilda....

yes, but please do remember
that we agreed to frobble the
twice in strictly alpha-
rather than in
hilda sug-
have to

THE LAW OF THE UNSTOPPABLE EMAIL SNOWBALL

AS MORE PEOPLE GET ADDED TO THE DISTRIBUTION LIST OF AN EMAIL, IT BECOMES INCREASINGLY UNLIKELY TO STOP.

AS MORE "IMPORTANT" PEOPLE GET ADDED (BECAUSE WE NEED MANAGERIAL INPUT TO MAKE THE DECISION), THE MORE PEOPLE WANT TO HAVE THEIR VOICE HEARD.

EVENTUALLY THE SNOWBALL BECOMES AN AVALANCHE. EVERYONE TRIES TO RUN OUT OF THE WAY, BUT NO ONE DARE STAND IN ITS PATH.

IT IS NO LONGER COMMUNICATION.

CHAPTER 37

Many-festos

Confusion of goals and perfection of means seems, in my opinion, to characterise our age.

— Albert Einstein

It's becoming an epidemic! They're springing up everywhere. We've got them coming out of our ears. It's as if you can't write a line of code, kick off a project, or even think about software development without signing up to one.

The manifestos are *everywhere.*

With all these different manifestos for software development, our profession is in danger of becoming more about politics than the actual art, craft, science, and trade of software development.

Of course, professional software development is largely a *people problem.* So it necessarily involves a certain amount of politics. But we're making even the foundational coding principles into a political battle.

Some of the developer manifestos are gloriously ambiguous; more akin to a development horoscope. And, sadly, when a manifesto becomes popular we see factions form around it, leading to disputes about what the manifesto really stands for. Whole debates spring up around the exegesis of particular manifesto items.

Software religion is alive and well.

Manifestos seem to spring up for any conceivable purpose. But I have a solution. In order to stem the flow, and make it easier for future software activists who'd like to pen their own, here I present the one, the overarching, generic software development manifesto. The `Manifesto<PET_SUBJECT>`, if you like.

A Generic Manifesto for Software Development

We, the undersigned, have an opinion about software development. We are concerned about the future of our profession, and our experience leads us to draw the following conclusions:

- *We believe in* a fixed set of immutable ideals *over* tailoring our approach to each specific situation.
- *We believe in* concentrating on and discussing only the things that interest us *over* the bigger problem.
- *We believe in* our opinion *over* the opinions and experiences of others.
- *We believe in* arbitrary black-and-white mandates *over* real-world scenarios with complex issues and delicate resolutions.
- *We believe that* when our approach is hard to follow *then* it only shows how much more important it is.
- *We believe in* crafting an arbitrary set of commandments over the realisation that it's just *never* that simple.
- *We believe in* trying to establish a movement to promote our view *over* something that will be genuinely useful.
- *We believe that* we are better developers than those who don't agree with us *because* they don't agree with us.

That is, we believe we're doing the right thing. And if you don't you're wrong. And if you don't do what we do, you're doing it wrong.

OK, OK

Alright. I'll admit it. My tongue *is* in my cheek. Mostly.

The Manyfestos

Perhaps the most famous developer manifesto is The Agile Manifesto (*http://agilema nifesto.org*) crafted in 2001 as a rally against the ineffectual heavyweight processes that had hindered software delivery in the preceding decade(s). The more recent Crafts-manship Manifesto (*http://manifesto.softwarecraftsmanship.org*) is, sadly, a response to the perceived degradation in importance of technical practices and responsibility for good code in Agile circles.

There are manifestos for other software movements, notably the GNU manifesto (*http:// www.gnu.org/gnu/manifesto.html*), The Refactoring Manifesto (*http://refactoringmani*

festo.org), and The Hacker Manifesto (*http://en.wikipedia.org/wiki/Hacker_Manifesto*). And still there are more.

Know the major manifestos. Form your own informed opinion about each.

> KEY ➤ Learn about development methodologies, trends, manifestos, and fads.

But, Really?

Good developers are passionate about their work. They become invested in what they are doing, and seek to constantly improve.

This is a good thing.

When they find a set of practices, ideals, or standards that work well, it is natural to want to capture them and share them with others to advance the profession. These days it has become popular to phrase this as a *manifesto*. As we've seen, there are many of them.

A manifesto is to our craft what coding standards are to code: useful guidelines, ideals to strive for, and pointers to best practice.

And, just like coding standards, unhelpful holy wars can brew around these documents. Some acolytes view them as invariants: mandates, indelibly carved on precious stone tablets by hallowed prophets. They shun those who do not follow the One True Way.

That is a far from useful attitude.

> KEY ➤ Subscribe to development manifestos that seem sensible. But don't blindly follow them, and don't treat them dogmatically.

Any manifesto can only be a broad statement of principles, *never* the One True Way. For example, the Agile evangelists explicitly state there are multiple ways to implement the goals of their manifesto; it's just an attempt to codify best practices.

If you care about becoming a better programmer, adopt a pragmatic approach to such things. Learn from them, and understand the views on development they each espouse. Use what works for you. Make sure that you keep up-to-date; learn about the new fashions and the en-vogue catechisms. Appreciate what's good about them, but don't follow them blindly. Appraise them with an open mind.

The Punchline

So, are manifestos silly and pointless? No. Are they helpful? Mostly. That is, when they contain good information and are used responsibly, to spark conversation, rather than as gospel. Can they be misused? Yes! Easily. But so can anything else in the software development world.

What would be on *your* Manifesto for Software Development? Here's a go at mine. But please don't write it in stone as *The Better Programmer Manifesto*. At least, not until I've formed a large enough movement behind it.

- Care about the code.
- Empower your team.
- Keep it simple.
- Use your brain.
- Nothing is set in stone.
- Learn. Constantly.
- Seek to improve. Constantly. (Yourself, your team, and your code.)
- Always deliver value, considering the long term.

Questions

1. What foundational development "principles" do you hold dear?
2. Do you sign up to, or align yourself with, development streams like "Agile," "craftsmanship," and so on? How closely do you agree with each of the items in their manifesto?
3. What do you think these manifestos have to offer the development community?
4. What kinds of harm might they *really* be able to do, if any?
5. Or do you keep your head down and ignore this kind of thing? *Should* you actually follow these software fashions and fads to maintain your personal development?

See also

- *Live to Love to Learn* Take time to learn about new fashions and fads in the industry.
- *Playing by the Rules* Write your own manifesto!

Try this....

Read the manifestos listed above. Consider your views on them. Consider what would be in your personal manifesto for software development.

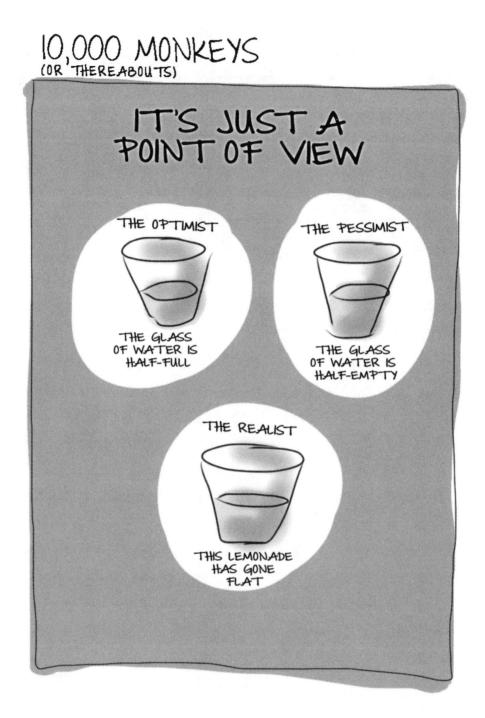

CHAPTER 38

An Ode to Code

> All bad poetry springs from genuine feeling.
>
> — Oscar Wilde

Gerald was a coder who worked in a small team.
The thing was: other coders coded code that was not clean.
The mess was detrimental, distracting, diabolic;
The inhumane detritus of an evil workaholic.

But Gerald had a conscience. He wouldn't let this lie.
He lay awake at night devising schemes to rectify
The awful internal structure, the confusing variable names,
And the contrived control flow that was consistently insane.

Those early days the "Boy Scout Rule" was how he planned to beat
The bugs and turgid software that had formed beneath his feet.
A tidy here, a bug fix there, refactors left and right.
Pretty soon, he thought, (with work) they'll all be out of sight.

But poor old Gerald, plan in action, missed one vital fact:
To make a dent, all programmers must enter in the pact.
His slapdash coding colleagues, just saw a rule to flout
And continued writing drivel whilst he tried to sort it out.

One step forwards, two steps back. Gerald danced this dance.
Until he learnt he needed a more militant stance.
Agile teams are excellent and clean code is the best.
To achieve this: the team, and not the code, would have to be addressed.

Conway's law describes to us how software follows team—
Sympathetic software is born from a well-oiled machine.
If cogs get stuck or grate, and stop doing what they ought.
Then there's only one option: to remove them, Gerald thought.

So the team refactor started, with the pattern: "Parameterise from Above":
The manager, on his cycle home, received a surprise shove.

He landed down a manhole. You might call it homocide.
Gerald called it team hygiene. One problem had then died.

One by one his team mates met with unusual fates.
The unsuspecting QA team were hit by flying plates.
(The lesson learned from this event was: never hold team meetings
In a diner with bad furniture, and poltergeisty leanings.)

The programmers who caused such ire each met a gory end.
One "caught his tie in the printer"; his face will never mend.
Another tripped atop the stairs on his way out for a break,
A pile of deadly Unix manuals flying in his wake.

Gerald's life was vastly better; the team was little more
Than one coder, a sys admin, and the guy who manned the door.
The problem with this setup, Gerald shortly found:
The code got no worse—good!—but it hardly changed, as no coders were around.

Progress was slow and tough, though heroic Gerald tried.
Deadlines made a "whooshing" sound as often they flew by.
With features sadly lacking, the project was a farce.
Then one day a policeman came, and put Gerald behind bars.

The moral of this simple tale is to react with care
When callous coder colleagues deign to drive you to despair.
The only sensible way there is to retaliate
Is British: maintain a healthy level of pent-up angst and hate.

Coding Is a People Problem

Hopefully you've read the chapter on ethics, so you probably agree that it is inadvisable to perform such a dramatic cull of the poorly performing members of your software team. However, how *should* you react when working with team members who do not perform adequately, or seem to willfully make the code worse?

What if the software team leaders do not notice or comprehend the problem? What if, heaven forbid, they are part of the problem itself?

Sadly, at the bleeding edge of the codeface, this is not entirely unusual. Although some teams are full of awesome codesmiths, many are not. Unless you are unusually blessed in your coding career, you will at some point find yourself in sticky situations that seem to have no solution.

> KEY ▶ Often, the tricky part of software development isn't in the technical aspects of the code; it's the people problems.

When the programmers just don't seem to get it, and fail to understand that they are making things worse, not better, you must respond.

Consider introducing practices that promote responsibility for the code and illustrate (in a way that avoids apportioning blame) how to work most effectively: introduce pair programming, mentoring, design review meetings, or the like.

Set an excellent example yourself. Do not fall into a trap of those bad habits; it's very easy to lose enthusiasm and cut corners because everyone else is. If you can't beat them, *don't* join them.

> KEY ➤ When surrounded by coders who do not care about the code, maintain healthy attitudes yourself. Beware of absorbing bad practices by osmosis.

It will not be simple or rapid to change a coding culture and steer development back towards healthy principles. But that doesn't mean that it can't be done.

Questions

1. How healthy is your current development team?

2. How can you quickly recognise when a developer is not performing as diligently as she should?

3. Which is most likely: people work sloppily on purpose, or they are sloppy because they don't appreciate how to work better?

4. How can you be sure that you're not adopting sloppy practices yourself? How can you prevent yourself from slipping into bad practices in the future?

See also

- *Care About the Code* You *have* to care about the code. But can you care *too much?*

- *The Ethical Programmer* Please reread this chapter, just in case you are about to go on a murderous rampage.

- *Wallowing in Filth* How to cope with the mess left by colleagues who don't know better.

Try this....

Consider whether you have adopted any bad habits recently. How can you rectify this?

Epilogue

Far out in the uncharted backwaters of the unfashionable end of the western spiral arm of the Galaxy lies a small unregarded yellow sun. Orbiting this at a distance of roughly 92 million miles is an utterly insignificant little blue-green planet whose ape-descended life-forms are so amazingly primitive that they still think computer programs are a pretty neat idea.

This planet has—or rather, had—a problem, which was this: most of the programmers on it wrote poor code pretty much all of the time, even when they were being paid to do a good job. Many solutions were suggested for this problem, but most of these were largely concerned with the education of programmers, which is odd because on the whole the programmers didn't want to be educated.

And so the problem remained; lots of the code produced was rubbish, and most of the users were miserable, even the ones who could write good computer programs.[1]

Well done: you got to the end of the book. That's a lot of chapters digested. (If you just skipped here to ruin the ending for yourself: *the butler did it.* Now go back and read why.)

Over the last few hundred pages you've seen techniques for writing technically elegant code, for creating beautiful designs, and for constructing pragmatic, maintainable systems. You've learnt approaches for dealing with legacy code and seen how to work effectively with other people.

---

1. With apologies to the late, great Douglas Adams.

But all of this head knowledge, the understanding of specific skills, won't help you at all unless you are driven by the correct *attitude*: the desire and passion to work well.

Do you have that?

Attitude

Attitude is what sets the *good* programmers apart from the *bad* ones; it's what distinguishes *exceptional* programmers from merely *adequate* ones.

Attitude trumps technical skill: intricate knowledge of a programming language does not guarantee maintainable code. Understanding many models of programming doesn't always lead to elegant designs. It's your attitude that determines whether your code is "good" and whether you are a pleasure to work with.

The dictionary definition of an *attitude* is:

Attitude: (n) *at-ti-tude*

1. A state of mind or a feeling; a disposition.
2. The position of an aircraft relative to a frame of reference.

That first definition isn't surprising, but the second is actually more revealing than the first.

There are three imaginary lines of axis running through an aircraft; one from wing to wing, one from nose to tail, and one running vertically where the other two cross. A pilot positions his aircraft around these axes; they define the aircraft's angle of approach. This is known as the *attitude* of the aircraft. If you apply a little power to the aircraft whilst it has the wrong attitude, it will end up missing the target massively. A pilot has to constantly monitor his vehicle's attitude, especially at critical times like takeoff and landing.

This parallels our software development experiences. The plane's attitude defines its angle of approach, and *our* attitude defines our angle of approach to coding. It doesn't matter how technically competent a programmer you are, if your abilities aren't tempered by healthy attitudes then your work will suffer.

With the wrong attitude you can shoot miles off in the wrong direction. A wrong attitude can make or break a software project, so it's vital we maintain the right angle of approach to programming. Your attitude will either hinder or promote your personal growth. To become better programmers, we need to ensure that we have the right attitudes.

Go Forth and Code

So *care* about good code, and seek to create it in better ways. Always learn. Learn to design, learn to code, learn to collaborate. Seek always to work alongside excellent engineers who will challenge and encourage you to improve. Be diligent, be conscientious, and be professional.

Enjoy programming. And more than anything else, enjoy becoming better!

Try this....

Read this book again in a few months. Revisit the material, and see what speaks to you next time around. Attempt the questions afresh; and observe how your perspectives, experience, and understanding have changed. If you are diligent, and concentrate on deliberate practice, you'll be amazed at how you've developed.

Index

We'd like to hear your suggestions for improving our indexes. Send email to index@oreilly.com.

exceptions, 64, 69
experience, 225
experts, 220, 301
eye strain, 267

F

fault, 190
fear, 157
feature complete, 196
feature freeze, 197
feature toggle, 179
feedback, 87
file structure, 48, 51, 175
fizzy milk, 131
Four Stages of Competence, 219, 225
fun, 137
functional languages, 254

G

geek, 313
Git, 173
Godwin's law, 7
gold master, 195

H

Heisenbug, 83
Hippocodic Oath, 249
Hippocratic Oath, 243
history, 110
holy wars, 7, 325

I

idioms, 40, 147, 257
imperative languages, 254
indirection, 147
integration tests, 90
interpreter, 313
invariants, 78
investing
    time, 57
investing time, 274, 275
ironed cutlery, 314

J

JIT, 313
job security, 244

K

KISS, 145, 276
knowledge, 221

L

languages, 216, 253
    code, 315
    data, 315
    dead, 254
    declarative, 254
    functional, 254
    imperative, 254
    libraries, 39
    Logic, 254
    natural, 315
last responsible moment, 208
latency, 83
layers, 49, 51
layout, 7, 10, 38, 57, 58
learning, 60, 136, 215
    code, 45
    languages, 254
    models, 219
legacy
    code, 26, 59, 94
    features, 31
legal issues, 245
libraries, 48, 167, 274
licenses, 245
lines, 107
little-and-often, 79, 176
logic, 18
Logic languages, 254
love, 183, 256

M

maintainability, 2
maintenance, 31
manager, 17, 247
manure, 184
meetings, 278, 319
memory corruption, 83
mental state, 218
mentoring, 300
Mercurial, 173
metaphors, 138, 259
mindlessness, 154, 225

mistakes, 154
    are OK, 159
mock objects, 99
modifiability, 106
motivation, 300
multi-tasking, 276

N

nagging wife, 314
names, 8, 12
navigating, 45, 56
network, 83
not invented here, 274
novice, 219

O

Oath
    Hippocodic, 249
    Hippocratic, 243
obfuscation, 147
optimisation, 149
ownership
    of code, 124, 159

P

pair programming, 307
parameterise from above, 98
people, 109, 299, 306
    attitude to, 56, 60
    employer, 248
    manager, 247
    team, 246, 319
    yourself, 248
politics, 115, 118
Pomodoro, 275
presentation, 7, 38, 147
pride, 293
prioritisation, 275
process, 135
    ownership of, 121
    release, 204
procrastination, 277
programming languages, 315
project size, 146

Q

QA, 160, 183, 184
    and TDD, 93
quality, 48
quicksand, 55

R

rcs, 173
README, 51
refactoring, 20, 59, 159, 167
release, 47, 175, 195, 203
release branch, 178, 198, 206
release candidate, 196
release notes, 189
removing code, 17
replacing code, 59
requirements, 48, 93
respect, 256
responsibility, 155, 159, 248
return value, 31, 64
reuse, 165, 274
revision control, 57
rigor mortis, 157
RTM, 195
rubber duck, 82

S

science, 133
scripting, 277
self-improvement, 231, 233
shutdown, 70
side effects, 64
simplicity, 104, 136, 145, 204, 276
singleton, 83
skills, 225
social, 299
software archaeology, 171
software license, 245
software release, 203
software stuff, 131
source control, 171
sport, 135
stability, 147
static analysis, 48
storage, 83
stub objects, 99
stupidity, 145, 153

style guide, 11
Subversion, 173
success, 285
sufficiency, 149
survey, 56
SUT, 89
system tests, 90

T

tag, 206
TDD, 87, 91
team, 246, 319
teamwork, 115, 133, 135, 187, 216, 221, 294
technical debt, 122, 161, 200
test-driven development, 91
test-first, 91
testing, 87, 116, 160–161, 184, 187, 207
tests, 47, 50, 59, 79, 201, 275, 278
    bad, 94
    change, 122
    code, 89
    doubles, 99
    good, 93
    integration tests, 90
    system tests, 90
    TDD, 87, 91
    test-first, 91
    unit tests, 90
threads, 56, 70, 83
tidying, 59
tidying code, 27, 58
to-do list, 276
tools, 47, 161, 278
town planning, 113

U

UI, 51

unexpected, 69
unit tests, 90, 187
use cases, 165

V

VCS, 171
VDU, 261
verbosity, 24
version control, 32–33, 46, 171, 275
    archaeology, 49, 79
    branches, 178
    centralised, 173
    distributed, 173
    presentation changes, 14
    release branch, 198, 206
    tag, 206

W

waterfall, 185, 192
whitespace, 10, 12, 26
wizards, 31, 104
work/life balance
    burnout, 278
    overtime, 278
working
    smart, 89, 274
    too hard, 284

Y

YAGNI, 29, 121, 150, 166
yak shaving, 276

About the Author

Pete Goodliffe is a programmer, software development columnist, musician, and author. He never stays at the same place in the software food chain; his projects range from OS implementation, to audio codecs, to multimedia applications; from embedded firmware, to iOS development, to desktop applications. He has a passion for curry and doesn't wear shoes.

Pete's popular development book, *Code Craft*, is a practical and entertaining investigation of the entire programming pursuit. In about 600 pages. No mean feat! It has been translated into many languages. He writes a magazine column called "Becoming a Better Programmer," has contributed to several software development books, and regularly speaks on software development topics.

Colophon

The animal on the cover of *Becoming a Better Programmer* is a two-winged flying fish (*Exocoetidae*). The flying fish can be distinguished by its unusually large pectoral fins. As the name suggests, it makes powerful, self-propelled leaps out of the water into the air by moving its tail up to 70 times per second. In the early 1900s, flying fish were studied as models for developing airplanes. Once in the air, it spreads its wing-like fins and tilts them upward, which enables it to glide for considerable distances. The pectoral fin, or "wing," has a similar aerodynamic shape as a bird wing. At the end of the glide, it either reenters the sea by folding the pectoral fins, or dropping its tail into the water to lift itself for another glide. The record is 45 seconds in flight, as recorded by a Japanese television crew in 2008.

Their ability to fly into the air is often used as a defense mechanism against predators, which include dolphins, tuna, marlin, birds, squids, and porpoises. They're commercially fished by gillnetting in Japan, Vietnam, and China, and by dipnetting in Indonesia and India. In the Solomon Islands, flying fish are caught during flight in nets from outrigger canoes. Commercial fishing of this species is done in complete darkness when no moonlight is available, as the fish are attracted to lit torches. Flying fish feed mainly on plankton, and live in all of the oceans, mostly in warm, tropical or subtropical waters.

Many of the animals on O'Reilly covers are endangered; all of them are important to the world. To learn more about how you can help, go to *animals.oreilly.com*.

The manuscript was prepared using asciidoc, love, and vim. The cover image is from loose plates. The cover fonts are URW Typewriter and Guardian Sans. The text font is Adobe Minion Pro; the heading font is Adobe Myriad Condensed; and the code font is Dalton Maag's Ubuntu Mono. Cartoons are drawn in AutoDesk SketchBook with layout in Adobe Photoshop.

Have it your way.